D0923252

COPYRIGHT CARTOGRAPHY BY PHILIP'S

PHILIP'S

POCKET
WORLD
ATLAS

PHILIP'S

POCKET WORLD ATLAS

Contents

vi–ix	World statistics
x–xi	Time zones
xii–xiii	Flight paths
xiv–xv	Climate
xvi–xvii	Wealth
xviii–xix	International organizations
xx–xxiv	World gazetteer

I	World Maps – general reference
2–3	Northern hemisphere 1:133.3M
4–5	Southern hemisphere 1:133.3M

EUROPE

6–7	Europe 1:26.7M
8–9	Scandinavia 1:13.3M
10–11	British Isles 1:6.7M
12–13	France 1:6.7M
14–15	Germany and Benelux 1:6.7M
16–17	Central Europe 1:6.7M

18–19	Spain and Portugal 1:6.7M
20–21	Italy and the Adriatic 1:6.7M
22–23	Greece and the Balkans 1:6.7M
24–25	Eastern Europe 1:13.3M

ASIA

26–27	Asia 1:67M
28–29	Western Russia and Central Asia 1:26.7M
30–31	Eastern Siberia 1:26.7M
32–33	Japan 1:6.7M Southern Honshu 1:13.3M
34–35	China 1:26.7M
36–37	South-east Asia 1:16.7M
38–39	Philippines and Eastern Indonesia 1:16.7M
40–41	Eastern India, Bangladesh and Burma 1:13.3M
42–43	Western India and Pakistan 1:13.3M

Published in Great Britain in 1999
by George Philip Limited,
a division of Octopus Publishing Group Limited,
2–4 Heron Quays, London E14 4JP

Cartography by Philip's

Copyright © 1999 George Philip Limited

ISBN 0-540-07832-8

Details of other Philip's titles and services can be found on
our website at: www.philips-maps.co.uk

A CIP catalogue record for this book is available from the
British Library.

All rights reserved. Apart from any fair dealing for the purpose
of private study, research, criticism or review, as permitted under
the Copyright, Designs and Patents Act, 1988, no part of this
publication may be reproduced, stored in a retrieval system, or
transmitted in any form or by any means, electronic, electrical,
chemical, mechanical, optical, photocopying, recording, or
otherwise, without prior written permission. All enquiries
should be addressed to the Publisher.

Printed in China

44 – 45	Iran, the Gulf and Afghanistan 1:13.3M
46 – 47	The Middle East and Turkey 1:13.3M
48 – 49	Arabia and the Horn of Africa 1:20M

AFRICA

50 – 51	Africa 1:56M
52 – 53	North-east Africa 1:20M
54 – 55	North-west Africa 1:20M
56 – 57	Central Africa 1:20M
58 – 59	Southern Africa 1:20M

AUSTRALASIA

60 – 61	Australia 1:26.7M
62 – 63	South-east Australia 1:10.7M
64 – 65	New Zealand, Central and South-west Pacific 1:8M

NORTH AMERICA

66 – 67	North America 1:46.7M
68 – 69	Eastern Canada 1:20M
70 – 71	Western Canada 1:20M
72 – 73	North-east USA 1:8M
74 – 75	South-east USA 1:8M
76 – 77	North-central USA 1:8M
78 – 79	Southern USA 1:8M
80 – 81	North-west USA 1:8M
82 – 83	South-west USA 1:8M
84 – 85	Mexico 1:20M
86 – 87	Caribbean and Central America 1:20M

SOUTH AMERICA

88 – 89	South America 1:46.7M
90 – 91	South America – North-west 1:21.3M
92 – 93	South America – North-east 1:21.3M
94 – 95	South America – South 1:21.3M

POLAR REGIONS

| 96 | Antarctica 1:46.7M |

INDEX

| 97 – 120 | Index to World Maps |

WORLD STATISTICS

Country / Territory	Area (1,000 sq km)	Area (1,000 sq mls)	Population (1,000s)	Capital City	Annual Income US$
AFGHANISTAN	652	252	19,509	KABUL	300
ALBANIA	28.8	11.1	3,458	TIRANA	670
ALGERIA	2,382	920	25,012	ALGIERS	1,600
AMERICAN SAMOA (US)	0.20	0.08	58	PAGO PAGO	3,500
ANDORRA	0.45	0.17	65	ANDORRA LA VELLA	14,000
ANGOLA	1,247	481	10,020	LUANDA	410
ANGUILLA (UK)	0.1	0.04	8	THE VALLEY	6,800
ANTIGUA & BARBUDA	0.44	0.17	67	ST JOHN'S	7,000
ARGENTINA	2,767	1,068	34,663	BUENOS AIRES	8,030
ARMENIA	29.8	11.5	3,603	YEREVAN	730
ARUBA (NETHS)	0.19	0.07	71	ORANJESTAD	16,000
AUSTRALIA	7,687	2,968	18,107	CANBERRA	18,720
AUSTRIA	83.9	32.4	8,004	VIENNA	26,890
AZERBAIJAN	86.6	33.4	7,559	BAKU	480
AZORES (PORT.)	2.2	0.87	238	PONTA DELGADA	4,500
BAHAMAS	13.9	5.4	277	NASSAU	11,940
BAHRAIN	0.68	0.26	558	MANAMA	7,840
BANGLADESH	144	56	118,342	DHAKA	240
BARBADOS	0.43	0.17	263	BRIDGETOWN	6,560
BELARUS	207.6	80.1	10,500	MINSK	2,070
BELGIUM	30.5	11.8	10,140	BRUSSELS	24,710
BELIZE	23	8.9	216	BELMOPAN	2,630
BENIN	113	43	5,381	PORTO-NOVO	370
BERMUDA (UK)	0.05	0.02	64	HAMILTON	27,000
BHUTAN	47	18.1	1,639	THIMPHU	420
BOLIVIA	1,099	424	7,900	LA PAZ/SUCRE	800
BOSNIA-HERZEGOVINA	51	20	3,800	SARAJEVO	2,600
BOTSWANA	582	225	1,481	GABORONE	3,020
BRAZIL	8,512	3,286	161,416	BRASÍLIA	3,640
BRUNEI	5.8	2.2	284	BANDAR SERI BEGAWAN	14,500
BULGARIA	111	43	8,771	SOFIA	1,330
BURKINA FASO	274	106	10,326	OUAGADOUGOU	230
BURMA (MYANMAR)	677	261	46,580	RANGOON	1,000
BURUNDI	27.8	10.7	6,412	BUJUMBURA	160
CAMBODIA	181	70	10,452	PHNOM PENH	270
CAMEROON	475	184	13,232	YAOUNDÉ	650
CANADA	9,976	3,852	29,972	OTTAWA	19,380
CANARY IS. (SPAIN)	7.3	2.8	1,494	LAS PALMAS/SANTA CRUZ	7,905
CAPE VERDE IS.	4	1.6	386	PRAIA	960
CAYMAN IS. (UK)	0.26	0.10	31	GEORGE TOWN	20,000
CENTRAL AFRICAN REPUBLIC	623	241	3,294	BANGUI	340
CHAD	1,284	496	6,314	NDJAMENA	180
CHILE	757	292	14,271	SANTIAGO	4,160
CHINA	9,597	3,705	1,226,944	BEIJING	620
COLOMBIA	1,139	440	34,948	BOGOTÁ	1,910
COMOROS	2.2	0.86	654	MORONI	470
CONGO	342	132	2,593	BRAZZAVILLE	680
CONGO (ZAÏRE)	2,345	905	44,504	KINSHASA	120
COOK IS. (NZ)	0.24	0.09	19	AVARUA	900
COSTA RICA	51.1	19.7	3,436	SAN JOSÉ	2,610
CROATIA	56.5	21.8	4,900	ZAGREB	3,250
CUBA	111	43	11,050	HAVANA	1,250
CYPRUS	9.3	3.6	742	NICOSIA	11,500
CZECH REPUBLIC	78.9	30.4	10,500	PRAGUE	3,870
DENMARK	43.1	16.6	5,229	COPENHAGEN	29,890

This alphabetical list includes all the countries and territories of the world. If a territory is not completely independent, then the country it is associated with is named. The area figures give the total area of land, inland water and ice. Units for areas and populations are thousands.

Country/Territory	Area (1,000 sq km)	Area (1,000 sq mls)	Population (1,000s)	Capital City	Annual Income US$
DJIBOUTI	23.2	9	603	DJIBOUTI	1,000
DOMINICA	0.75	0.29	89	ROSEAU	2,990
DOMINICAN REPUBLIC	48.7	18.8	7,818	SANTO DOMINGO	1,460
ECUADOR	284	109	11,384	QUITO	1,390
EGYPT	1,001	387	64,100	CAIRO	790
EL SALVADOR	21	8.1	5,743	SAN SALVADOR	1,610
EQUATORIAL GUINEA	28.1	10.8	400	MALABO	380
ERITREA	94	36	3,850	ASMARA	500
ESTONIA	44.7	17.3	1,531	TALLINN	2,860
ETHIOPIA	1,128	436	51,600	ADDIS ABABA	100
FALKLAND IS. (UK)	12.2	4.7	2	STANLEY	–
FAROE IS. (DEN.)	1.4	0.54	47	TÓRSHAVN	23,660
FIJI	18.3	7.1	773	SUVA	2,440
FINLAND	338	131	5,125	HELSINKI	20,580
FRANCE	552	213	58,286	PARIS	24,990
FRENCH GUIANA (FR.)	90	34.7	154	CAYENNE	6,500
FRENCH POLYNESIA (FR.)	4	1.5	217	PAPEETE	7,500
GABON	268	103	1,316	LIBREVILLE	3,490
GAMBIA, THE	11.3	4.4	1,144	BANJUL	320
GEORGIA	69.7	26.9	5,448	TBILISI	440
GERMANY	357	138	82,000	BERLIN/BONN	27,510
GHANA	239	92	17,462	ACCRA	390
GIBRALTAR (UK)	0.007	0.003	28	GIBRALTAR TOWN	7,500
GREECE	132	51	10,510	ATHENS	8,210
GREENLAND (DEN.)	2,176	840	59	GODTHÅB (NUUK)	12,000
GRENADA	0.34	0.13	94	ST GEORGE'S	2,980
GUADELOUPE (FR.)	1.7	0.66	443	BASSE-TERRE	9,500
GUAM (US)	0.55	0.21	155	AGANA	6,000
GUATEMALA	109	42	10,624	GUATEMALA CITY	1,340
GUINEA	246	95	6,702	CONAKRY	550
GUINEA-BISSAU	36.1	13.9	1,073	BISSAU	250
GUYANA	215	83	832	GEORGETOWN	590
HAITI	27.8	10.7	7,180	PORT-AU-PRINCE	250
HONDURAS	112	43	5,940	TEGUCIGALPA	600
HONG KONG (CHINA)	1.1	0.40	6,000	–	22,990
HUNGARY	93	35.9	10,500	BUDAPEST	4,120
ICELAND	103	40	269	REYKJAVIK	24,950
INDIA	3,288	1,269	942,989	NEW DELHI	340
INDONESIA	1,905	735	198,644	JAKARTA	980
IRAN	1,648	636	68,885	TEHRAN	4,800
IRAQ	438	169	20,184	BAGHDAD	1,800
IRELAND	70.3	27.1	3,589	DUBLIN	14,710
ISRAEL	27	10.3	5,696	JERUSALEM	15,920
ITALY	301	116	57,181	ROME	19,020
IVORY COAST	322	125	14,271	YAMOUSSOUKRO	660
JAMAICA	11	4.2	2,700	KINGSTON	1,510
JAPAN	378	146	125,156	TOKYO	39,640
JORDAN	89.2	34.4	5,547	AMMAN	1,510
KAZAKSTAN	2,717	1,049	17,099	AQMOLA	1,330
KENYA	580	224	28,240	NAIROBI	280
KIRIBATI	0.72	0.28	80	TARAWA	920
KOREA, NORTH	121	47	23,931	PYONGYANG	1,000
KOREA, SOUTH	99	38.2	45,088	SEOUL	9,700
KUWAIT	17.8	6.9	1,668	KUWAIT CITY	17,390
KYRGYZSTAN	198.5	76.6	4,738	BISHKEK	700

The annual income is the Gross National Product per capita in US dollars. The figures are the latest available, usually 1995.

WORLD STATISTICS

Country/Territory	Area (1,000 sq km)	Area (1,000 sq mls)	Population (1,000s)	Capital City	Annual Income US$
LAOS	237	91	4,902	VIENTIANE	350
LATVIA	65	25	2,558	RIGA	2,270
LEBANON	10.4	4	2,971	BEIRUT	2,660
LESOTHO	30.4	11.7	2,064	MASERU	770
LIBERIA	111	43	3,092	MONROVIA	850
LIBYA	1,760	679	5,410	TRIPOLI	7,000
LIECHTENSTEIN	0.16	0.06	31	VADUZ	34,000
LITHUANIA	65.2	25.2	3,735	VILNIUS	1,900
LUXEMBOURG	2.6	1	408	LUXEMBOURG	41,210
MACAU (PORT.)	0.02	0.006	409	MACAU	16,000
MACEDONIA	25.3	9.8	2,173	SKOPJE	860
MADAGASCAR	587	227	15,206	ANTANANARIVO	230
MADEIRA (PORT.)	0.81	0.31	253	FUNCHAL	4,400
MALAWI	118	46	9,800	LILONGWE	170
MALAYSIA	330	127	20,174	KUALA LUMPUR	3,890
MALDIVES	0.30	0.12	254	MALÉ	990
MALI	1,240	479	10,700	BAMAKO	250
MALTA	0.32	0.12	367	VALLETTA	11,000
MARSHALL IS.	0.18	0.07	55	DALAP-ULIGA-DARRIT	1,500
MARTINIQUE (FR.)	1.1	0.42	384	FORT-DE-FRANCE	10,000
MAURITANIA	1,025	396	2,268	NOUAKCHOTT	460
MAURITIUS	2.0	0.72	1,112	PORT LOUIS	3,380
MAYOTTE (FR.)	0.37	0.14	101	MAMOUNDZOU	1,430
MEXICO	1,958	756	93,342	MEXICO CITY	3,320
MICRONESIA, FED. STATES OF	0.70	0.27	125	PALIKIR	1,560
MIDWAY IS. (US)	0.005	0.002	2	–	–
MOLDOVA	33.7	13	4,434	CHISINAU	920
MONACO	0.002	0.0001	32	MONACO	-
MONGOLIA	1,567	605	2,408	ULAN BATOR	310
MONTSERRAT (UK)	0.10	0.04	11	PLYMOUTH	4,500
MOROCCO	447	172	26,857	RABAT	1,110
MOZAMBIQUE	802	309	17,800	MAPUTO	80
NAMIBIA	825	318	1,610	WINDHOEK	2,000
NAURU	0.02	0.008	12	YAREN DISTRICT	10,000
NEPAL	141	54	21,953	KATMANDU	200
NETHERLANDS	41.5	16	15,495	AMSTERDAM/THE HAGUE	24,000
NETHS ANTILLES (NETHS)	0.99	0.38	199	WILLEMSTAD	10,500
NEW CALEDONIA (FR.)	19	7.3	181	NOUMÉA	16,000
NEW ZEALAND	269	104	3,567	WELLINGTON	14,340
NICARAGUA	130	50	4,544	MANAGUA	380
NIGER	1,267	489	9,149	NIAMEY	220
NIGERIA	924	357	88,515	ABUJA	260
NORTHERN MARIANA IS. (US)	0.48	0.18	47	SAIPAN	11,500
NORWAY	324	125	4,361	OSLO	31,250
OMAN	212	82	2,252	MUSCAT	4,820
PAKISTAN	796	307	143,595	ISLAMABAD	460
PALAU	0.46	0.18	17	KOROR	2,260
PANAMA	77.1	29.8	2,629	PANAMA CITY	2,750
PAPUA NEW GUINEA	463	179	4,292	PORT MORESBY	1,160
PARAGUAY	407	157	4,979	ASUNCIÓN	1,690
PERU	1,285	496	23,588	LIMA	2,310
PHILIPPINES	300	116	67,167	MANILA	1,050
PITCAIRN IS. (UK)	0.03	0.01	0.07	ADAMSTOWN	–
POLAND	313	121	38,587	WARSAW	2,290
PORTUGAL	92.4	35.7	10,600	LISBON	9,740
PUERTO RICO (US)	9	3.5	3,689	SAN JUAN	7,500
QATAR	11	4.2	594	DOHA	11,600
RÉUNION (FR.)	2.5	0.97	655	SAINT-DENIS	4,500
ROMANIA	238	92	22,863	BUCHAREST	1,480

Country/Territory	Area (1,000 sq km)	Area (1,000 sq mls)	Population (1,000s)	Capital City	Annual Income US$
RUSSIA	17,075	6,592	148,385	MOSCOW	2,240
RWANDA	26.3	10.2	7,899	KIGALI	180
ST HELENA (UK)	0.12	0.04	6	JAMESTOWN	–
ST KITTS-NEVIS	0.36	0.14	45	BASSETERRE	5,170
ST LUCIA	0.62	0.24	147	CASTRIES	3,370
ST VINCENT & GRENADINES	0.39	0.15	111	KINGSTOWN	2,280
SAN MARINO	0.06	0.02	26	SAN MARINO	20,000
SÃO TOMÉ & PRÍNCIPE	0.96	0.37	133	SÃO TOMÉ	350
SAUDI ARABIA	2,150	830	18,395	RIYADH	7,040
SENEGAL	197	76	8,308	DAKAR	600
SEYCHELLES	0.46	0.18	75	VICTORIA	6,620
SIERRA LEONE	71.7	27.7	4,467	FREETOWN	180
SINGAPORE	0.62	0.24	2,990	SINGAPORE	26,730
SLOVAK REPUBLIC	49	18.9	5,400	BRATISLAVA	2,950
SLOVENIA	20.3	7.8	2,000	LJUBLJANA	8,200
SOLOMON IS.	28.9	11.2	378	HONIARA	910
SOMALIA	638	246	9,180	MOGADISHU	500
SOUTH AFRICA	1,220	471	44,000	C. TOWN/PRET./BLOEM.	3,160
SPAIN	505	195	39,664	MADRID	13,580
SRI LANKA	65.6	25.3	18,359	COLOMBO	700
SUDAN	2,506	967	29,980	KHARTOUM	750
SURINAM	163	63	421	PARAMARIBO	880
SWAZILAND	17.4	6.7	849	MBABANE	1,170
SWEDEN	450	174	8,893	STOCKHOLM	23,750
SWITZERLAND	41.3	15.9	7,268	BERN	40,630
SYRIA	185	71	14,614	DAMASCUS	1,120
TAIWAN	36	13.9	21,100	TAIPEI	12,000
TAJIKISTAN	143.1	55.2	6,102	DUSHANBE	340
TANZANIA	945	365	29,710	DODOMA	120
THAILAND	513	198	58,432	BANGKOK	2,740
TOGO	56.8	21.9	4,140	LOMÉ	310
TONGA	0.75	0.29	107	NUKU'ALOFA	1,630
TRINIDAD & TOBAGO	5.1	2	1,295	PORT OF SPAIN	3,770
TRISTAN DA CUNHA (UK)	0.11	0.04	0.33	EDINBURGH	–
TUNISIA	164	63	8,906	TUNIS	1,820
TURKEY	779	301	61,330	ANKARA	2,780
TURKMENISTAN	488.1	188.5	4,100	ASHKHABAD	920
TURKS & CAICOS IS. (UK)	0.43	0.17	15	COCKBURN TOWN	5,000
TUVALU	0.03	0.01	10	FONGAFALE	600
UGANDA	236	91	21,466	KAMPALA	240
UKRAINE	603.7	233.1	52,027	KIEV	1,630
UNITED ARAB EMIRATES	83.6	32.3	2,800	ABU DHABI	17,400
UNITED KINGDOM	243.3	94	58,306	LONDON	18,700
UNITED STATES OF AMERICA	9,373	3,619	263,563	WASHINGTON, DC	26,980
URUGUAY	177	68	3,186	MONTEVIDEO	5,170
UZBEKISTAN	447.4	172.7	22,833	TASHKENT	970
VANUATU	12.2	4.7	167	PORT-VILA	1,200
VATICAN CITY	0.0004	0.0002	1	–	–
VENEZUELA	912	352	21,810	CARACAS	3,020
VIETNAM	332	127	74,580	HANOI	240
VIRGIN IS. (UK)	0.15	0.06	20	ROAD TOWN	–
VIRGIN IS. (US)	0.34	0.13	105	CHARLOTTE AMALIE	12,000
WALLIS & FUTUNA IS. (FR.)	0.20	0.08	13	MATA-UTU	–
WESTERN SAHARA	266	103	220	EL AAIÚN	300
WESTERN SAMOA	2.8	1.1	169	APIA	1,120
YEMEN	528	204	14,609	SANA	260
YUGOSLAVIA	102.3	39.5	10,881	BELGRADE	1,400
ZAMBIA	753	291	9,500	LUSAKA	400
ZIMBABWE	391	151	11,453	HARARE	540

TIME ZONES

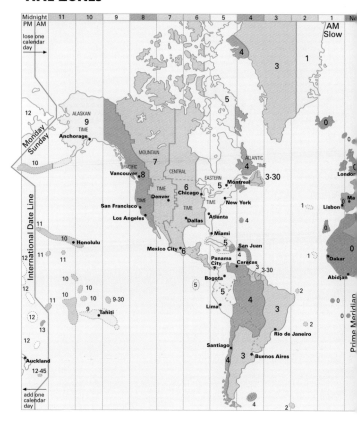

The world is divided into 24 time zones, each centred on meridians at 15° intervals, which is the longitudinal distance the sun travels every hour. The meridian running through Greenwich in London, England, passes through the middle of the first time zone. Zones to the east of Greenwich are ahead of Greenwich Mean Time (GMT) by one hour for every 15° of longitude, while zones to the west are behind GMT by one hour.

When it is 12 noon at the Greenwich meridian, 180° east it is midnight on the same day, while at 180° west the day is only just beginning. To overcome this, the International Date Line was established in 1883 – an imaginary line which approximately follows the 180th meridian. Therefore, if one travelled eastwards from Japan (140° East) towards Samoa (170° West), one would pass from Sunday night straight into Sunday morning.

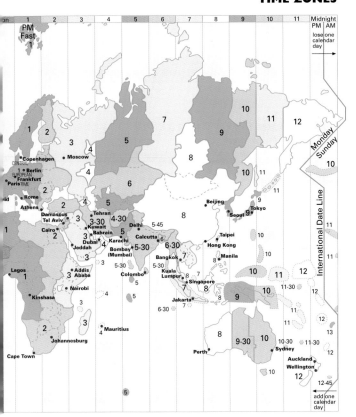

TIME DIFFERENCES FROM GMT (LONDON)

BEIJING	+8	BANGKOK	+7
CHICAGO	−6	DELHI	+5.30
JO'BURG	+2	LAGOS	+1
LOS ANGELES	−8	MEXICO CITY	−6
MOSCOW	+3	NEW YORK	−5
PARIS	+1	ROME	+1
SYDNEY	+10	TEHRAN	+3.30
TOKYO	+9	TORONTO	−5

KEY TO TIME ZONES MAP

	Zones using GMT		Zones fast of GMT
	Zones slow of GMT		Half-hour zones
− − −	International boundaries		Time zone boundaries
10	Hours slow or fast of GMT		International Date Line

Actual Solar Time, when it is noon at Greenwich, is shown along the top of the map.

Note: Certain time zones are affected by the incidence of 'summer' time' in countries where it is adopted.

FLIGHT PATHS

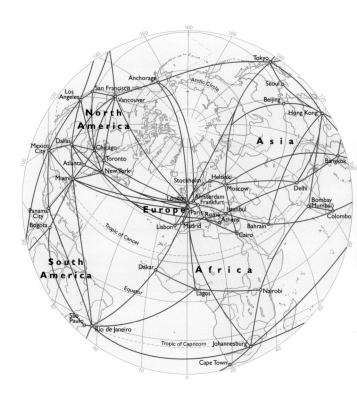

BUSIEST AIRPORTS

(NUMBER OF PASSENGERS, 1996)

CHICAGO O'HARE	67,253,000
ATLANTA HARTSFIELD	57,735,000
DALLAS/FORT WORTH	56,491,000
LONDON HEATHROW	54,453,000
LOS ANGELES INTL.	53,909,000
TOKYO HANEDA	45,823,000
FRANKFURT/MAIN	38,178,000
SAN FRANCISCO INTL.	36,263,000

The flight paths shown on the maps above usually follow the shortest, most direct route from A to B, known as the *great-circle route*. A great circle is any circle that divides the globe into equal halves. Aircraft do not always fly along great-circle routes, however. Lack of search and rescue and emergency landing provisions, together with limits on fuel consumption and minimum flying altitudes, mean that commercial aircraft do not usually fly across Antarctica.

FLIGHT PATHS

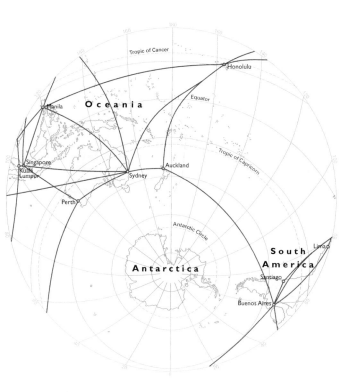

FLIGHT TIMES FROM LONDON		FLIGHT TIMES FROM NEW YORK	
ATHENS	4hrs 05mins	FRANKFURT	8hrs 35mins
AUCKLAND	24hrs 20mins	JOHANNESBURG	17hrs 45mins
BANGKOK	14hrs 30mins	MEXICO CITY	5hrs 45mins
BOMBAY (MUMBAI)	11hrs 15mins	PARIS	8hrs 15mins
BUENOS AIRES	14hrs 20mins	ROME	9hrs 35mins
HONG KONG	14hrs 10mins	SANTIAGO	12hrs 55mins
LOS ANGELES	12hrs 00mins	SINGAPORE	23hrs 10mins
MOSCOW	3hrs 50mins	TOKYO	14hrs 35mins
NEW YORK	6hrs 50mins	VANCOUVER	7hrs 25mins

CLIMATE

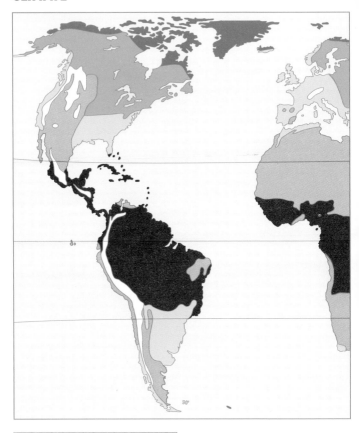

SEASONAL WEATHER EXTREMES

- **Caribbean**
  Hurricanes – August to October

- **Northern Latitudes**
  Blizzards – November to March

- **Southern Asia**
  Cyclones and typhoons – June to November

- **Southern Asia**
  Monsoon rains – July to October

Climate is weather in the long term: the seasonal pattern of temperature and precipitation averaged over a period of time. Temperature roughly follows latitude, warmest near the equator and coldest near the poles. The interplay of various factors, however, namely the differential heating of land and sea, the influence of landmasses and mountain ranges on winds and ocean currents, and the effect of vegetation,

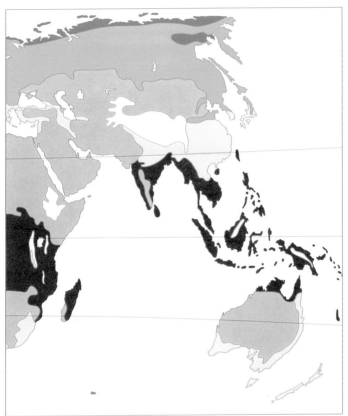

combine to add complexity. Thus New York, Naples and the Gobi Desert share almost the same latitude, but their resulting climates are very different.

Most scientists are now in agreement that the world's climate is changing, due partly to atmospheric pollution. By the year 2050 average world temperatures are predicted to rise by 1.5–2.8°C to make it hotter than at any time during the last 120,000 years.

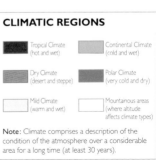

CLIMATIC REGIONS

Tropical Climate (hot and wet)

Continental Climate (cold and wet)

Dry Climate (desert and steppe)

Polar Climate (very cold and dry)

Mild Climate (warm and wet)

Mountainous areas (where altitude affects climate types)

Note: Climate comprises a description of the condition of the atmosphere over a considerable area for a long time (at least 30 years).

The most commonly used method of classifying countries according to economic well-being is to calculate the Gross National Product (GNP) per capita (a measure of average income). The World Bank identifies three main groups according to GNP. These are known as high-income, middle-income and low-income economies. Sometimes low- and middle-income economies are referred to as developing countries.

Poverty in developing countries is often exacerbated by crippling debts. In these cases aid from abroad is vital to the population and the economy. The latest figures show that aid to Mozambique (the poorest country in the world with a GNP per capita of only US$80) amounts to more than 70% of its total GNP. In contrast, the country with the world's highest GNP per capita is Luxembourg with US$41,210.

EXCHANGE RATES 1997

(UNITS PER US$)

ARGENTINA	1.00	ITALY	1,722
AUSTRALIA	1.38	JAPAN	121
BELGIUM	36.4	MEXICO	7.82
CANADA	1.39	RUSSIA	5,866
FRANCE	5.92	S. AFRICA	4.68
GERMANY	1.76	SPAIN	149
HONG KONG	7.74	SWEDEN	7.58
INDIA	36.2	UK	0.62

LEVELS OF INCOME

Gross National Product per capita: the value of total production divided by the population (1995)

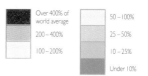

Over 400% of world average

200 – 400%

100 – 200%

50 – 100%

25 – 50%

10 – 25%

Under 10%

[World average wealth per person US$5,714]

INTERNATIONAL ORGANIZATIONS

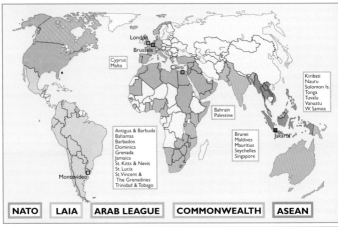

London
Brussels
Cyprus
Malta
Cairo

Kiribati
Nauru
Solomon Is.
Tonga
Tuvalu
Vanuatu
W. Samoa

Bahrain
Palestine

Antigua & Barbuda
Bahamas
Barbados
Dominica
Grenada
Jamaica
St. Kitts & Nevis
St. Lucia
St. Vincent &
The Grenadines
Trinidad & Tobago

Brunei
Maldives
Mauritius
Seychelles
Singapore

Jakarta

Montevideo

| NATO | LAIA | ARAB LEAGUE | COMMONWEALTH | ASEAN |

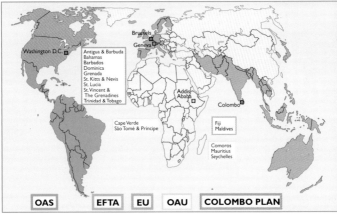

Brussels
Geneva

Washington D.C.

Antigua & Barbuda
Bahamas
Barbados
Dominica
Grenada
St. Kitts & Nevis
St. Lucia
St. Vincent &
The Grenadines
Trinidad & Tobago

Addis
Ababa

Colombo

Cape Verde
São Tomé & Principe

Fiji
Maldives

Comoros
Mauritius
Seychelles

| OAS | EFTA | EU | OAU | COLOMBO PLAN |

GLOSSARY OF ACRONYMS

ACP	African-Caribbean-Pacific	**NATO**	North Atlantic Treaty Organization
ASEAN	Association of South-east Asian Nations	**OAS**	Organization of American States
CIS	Commonwealth of Nations	**OAU**	Organization of African Unity
EFTA	European Free Trade Association	**OECD**	Organization for Economic Co-operation and Development
EU	European Union	**OPEC**	Organization for Petroleum Exporting Countries
LAIA	Latin American Integration Association		

INTERNATIONAL ORGANIZATIONS

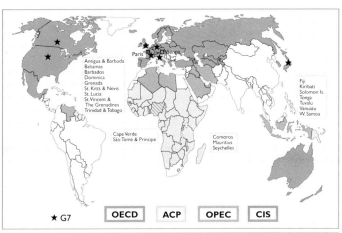

Antigua & Barbuda
Bahamas
Barbados
Dominica
Grenada
St. Kitts & Nevis
St. Lucia
St. Vincent &
The Grenadines
Trinidad & Tobago

Paris

Vienna

Fiji
Kiribati
Solomon Is.
Tonga
Tuvalu
Vanuatu
W. Samoa

Cape Verde
São Tomé & Príncipe

Comoros
Mauritius
Seychelles

★ G7

| OECD | ACP | OPEC | CIS |

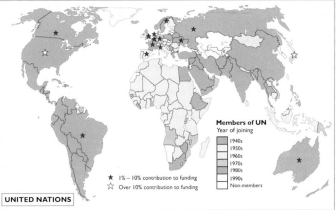

Members of UN
Year of joining

1940s
1950s
1960s
1970s
1980s
1990s
Non-members

★ 1% – 10% contribution to funding
☆ Over 10% contribution to funding

UNITED NATIONS

THE UNITED NATIONS

Created in 1945 to promote peace and co-operation and based in New York, the UN is the world's largest international organization. The UN budget for 1996–7 was US$2.61 billion; the US contributed the most with 25%, followed by Japan 12.5%, then Germany 8.9%. From the original 51, membership of the UN has grown to 185. Recent additions include Andorra, Bosnia-Herzegovina, Moldova, Palau, San Marino and the Slovak Republic. There are only seven independent states which are not members – Kiribati, Nauru, Switzerland, Taiwan, Tonga, Tuvalu and the Vatican City.

WORLD GAZETTEER

AUSTRALIA

AREA 7,686,850 sq km / 2,967,893 sq mls
POPULATION 18,107,000
CAPITAL Canberra
GOVERNMENT Federal constitutional monarchy
LANGUAGES English (official)
CURRENCY Australian dollar
EMPLOYMENT Agriculture 5%, industry 16%, services 78%

CANADA

AREA 9,976,140 sq km / 3,851,788 sq mls
POPULATION 29,972,000
CAPITAL Ottawa
GOVERNMENT Federal constitutional monarchy
LANGUAGES English and French (official)
CURRENCY Canadian dollar
EMPLOYMENT Agriculture 3%, industry 19%, services 77%

BELGIUM

AREA 30,510 sq km / 11,780 sq mls
POPULATION 10,140,000
CAPITAL Brussels
GOVERNMENT Constitutional monarchy
LANGUAGES Dutch, French, German (all official)
CURRENCY Belgian franc
EMPLOYMENT Agriculture 3%, industry 20%, services 78%

CHINA

AREA 9,596,960 sq km / 3,705,386 sq mls
POPULATION 1,226,944,000
CAPITAL Beijing (Peking)
GOVERNMENT Single-party Communist state
LANGUAGES Mandarin Chinese (official)
CURRENCY Renminbi yuan
EMPLOYMENT Agriculture 74%, industry 14%, services 13%

BRAZIL

AREA 8,511,970 sq km / 3,286,472 sq mls
POPULATION 161,416,000
CAPITAL Brasília
GOVERNMENT Federal multiparty republic
LANGUAGES Portuguese (official)
CURRENCY Cruzeiro real
EMPLOYMENT Agriculture 29%, industry 16%, services 55%

CZECH REPUBLIC

AREA 78,864 sq km / 30,449 sq mls
POPULATION 10,500,000
CAPITAL Prague
GOVERNMENT Multiparty democratic republic
LANGUAGES Czech (official)
CURRENCY Czech koruna
EMPLOYMENT Agriculture 13%, industry 49%, services 37%

DENMARK

AREA 43,070 sq km/16,629 sq mls
POPULATION 5,229,000
CAPITAL Copenhagen
GOVERNMENT Democratic constitutional monarchy
LANGUAGES Danish (official)
CURRENCY Danish krone
EMPLOYMENT Agriculture 5%, industry 22%, services 60%

EGYPT

AREA 1,001,450 sq km/386,660 sq mls
POPULATION 64,100,000
CAPITAL Cairo (El Qâhira)
GOVERNMENT Multiparty republic
LANGUAGES Arabic (official), French, English
CURRENCY Egyptian pound
EMPLOYMENT Agriculture 34%, industry 22%, services 60%

FRANCE

AREA 551,500 sq km/212,934 sq mls
POPULATION 58,286,000
CAPITAL Paris
GOVERNMENT Multiparty democratic republic
LANGUAGES French (official)
CURRENCY French franc
EMPLOYMENT Agriculture 7%, industry 20%, services 74%

GERMANY

AREA 356,910 sq km/137,803 sq mls
POPULATION 82,000,000
CAPITAL Berlin/Bonn
GOVERNMENT Federal multiparty republic
LANGUAGES German (official)
CURRENCY Deutsche mark
EMPLOYMENT Agriculture 4%, industry 30%, services 66%

GREECE

AREA 131,990 sq km/50,961 sq mls
POPULATION 10,510,000
CAPITAL Athens
GOVERNMENT Multiparty democratic republic
LANGUAGES Greek (official)
CURRENCY Greek drachma
EMPLOYMENT Agriculture 25%, industry 19%, services 56%

HUNGARY

AREA 93,030 sq km/35,919 sq mls
POPULATION 10,500,000
CAPITAL Budapest
GOVERNMENT Multiparty democratic republic
LANGUAGES Hungarian (official)
CURRENCY Hungarian forint
EMPLOYMENT Agriculture 6%, industry 28%, services 66%

INDIA

AREA 3,287,590 sq km/1,269,338 sq mls
POPULATION 942,989,000
CAPITAL New Delhi
GOVERNMENT Federal multiparty republic
LANGUAGES Hindi and English (both official)
CURRENCY Indian rupee
EMPLOYMENT Agriculture 63%, industry 11%, services 27%

JAPAN

AREA 377,800 sq km/145,869 sq mls
POPULATION 125,156,000
CAPITAL Tokyo
GOVERNMENT Democratic constitutional monarchy
LANGUAGES Japanese (official)
CURRENCY Japanese yen
EMPLOYMENT Agriculture 7%, industry 24%, services 69%

IRELAND

AREA 70,280 sq km/27,135 sq mls
POPULATION 3,589,000
CAPITAL Dublin
GOVERNMENT Multiparty democratic republic
LANGUAGES Irish and English (both official)
CURRENCY Irish pound (Punt)
EMPLOYMENT Agriculture 13%, industry 18%, services 69%

MEXICO

AREA 1,958,200 sq km/756,061 sq mls
POPULATION 93,342,000
CAPITAL Mexico City
GOVERNMENT Multiparty democratic republic
LANGUAGES Spanish (official)
CURRENCY Mexican peso
EMPLOYMENT Agriculture 23%, industry 20%, services 57%

ITALY

AREA 301,270 sq km/116,320 sq mls
POPULATION 57,181,000
CAPITAL Rome
GOVERNMENT Multiparty democratic republic
LANGUAGES Italian (official)
CURRENCY Italian lira
EMPLOYMENT Agriculture 9%, industry 20%, services 71%

NETHERLANDS

AREA 41,526 sq km/16,033 sq mls
POPULATION 15,495,000
CAPITAL Amsterdam/The Hague
GOVERNMENT Democratic constitutional monarchy
LANGUAGES Dutch (official)
CURRENCY Dutch guilder (florin)
EMPLOYMENT Agriculture 4%, industry 17%, services 78%

NEW ZEALAND

AREA 268,680 sq km/103,737 sq mls
POPULATION 3,567,000
CAPITAL Wellington
GOVERNMENT Parliamentary democracy
LANGUAGES English and Maori (both official)
CURRENCY New Zealand dollar
EMPLOYMENT Agriculture 10%, industry 20%, services 70%

RUSSIA

AREA 17,075,000 sq km/6,592,000 sq mls
POPULATION 148,385,000
CAPITAL Moscow
GOVERNMENT Federal multiparty republic
LANGUAGES Russian (official), Ukrainian, Belarussian and others
CURRENCY Russian rouble
EMPLOYMENT Agriculture 13%, industry 28%, services 59%

NIGERIA

AREA 923,770 sq km/356,668 sq mls
POPULATION 88,515,000
CAPITAL Abuja (Federal Capital Territory)
GOVERNMENT Transitional government
LANGUAGES English (official)
CURRENCY Nigerian naira
EMPLOYMENT Agriculture 45%, industry 4%, services 51%

SAUDI ARABIA

AREA 2,149,690 sq km/829,995 sq mls
POPULATION 18,395,000
CAPITAL Riyadh
GOVERNMENT Absolute monarchy (with a consultative assembly)
LANGUAGES Arabic (official)
CURRENCY Saudi riyal
EMPLOYMENT Agriculture 49%, industry 14%, services 37%

POLAND

AREA 312,680 sq km/120,726 sq mls
POPULATION 38,587,000
CAPITAL Warsaw
GOVERNMENT Multiparty democratic republic
LANGUAGES Polish (official)
CURRENCY Polish zloty
EMPLOYMENT Agriculture 28%, industry 28%, services 44%

SINGAPORE

AREA 618 sq km/239 sq mls
POPULATION 2,990,000
CAPITAL Singapore City
GOVERNMENT Multiparty republic
LANGUAGES Chinese, Malay, Tamil and English (all official)
CURRENCY Singapore dollar
EMPLOYMENT Agriculture 1%, industry 29%, services 71%

WORLD GAZETTEER

SOUTH AFRICA

AREA 1,219,916 sq km/470,566 sq mls
POPULATION 44,000,000
CAPITAL Cape Town/Pretoria/
Bloemfontein
GOVERNMENT Multiparty republic
LANGUAGES Afrikaans, English, 9 others
CURRENCY South African rand
EMPLOYMENT Agriculture 3%, industry
24%, services 68%

SWITZERLAND

AREA 41,290 sq km/15,942 sq mls
POPULATION 7,268,000
CAPITAL Bern
GOVERNMENT Federal republic
LANGUAGES French, German, Italian and
Romansch (all official)
CURRENCY Swiss franc
EMPLOYMENT Agriculture 6%, industry
30%, services 64%

SPAIN

AREA 504,780 sq km/194,896 sq mls
POPULATION 39,664,000
CAPITAL Madrid
GOVERNMENT Constitutional monarchy
LANGUAGES Castilian Spanish (official),
Catalan, Galician, Basque
CURRENCY Spanish peseta
EMPLOYMENT Agriculture 11%, industry
21%, services 68%

UNITED KINGDOM

AREA 243,368 sq km/94,202 sq mls
POPULATION 58,306,000
CAPITAL London
GOVERNMENT Democratic constitutional
monarchy
LANGUAGES English (official)
CURRENCY Pound sterling
EMPLOYMENT Agriculture 2%, industry
20%, services 78%

SWEDEN

AREA 449,960 sq km/173,730 sq mls
POPULATION 8,893,000
CAPITAL Stockholm
GOVERNMENT Democratic constitutional
monarchy
LANGUAGES Swedish (official), Finnish
CURRENCY Swedish krona
EMPLOYMENT Agriculture 3%, industry
22%, services 75%

UNITED STATES

AREA 9,372,610 sq km/3,618,765 sq mls
POPULATION 263,563,000
CAPITAL Washington, DC
GOVERNMENT Federal republic
LANGUAGES English (official) and over
30 others
CURRENCY US dollar
EMPLOYMENT Agriculture 3%, industry
18%, services 79%

WORLD MAPS – GENERAL REFERENCE

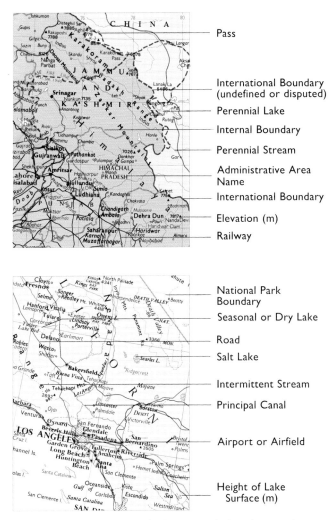

Pass

International Boundary
(undefined or disputed)

Perennial Lake

Internal Boundary

Perennial Stream

Administrative Area
Name

International Boundary

Elevation (m)

Railway

National Park
Boundary

Seasonal or Dry Lake

Road

Salt Lake

Intermittent Stream

Principal Canal

Airport or Airfield

Height of Lake
Surface (m)

Settlements

Settlement symbols and type styles vary
according to the scale of each map and
indicate the importance of towns rather
than specific population figures.

TIME ZONES

Zones using Greenwich Mean Time

Zones fast of Greenwich Mean Time

Zones slow of Greenwich Mean Time

Standard Time not the Zone hour

No Official Time

Projection: Oblique Azimuthal Equidistant

PROJECTION CENTRED ON SAN FRANCISCO

PROJECTION CENTRED ON CAPE TOWN

CARTOGRAPHY BY PHILIP'S. COPYRIGHT REED INTERNATIONAL BOOKS LTD

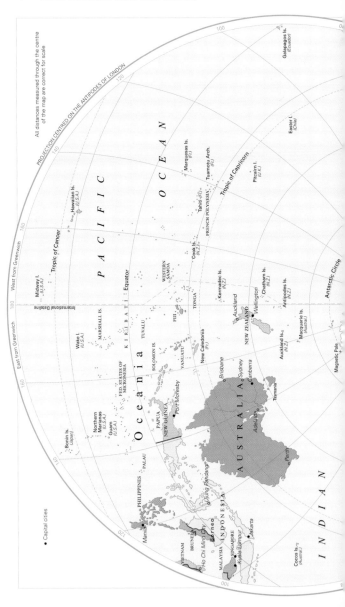

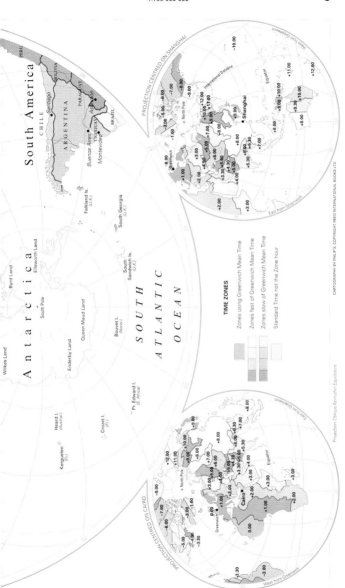

PROJECTION CENTRED ON SHANGHAI

South America

PERU
CHILE
BOLIVIA
PARAGUAY
ARGENTINA
BRAZIL
URUGUAY
Santiago
Buenos Aires
Montevideo
Asunción

Falkland Is.
(U.K.)

South Georgia
(U.K.)

South Sandwich Is.
(U.K.)

Wilkes Land
Byrd Land
Ellsworth Land

A n t a r c t i c a
+ South Pole

Enderby Land
Queen Maud Land

Bouvet I.
(Norw.)

S O U T H

A T L A N T I C

O C E A N

Pr. Edward I.
(S. African)

Crozet I.
(Fr.)

Heard I.
(Austral.)

Kerguelen
(Fr.)

International Dateline
+ North Pole
Greenwich
Equator
Shanghai

East from Greenwich
West from Greenwich
Mean from Greenwich

TIME ZONES

Zones using Greenwich Mean Time

Zones fast of Greenwich Mean Time

Zones slow of Greenwich Mean Time

Standard Time not the Zone hour

PROJECTION CENTRED ON CAIRO

Projection Oblique Azimuthal Equidistant

Greenwich
Equator
+ North Pole
Cairo

CARTOGRAPHY BY PHILIP'S, COPYRIGHT REED INTERNATIONAL BOOKS LTD

C

1 30 25 2 20 3 15 4 10 5 6 5 7 10 8 15 S

ICELAND
Reykjavik

Arctic Circle

N o r w e g i a n

S e a

Trom

60

Faroe Is.
(Den.)

D

SWEDE

Trondheim

Shetland
Is.

NORWAY

Bergen   Oslo

Örebro

Uppsala

55

Hebrides

Orkney
Is.

Stavanger

Gd

A T L A N T I C

**UNITED
KINGDOM**

SCOTLAND
Glasgow   Dundee
Edinburgh

Aberdeen

Skagerrak

Kattegat

Yttran

Vättern

Jönköping

E

IRELAND
Belfast

N o r t h

DENMARK
Ålborg

Go

Gothenburg

Malmö

IRELAND

Dublin

Manchester
Liverpool
Cork

Newcastle-
upon-Tyne
Leeds
Sheffield

S e a

Århus

Copenhagen

Ba

50

WALES
Cardiff

Birmingham
ENGLAND
Bristol

Kiel

Hamburg

Gdańsk

Szczecin

P O

Bydgoszcz

Plymouth

Southampton

LONDON

Amsterdam
The Hague
Rotterdam

**NETHER-
LANDS**

Bremen

Hannover

Elbe

Magdeburg

Berlin

Oder

Poznań

F

O C E A N

English Channel

Antwerp

BELGIUM

Essen
Dortmund

GERMANY

Halle

Leipzig

Dresden

Wrocł

Channel Is.
(U.K.)
Brest

Le Havre

Rouen

Brussels

Cologne
Bonn

Wiesbaden

Frankfurt

Chemnitz

Prague

Katowice

Ostrava

Seine

PARIS

LUX.
Luxembourg

am Main

CZECH REP.

S

45

F R A N C E

Strasbourg

Rhine

Nuremberg

Nantes

Loire

Dijon

Stuttgart

Munich

Vienna

Bratisl

G

Limoges

Lyons

SWITZERLAND
Geneva

Zürich
LIECH

Innsbruck

Salzburg

AUSTRIA

Linz

Graz

HUN

B a y   o f

B i s c a y

Bordeaux

St-Étienne

Garonne

Toulouse

Grenoble

Rhône

Milan

SLOVENIA
Ljubljana

Zagreb

Vaduz

Venice

Trieste

CROATIA

Vigo

La Coruña

Bilbao

ANDORRA
Andorra
la Vella

Ebro

Nice

MONACO

Turin

Genoa

Bologna

Florence

**SAN
MARINO**

**BOSNIA
HERZ.**

Adriatic

Split

Sarajevo

Porto

Douro

Valladolid

Zaragoza

Marseilles

Toulon

Corsica

ITALY

Sea

H

PORTUGAL

Lisbon

Tagus

Madrid

SPAIN

Barcelona

Valencia

Ajaccio

Rome

Naples

Bari

Taranto

Guadiana

Seville

Córdoba
Guadalquivir

Granada

Murcia

Alicante

Balearic
Is.
Ibiza

Palma
Minorca
Majorca

Sardinia

Tyrrhenian

35

Cádiz

Str. of Gibraltar
Tangier

Málaga
Gibraltar (U.K.)
Ceuta (Sp.)

Melilla (Sp.)

Algiers

M e d i t e r r a n e a n

Cagliari

Sea

Palermo

Messina

Sicily

Catania

Ion i

Se

J

MOROCCO

A f r i c a

ALGERIA

Annaba

Constantine

TUNISIA

Tunis

Pantelleria
(Italy)

MALTA

Valletta

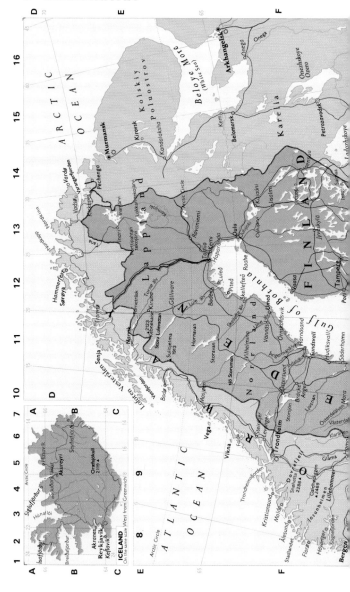

ARCTIC OCEAN

Kolskiy Poluostrov

Beloye More (White Sea)

Murmansk

Kirovsk

Kandalaksha

Karelia

Kem

Belomorsk

Arkhangelsk

Onega

Onezhskoye Ozero

Petrozavodsk

Vardø

Vadsø Varangerfjorden

Pechenga

Nordkapp

Nordkinn

Hammerfest

Sørøya

Inari

Ivalo

Inarijärvi

Lakselv

Karasjok

Arctic Circle

Kautokeino

Enontekiö

Kittilä

Rovaniemi

LAPPLAND

Kemijärvi

Isalmi

Oulujärvi

Oulu

Oulujoki

Kajaani

Oulu

Kemi

Tornio

Haparanda

Raahe

Kokkola

FINLAND

Tampere

Pori

Senja

Narvik

2123

Vesterålen

Lofoten

Kiruna

Fjällfjäll

Gällivare

Stora Lulevatn

Sulitjelma 1913

Suitjelma

Torne älv

Luleå

Boden

Piteå

Skellefteå

Luleälven

Umeälven

Vindelälven

Umeå

NORRLAND

Vaasa

Gulf of Bothnia

Jyväskylä

Vega

Vefsna

Bodø

Mo i Rana

Hornavan

Storavan

Storuman

Storuman

Skellefte älv

Ångermanälven

Härnösand

Sundsvall

Hudiksvall

Söderhamn

Vesterålen

Vestfjorden

Vega

Vikna

Namsos

Steinkjer

Trondheim

Stjørdal

Orkla

Østersund

Storsjön

Brakke

Ange

Ljusnan

Östersund

Mora

Österdalälven

Västerdal

Klara älv

Kristiansund

Trondheimsfjorden

Molde

Dovrefjell

Snøhetta 2286

Galdhøpiggen 2469

Jotunheimen

Dovre

Lillehammer

Glåma

Ålesund

Stadlandet

Florø

Høyanger

Sognefjorden

Bergen

ATLANTIC OCEAN

Arctic Circle

ICELAND
On the same scale West from Greenwich

Ísafjörður

Breiðafjörður

Húnaflói

Arctic Circle

Siglufjörður

Hófsós

Sauðárkrókur

Blönduós

Akureyri

Seyðisfjörður

Öræfajökull 2119

Akranes

Reykjavík

Keflavík

1: 13 300 000

CARTOGRAPHY BY PHILIP'S. COPYRIGHT REED INTERNATIONAL BOOKS LTD.

Projection: Conical with two standard parallels

East from Greenwich

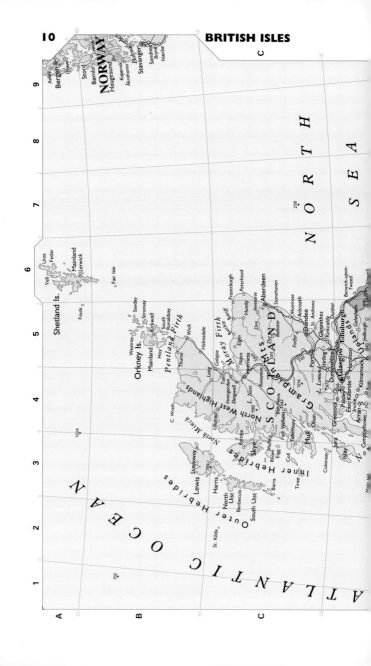

NORWAY

Bergen
Askøy
Øygar
Stord
Bømlo
Haugesund
Kopervik
Åkrahamn
Stavanger
Sandnes
Bryne
Nærbø

Shetland Is.
Yell
Unst
Fetlar
Mainland
Lerwick
Fair Isle
Foula

Orkney Is.
Westray
Sanday
Stronsay
Mainland
Kirkwall
Hoy
South Ronaldsay

Pentland Firth
Thurso
Wick
Helmsdale
Golspie

Moray Firth
Tain
Inverness
Lairg
L. Ness
Elgin
Nairn

C. Wrath
Ullapool
Dingwall
Invergordon

North West Highlands
Aviemore

Stornoway
Lewis
Harris
North Uist
Benbecula
South Uist
Barra
St. Kilda

Outer Hebrides

North Minch

Skye
Portree
Mallaig
Rhum
Eigg
Ben Nevis 1342
Fort William

Inner Hebrides

Tiree
Coll
Mull
Tobermory
Oban
Colonsay
Jura
Islay
N. of Kintyre
Campbeltown

SCOTLAND

Grampian Mts.
1224

Fraserburgh
Peterhead
Aberdeen
Banff
Huntly
Stonehaven
Don
Inverurie
Ballater
Brechin
Montrose
Arbroath
Forfar
Dundee
St. Andrews
Perth
Kirkcaldy
Glenrothes
Dunfermline
Stirling
L. Lomond
Greenock
Paisley
Glasgow
Hamilton
East Kilbride
Irvine
Kilmarnock
Arran
Ayr

Edinburgh
Dunbar
Berwick-upon-Tweed
Galashiels
Jedburgh 840
Hawick
Alnwick

NORTH SEA
238

ATLANTIC OCEAN
396
1224

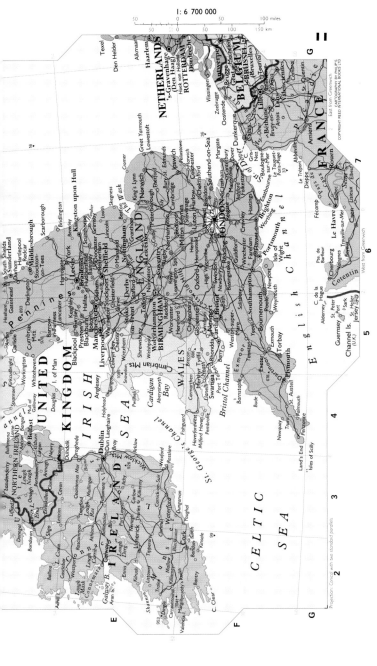

1: 6 700 000

50   0   100 miles
50   0   50   100 150 km

Projection: Conical with two standard parallels

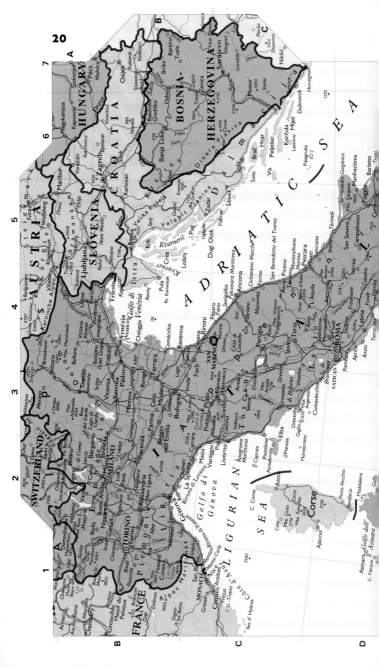

1: 6 700 000

50   0   50   100 miles

50   0   50   100   150 km

E   **F**   **G**

CARTOGRAPHY BY PHILIP'S. COPYRIGHT REED INTERNATIONAL BOOKS LTD.

East from Greenwich

Projection: Conical with two standard parallels

I O N I A N   S E A

Golfo di Táranto

Rossano Calabro
Crotone
Catanzaro
C. Rizzuto

Str. di Messina

Reggio di Calàbria
C. Spartivento

Messina
Milazzo
Ísole Eòlie
Strómboli
Lípari
Salina
Vulcano

Cefalù
Monti Nèbrodi
Barcellona
Pozzo di Gotto
Patti
Giarre
Acireale
Etna 3340
Catània
Augusta
Siracusa
Avola
C. Passero

Paternò
Adrano
Enna
Lentini
Módica
Ragusa
Vittòria
Gela
Licata
Caltagirone
Caltanissetta
Canicattì
Favara
Agrigento

Sciacca
Porto Empèdocle

Palermo
Monreale
Golfo di Castellammare
Alcamo
Partinico
Castelvetrano
Mazara del Vallo
Marsala
Trápani
Érice
Ísole Ègadi
Favignana

S I C I L I A (SICILY)

Ústica (Italy)

Valletta
MALTA
Gozo
Rabat

Pantelleria (Italy)

M E D I T E R R A N E A N   S E A

J. Linosa
Lampione
Ísole Pelagie (Italy)
Lampedusa

T Y R R H E N I A N

S E A

3580

Sardegna

C. Comino
C. di Monte Santu
Arbatax
Tortolì

Mte. di Gennargentu
1834

C. Carbonara
Cagliari
Quartu Sant' Elena
Sant' Elena

San Pietro
Sant' Antioco
Carbònia
G. di Palmas
C. Spartivento
C. Teulada

Iglésias
Oristano
G. di Oristano

Bosa
Macomer

NÀPOLI
Ischia
Torre del Greco
Castellammare
Capri
Sorrento

Salerno
Battipaglia
Agrópoli
Piscotta

Eboli
Potenza
Matera

Lecce
Brindisi
Gallìpoli
Otranto
Nardò

Táranto

Martina Franco

Cosenza
Nicastro
Vibo Valéntia
Pàola
Palmi
Cetraro

T U N I S I A

Tunis
Golfe de Tunis
C. Bon
Kélibia
Ras Mostefa
Menzel-Temime
Nabeul
Hammamet
Golfe de Hammamet
Soliman
Ben Arous
Bizerte
Menzel-Bourguiba
Mateur
Tébourba
Manouba
Bardo
La Goulette
Zaghouan
Grombalia
Korba
Sousse
Monastir
Kalaa-Kebira
Moknine
Mahdia
Medjez-el-Bab
Téboursouk
El Fahs
Testour
Kairouan
Hamman Sousse
Maktar
C. Blanc
C. Serrat
Is. de la Galite (Tunisia)

A L G E R I A
Souk Ahras
Guelma
Tébessa
Ain Beïda
Kasserine
Thala
Sbeïtla
Sfax
Sidi Bou Zid
Feriana
Sbiba
Gafsa
Metlaoui
Haïdra

Oued Mellègue

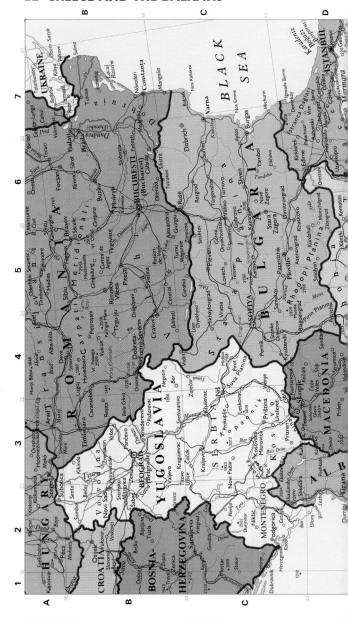

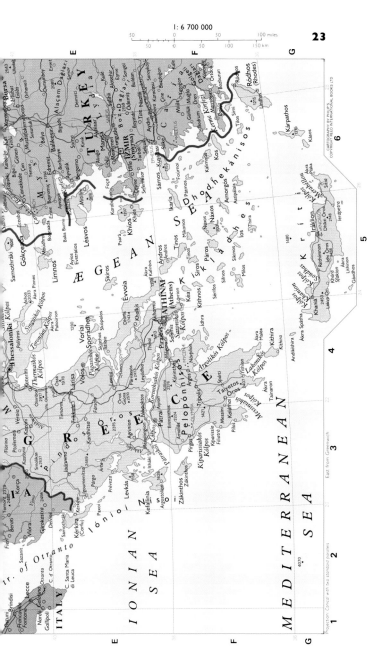

1: 13 300 000

CARTOGRAPHY BY PHILIP'S. COPYRIGHT REED INTERNATIONAL BOOKS LTD.

35 East from Greenwich

Projection: Conical with two standard parallels

1. Karachey-Cherkessia
2. Kabardino-Balkaria
3. North Ossetia
4. Ingusheta

Projection: Bonne 30
Hanoi ● Capital Cities
East from Greenwich

1 : 67 000 000

200   0   200   400   600   800   1000   1200 miles
200   0   400   800   1200   1600   2000 km

OCEAN

Laptev   New
Sea   Siberian Is.

Wrangel I.   ALASKA (USA)

Bering

Sea

Khatanga   Verkhoyansk   Gizhiga   Aleutian Is. (USA)

Lena   Sea of
Okhotsk

A   Yakutsk   Okhotsk   Petropavlovsk-
Kamchatskiy

S   I   A

Angara   Yuzhno-
Sakhalinsk   Kuril Is.

Krasnoyarsk   Bratsk   L. Baikal   Chita   Blagoveshchensk   Khabarovsk   Hokkaidō
Irkutsk   Ulan Ude   Hailar   Qiqihar   Komsomolsk   Sapporo

birsk
ovokuznetsk   Harbin   Vladivostok   Sea of   Honshū

Changchun   Japan   TŌKYŌ

Ūrümqi   Ulan Bator   Jilin   Yokohama

MONGOLIA   SHENYANG   NORTH   JAPAN
Jinzhou   Anshan   KOREA   Nagoya

Hami   Baotou   BEIJING   Dalian   Pyongyang   SOUTH   Kyōto   Ōsaka
TIANJIN   SEOUL   KOREA   Hiroshima

Yumen   Taiyuan   Jinan   Pusan   Kitakyūshū   Kyūshū
Lanzhou   Yellow

Hoang-ho   Bonin Is.
Xian   Sea   (Japan)

C H I N A   Nanjing   SHANGHAI   East   Volcano Is.
(Japan)

Wuhan   HANGZHOU   China   Tropic of Cancer

E   Chengdu   Yangtze   Nanchang   Sea
T   Changsha   Fuzhou   Ryukyu Is.

Lhasa   CHONGQING   Taipei

BHUTAN   Kunming   GUANGZHOU   TAIWAN   GUAM
(USA)

BANGLADESH   Brahmaputra   Si Kiang   HONG KONG
DAOCA   Macau

CUTTA   Chittagong   (Port.)   FED. STATES
OF MICRONESIA

BURMA   Hanoi   Hainan   Luzon   PALAU
(MYANMAR)   Haiphong

Bay   LAOS   VIETNAM   South China Sea   MANILA   PHILIPPINES

of   Irrawaddy   Mekong
Bengal   Rangoon   THAILAND   Cebu   Mindanao

Andaman Is.   BANGKOK   CAMBODIA   Palawan   Davao
(India)   Phnom Penh   Sulu   Zamboanga

G. of   Ho Chi Minh   Sea
Thailand   City   Manado   Halmahera

Nicobar Is.   Str. of Malacca   BRUNEI   SABAH   Celebes
(India)   PEN.   Bandar Seri Begawan   Sea   IRIAN
Medan   MALAYSIA   SARAWAK   JAYA

KA   Kuala Lumpur   MALAYSIA   Ceram
AN   SINGAPORE   Borneo   Celebes   Ambon   Ceram

Sumatra   Banjarmasin   Banda   Sea
Palembang   I N D O N E S I A   Ujung Pandang   Arafura Sea

Java Sea   Flores   Timor
JAKARTA   Semarang   Sumba   Timor Sea
Bandung   Surabaya   AUSTRALIA
Java

12   13   14   15   16   17

CARTOGRAPHY BY PHILIP'S. COPYRIGHT REED INTERNATIONAL BOOKS LTD.

RUSSIA
1. Adyhea
2. Karachev-Cherkessia
3. Kabardino-Balkaria
4. North Ossetia
5. Ingushetia
6. Chechenia
7. Dagestan
8. Mordovia
9. Chuvashia
10. Mari El
11. Tatarstan
12. Udmurtia
13. Khakassia

AZERBAIJAN
14. Naxçıvan

GEORGIA
15. Ajaria
16. Abkhazia

UKRAINE
17. Crimea

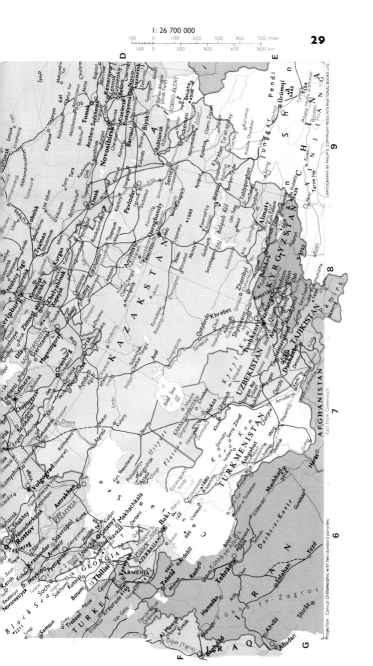

1: 26 700 000

100   0   100   200   300   400   500 miles

100   0   200   400   600   800 km

CARTOGRAPHY BY PHILIP'S COPYRIGHT REED INTERNATIONAL BOOKS LTD.

East from Greenwich

Projection: Conical Orthomorphic with two standard parallels

Projection: Conical Orthomorphic with two standard parallels

1 : 26 700 000

100   0   100   200   300   400   500 miles
100   0   200   400   600   800 km

C
Mys Dezhneva
(East C.)

14   **15**   **16**

Ostrova Henrietta
Ostrov Zhokhova
Ostrova Delong

East Siberian Sea

Ostrov Vrangelya

Chukotskoye Nagorye

St. Lawrence I.
(U.S.A.)

Anadyrskiy Zaliv

Ostrova Molyy
Lyakhovskiy

Proliv Dmitriya Lapteva

Ostrov
Medvezhi

Chaun

Pevek

Ust Chaun

Anadyr

Koryakskoye Nagorye

D

Bering Sea

Srednekolymsk

Kolyma

Khrebet Cherskogo

Verkhoyansk

Khrebet Dzhugdzhur

Gizhiginskaya Guba

Sredinnyy
Khrebet

Poluostrov
Kamchatka

Magadan

Okhotsk

Petropavlovsk-
Kamchatskiy

Yakutsk

Ust Maya

*Sea of
Okhotsk*

Olekminsk

Ust-Mila

Ostrov Paramushir

Stanovoy Khrebet

Ostrov
Bolshoy
Shantar

Sakhalinskiy
Zaliv

Sakhalin

Nikolayevsk
na-Amure

Kurilskiye Ostrova

Komsomolsk

E

Khabarovsk

Yuzhno-Sakhalinsk

Sovetskaya Gavan

Blagoveshchensk

Sikhote Alin

Birobidzhan

Amur

Khrebet

Da Hingan Ling

Sapporo

Hokkaido

Hakodate

Qiqihar

Harbin

Jamusi

JAPAN

Ussuriysk

Vladivostok

Nakhodka

Unggi

9   **10**   **11**

CARTOGRAPHY BY PHILIP'S.
COPYRIGHT REED INTERNATIONAL BOOKS LTD.

East from Greenwich

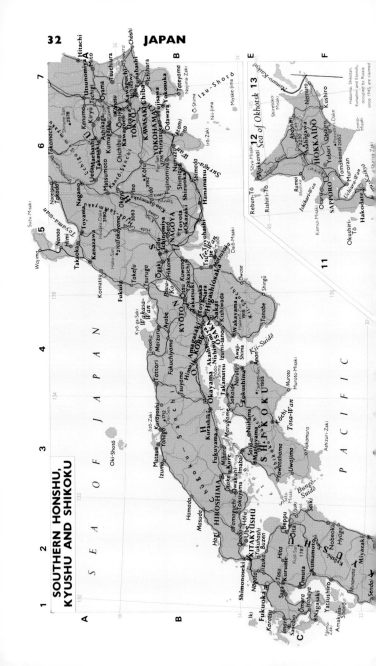

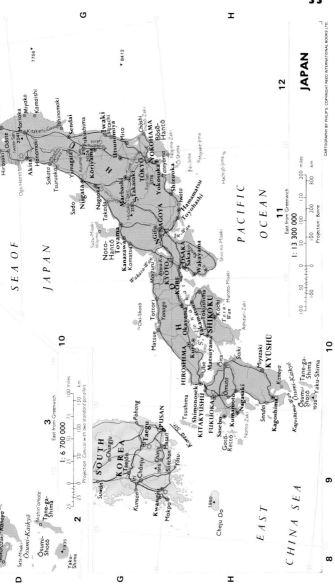

33

SEA OF

JAPAN

PACIFIC

OCEAN

EAST

CHINA SEA

JAPAN

SOUTH
KOREA

Hiroaki Odate Miyako
Akita Morioka Kamaishi
Hinomaki Iwaki
Sakata Yamagata Kōriyama Hitachi
Tsuruoka Utsunomiya
Niigata Takasaki Mito
Sado Nagaoka Maebashi TOKYO YOKOHAMA
Toyama Gifu Yokosuka
Noto-Hantō NAGOYA Shizuoka
Kanazawa Toyohashi
Komatsu Hamamatsu
KYOTO OSAKA
KOBE Sakai Wakayama
Tottori
Matsue Okayama SHIKOKU
HIROSHIMA Kure Takamatsu Tokushima
Ube Matsuyama Kōchi
Shimonoseki Ōita
KITAKYUSHU Saiki
FUKUOKA Ōmuta Miyazaki KYUSHU
Sasebo Kumamoto Kanoya
Nagasaki Sendai
Kagoshima

Pohang
Chungju
Taegu PUSAN
Chinju Masan
Suwŏn Kumsan
Taejŏn
Kwangju
Mokpo

Cheju Do

Yaku-Shima

Kanoya

Ōsumi-Shotō
Tane-ga-Shima
Yaku-Shima

1:6 700 000
East from Greenwich

1:13 300 000
East from Greenwich
Projection: Bonne

CARTOGRAPHY BY PHILIP'S. COPYRIGHT REED INTERNATIONAL BOOKS LTD.

G   H

10   11   12

8   9   10

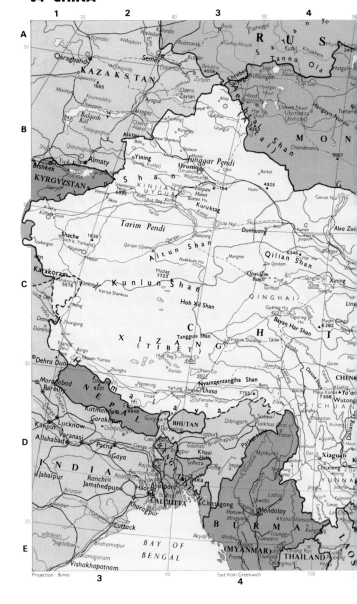

East from Greenwich

1 : 26 700 000

CARTOGRAPHY BY PHILIP'S. COPYRIGHT REED INTERNATIONAL BOOKS LTD.

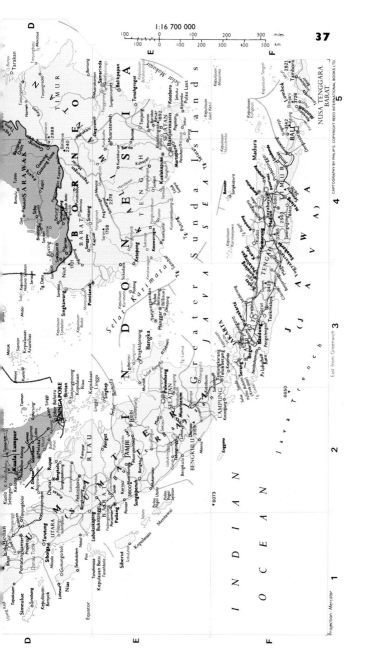

1:16 700 000

East from Greenwich

Projection: Mercator

CARTOGRAPHY BY PHILIP'S. COPYRIGHT REED INTERNATIONAL BOOKS LTD.

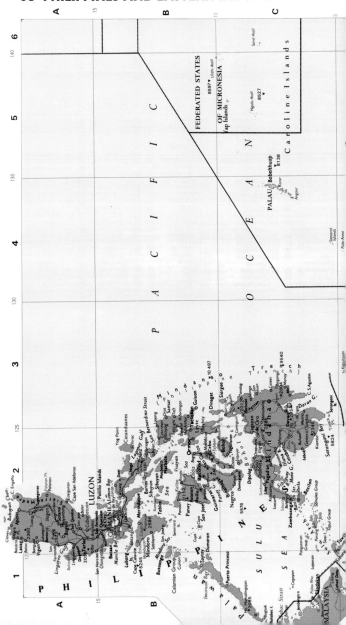

FEDERATED STATES
OF MICRONESIA
Yap Islands

PALAU

Caroline Islands

PACIFIC OCEAN

LUZON

PHILIPPINE SEA

Mindanao

SULU SEA

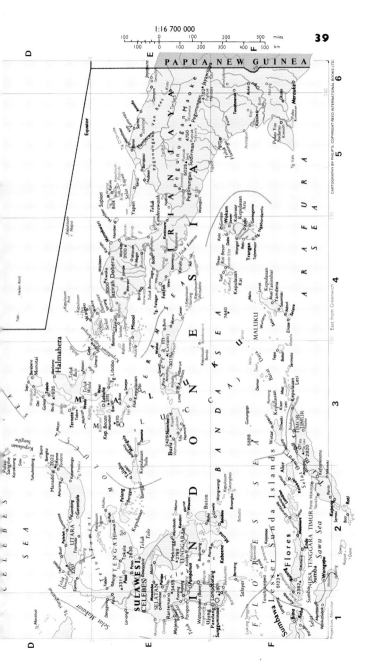

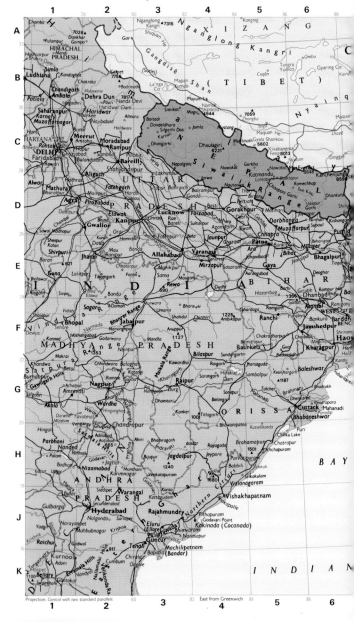

1: 13 300 000

50 0 50 100 150 200 250 miles
0 50 100 150 200 250 300 350 400 km

CARTOGRAPHY BY PHILIP'S. COPYRIGHT REED INTERNATIONAL BOOKS LTD.

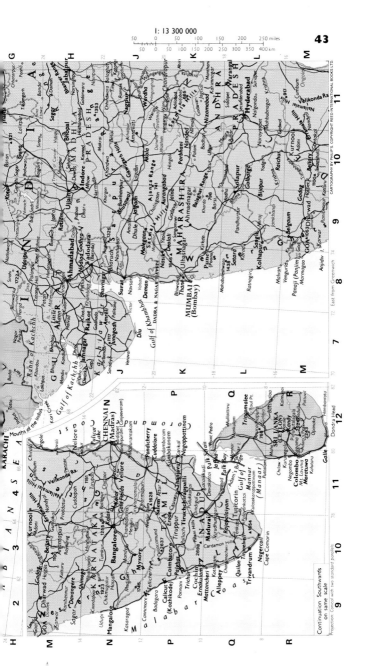

1: 13 300 000

50 0 50 100 150 200 250 miles
50 0 50 100 150 200 250 300 350 400 km

CARTOGRAPHY BY PHILIP'S COPYRIGHT REED INTERNATIONAL BOOKS LTD.

Continuation Southwards
on same scale

Projection: Conical with two standard parallels

East from Greenwich

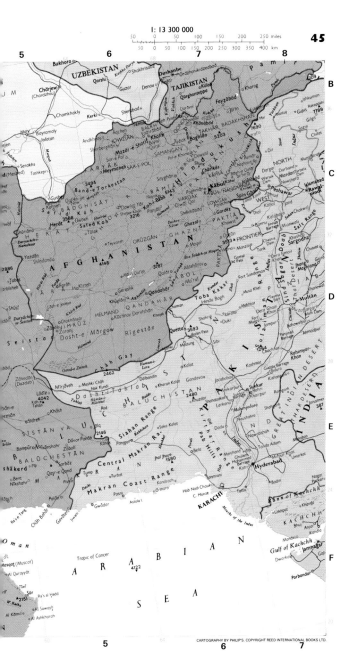

1: 13 300 000

50   0   50   100   150   200   250 miles
50   0   50   100 150 200 250 300 350 400 km

UZBEKISTAN

Bukhoro

Qarshi

Chärjew
(Chardzhou)

Chamkhakly

Maty   Bayramaly
Iolotan

Kerki

Andkhvoy

TAJIKISTAN

Dushanbe   Ordzhonikidzeabad

Denau

Sherabad

Qūrghonteppa

Kholm

Feyzābād

BADAKHSHĀN

Pamir

HINDU KUSH

Kābul

AFGHANISTAN

Herāt

Safēd Kōh

Ghazni

ORŪZGĀN

GHAZNI

PAKTIA

Peshawar

Rāwal-pindi

WEST

FRONTIER

QANDAHĀR

HELMAND

NĪMRŪZ

Rigestān

Dasht-e Mārgow

Quetta

Toba Kakar

BALUCHISTAN

KĪRTHAR RANGE

Multan

INDIA

GREAT INDIAN DESERT

Zāhedān
(Duzdab)

SISTĀN VA

BALŪCHESTĀN

Makran Coast Range

Central Makran Range

Sīstan

KARACHI

Hyderabad

Rann of Kachchh

KACHCHH

Gulf of Kachchh

Jāmnagar

Porbandar

Masqaţ (Muscat)

Tropic of Cancer

A R A B I A N

S E A

O m a n

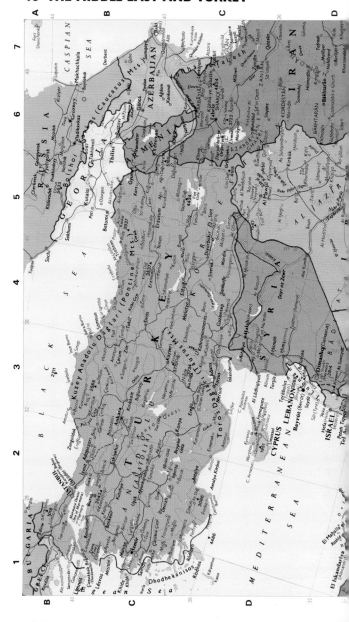

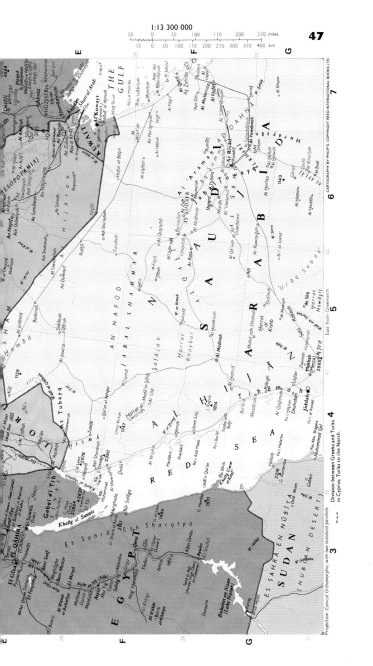

1:13 300 000

50 0 50 100 150 200 250 miles
50 0 50 100 150 200 250 300 350 400 km

Projection: Conical Orthomorphic, with two standard parallels

Division between Greeks and Turks
in Cyprus; Turks to the North.

East from Greenwich

CARTOGRAPHY BY PHILIP'S. COPYRIGHT REED INTERNATIONAL BOOKS LTD.

THE GULF

KUWAYT

K U W A I T

MESOPOTAMIA

H I L L A H

A N   N A F U D

J A B A L   S H A M M A R

AL HIJAZ

AL HIJĀZ

S A U D I   A R A B I A

DAHNA

N E J D

Ar Riyad (Riyadh)

TIHAMA

R E D   S E A

E G Y P T

S U D A N

ES SAHRA EN NUBIYA

(NUBIAN DESERT)

Buheirat en Nasser (Lake Nasser)

El Qahira (Cairo)

Sharqiya

Es Sahra esh Sharqiya

Gebel Elba

Muhammad Qol

Jiddah

Makkah (Mecca)

Al Madinah

Harrat Khaybar

Harrat 'Uwairidh

Mt. Tubayq

S I N A I

Khalig el Suweis

Khalig el 'Aqaba

AFGHANISTAN

I R A N

Dasht-e Lūt

Gulf of Oman

Str. of Hormuz

Bandar 'Abbās

O M A N

Masīrah

Ṣūr

Maṭraḥ (Masqaṭ)

Muscat

Wudham 'Alwā

3019▲

Dubai

Abū Ẓaby (Abu Dhabi)

UNITED ARAB EMIRATES

Ash Shāriqah

205▲

Ḥofūf

192

THE GULF

Ad Dawhah

BAHRAIN

Al Manāmah

Ad Dammām

Al Mubarraz

Ḥalūl

Shīrāz

Eṣfahān

4548▲

Būshehr

Būbiyān

Faylakah

Al Kuwayt (Kuwait)

KUWAIT

Al Baṣrah

Baghdād (Mesopotamia)

Karbalā'

Al Ḥillah

I R A Q

S y r i a n D e s e r t

An Nafūd

S A U D I   A R A B I A

Ar Riyāḍ (Riyadh)

Ḥā'il

Al Madīnah

Makkah (Mecca)

At Ṭā'if

Jiddah

SYRIA

Dimashq (Damascus)

LEBANON

Bayrūt

ISRAEL

Tel Aviv–Yafo

JORDAN

'Ammān

Tropic of Cancer

Birkat Qārūn (Lake Nasser)

EGYPT

Eṣ Ṣaḥrā' en Nūbīya (Nubian Desert)

Bur Sūdān

Rub' al Khālī

Gulf of Oman

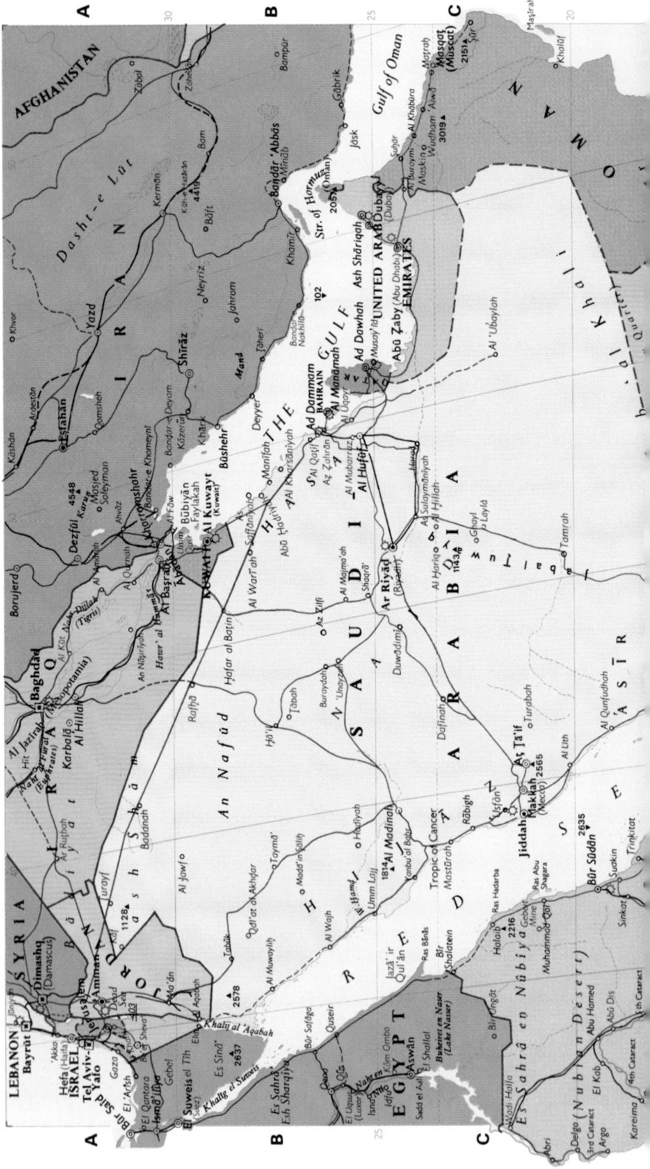

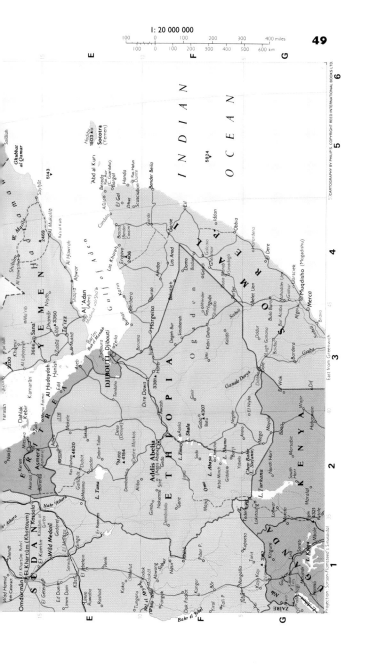

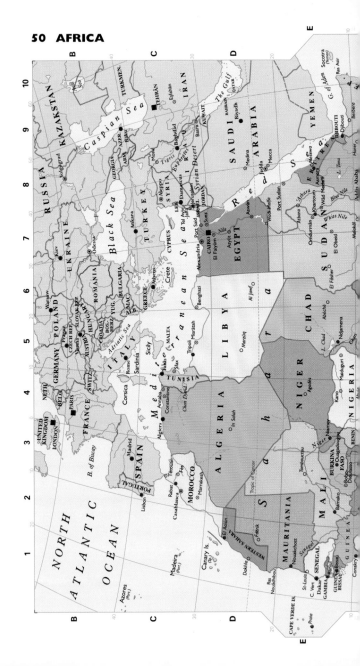

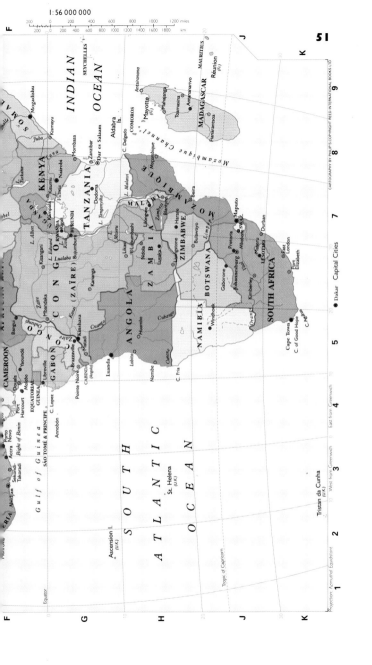

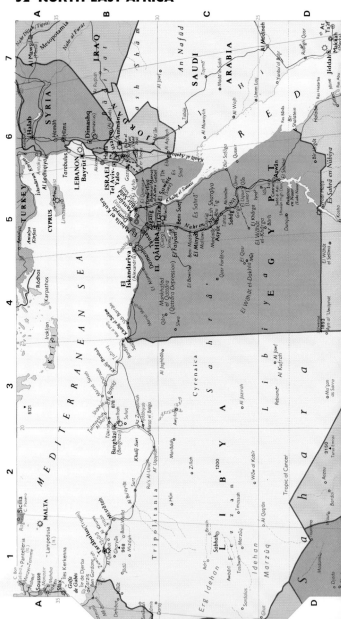

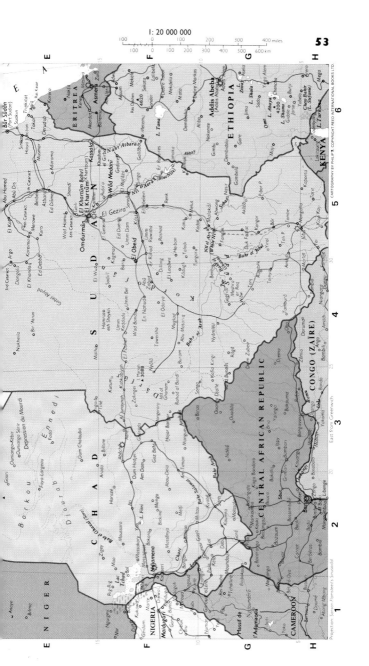

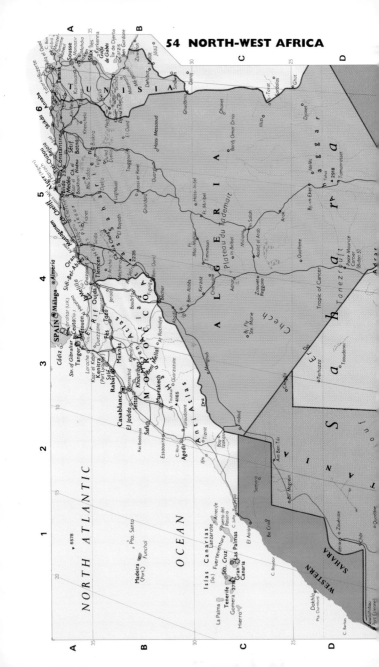

NORTH ATLANTIC OCEAN

SPAIN

Málaga○ ●Almería

Cádiz○

Str. of Gibraltar ○Gibraltar (U.K.)
Tangier ●Ceuta (Sp.) Melilla (Sp.)
●Tetouan (Port Lyautey)

El Rif

Ksar el Kebir
Laroche

Kenitra
Rabat Meknès ○Fès ○Taza

Oujda○

Casablanca Settat

El Jadida ○Khouribga

Safi Beni Mellal ○Marrakech

Essaouira ○C. Rhir ○Ouarzazate

Agadir Anti Atlas

Ifni

MOROCCO

Haut Atlas

Middle Atlas

High Atlas

Tafilalet

WESTERN SAHARA

Smara

Bir Mogrein○

El Aaiún

C. Bojador

Bu Craa

Dakhla
(Pta. Durnford)

C. Barbas

Villa Cisneros
Port Etienne

Islas Canarias (Sp.)
La Palma
Tenerife
Gomera
Hierro
Fuerteventura
Lanzarote
Arrecife
Puerto del Rosario
Sta. Cruz
Gran Canaria
Las Palmas

Madeira (Port.)
Pto. Santo
Funchal

TUNISIA
Bizerte
Tunis
Sousse
Monastir
Sfax
Kairouan
Gabès
Golfe de Gabès
Île de Djerba
Ben Gardane
Gafsa
Kasserine

ALGERIA
Annaba
Constantine
Sétif
Bône
Algiers
Médéa
Blida
Bou Saâda
Biskra
Touggourt
Ghardaïa
Laghouat
El Oued
Ouargla
Hassi Messaoud

Ouahran (Oran)
Mostaganem
Tlemcen
Mascara
Tiaret
Saïda
El Bayadh

Sahara Atlas

Béchar
Colomb-Béchar
Béni Abbès
Adrar
Reggane
Aoulef
In Salah
Timimoun

Plateau du Tademaït

Tropic of Cancer

Hoggar

Tamanrasset
●2918

In Amenas
Illizi
Djanet
Ghadamès
Ghat

Erg Chech

Tanezrouft

MALI

Taoudenni

Tessalit

Aïr
Tanout

1: 20 000 000

0   100   200 miles
0   100   200   300 km

E

F   G   H

CARTOGRAPHY BY PHILIP'S.
COPYRIGHT REED INTERNATIONAL BOOKS LTD.

Projection: Sanson-Flamsteed's Sinusoidal

East from Greenwich

West from Greenwich

MAURITANIA

SENEGAL

GAMBIA

GUINEA BISSAU

GUINEA

SIERRA LEONE

LIBERIA

IVORY COAST

MALI

BURKINA FASO

GHANA

TOGO

BENIN

NIGER

NIGERIA

CAMEROON

AïR ou Azbine
Monts Tamgak
1900

Bight of Benin

Lake Volta

Black Volta

White Volta

Niger

Fouta Djalon

Arquipélago dos Bijagós

Nouakchott

Dakar

Thiès

St. Louis

Conakry

Freetown

Monrovia

Abidjan

Bouaké

Yamoussoukro

Kumasi

Tamale

Accra

Sekondi-Takoradi

Lomé

Cotonou

Porto-Novo

Lagos

Ibadan

Abeokuta

Oyo

Ogbomosho

Ife

Ado-Ekiti

Ondo

Benin City

Warri

Port Harcourt

Onitsha

Enugu

Aba

Calabar

Douala

Yaoundé

Bioko

Maiduguri

Kano

Katsina

Zaria

Kaduna

Sokoto

Ilorin

Niamey

Ouagadougou

Bobo-Dioulasso

Bamako

Timbuktu

Man

Daloa

Cape Coast

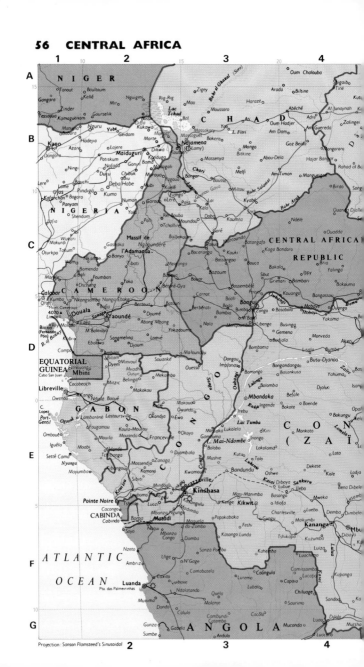

1: 20 000 000

100   0   100   200   300   400 miles
100   0   100 200 300 400   500 600 km

5   6   7   8

Omdurmân El Khartûm Bahri
Malha   El Wuz   El Khartûm (Khartoum)   Kassala   Akordat   Massawa   Dahlak Kebir   A
Hamrat   Sodirî   El Kámlin   Barentu   ERITREA   Zula   Mersa Fatma
esh Sheykh   El Geteina   Rufa'a   Khashm   Gedaref   Asmera
El Fâsher   Umm   Kagmar   Ed Dueim   el Girba   Edd
Keddada   Umm Bel   Bara   Umm Dam   El Matabiq   Aksum   -116   Mekele
Wad Banda   Abû   Senâr   Singa   Gallâbât   Metema   Ras Dashen   4620
En Nahud   Zabad   El Obeid   Kôsti   Gônder   Debre   Sekota   B
Taweisha   El Odaiya   Er Rahad   El   Renk   Er Roseires   Tabor   Lalibela
S U   Dilling   Rashad   Jebelein   L. Tana   Tendaho
Muglad   Heiban   Kôdugli   Talodi   Kaka   Dembecha   (Blue Nile)   Mota   Debre Markos   Dese
Bahr el 'Arab   Tungaru   Melut   Kodok   Nekemte   Abbay)   Alibo   Nila
Nyamlell   Bentiu   Nil el Abyad   Malakâl   Abwong   Gimbi   Addis Abeba   Awash   Ankober
Gogrial   Jur   (White Nile)   Sobat   Nasir   Dembidolo   Addis Alem   Asela
Meshra   Bahr el Ghazal   Fangak   Gambela   Gore   Jima   L. Ziway   Ginir
er Req   Wow   Tonj   Duk Fadiat   Pibor P.   Maji   Omo   Sodo   L. Shala   Gobā   C
Rumbek   Kongor   Bôr   Chencha   Yirga Alem   4307
Tombura   Amadi   Yirol   Tali P.   L. Abaya   Negele
Doruma   Tombe   Mongalla   Kapoeta   Gidole   L. Shamo   Burji   Yabelo   Arero   El Niybo
Ango   Bambili   Maridi   Juba   Chew Bahir   Mega
Titule   Faradje   Namule   Torit   Lokichaggio   Todenyang   (L. Stefanie)
Poko   Watsa   Kitgum   L.   Moyale
Isiro   Gulu   Turkana   Buna   El Wak   D
Wamba   Mungbere   Kabalega   Lira   Soroti   (L. Rudolf)   Marsabit
Bomili   Falls   Morato   Dodwar   South Horr   Wajir
Banalia   Irumu   Masindi   U G A N D A   Kitale   Isiolo   Habaswein   Dif
Kisangani   Ruwenzori   L. Albert   L. Kyoga   Mt Elgon   Eldoret   K E N Y A
Butembo   5109   321   Tororo   Nyahururu   Meru   Garissa
Equator   Kasese   Fort-Portal   Hoima   Mubende   Jinja   Kakamega   4199   Embu
Lubutu   L. Edward   George   Masaka   Kampala   Kisumu   Kericho   Nakuru   Thika   Kitui   Lamu
Kalima   Rutshuru   Mbarara   Entebbe   Kisii   Nyeri   Murang'a   Machakos   Formosa
L.   RWANDA   Bukoba   Victoria   Musoma   Loliondo   Nairobi   Garsen   Bay   E
Kindu   Kigali   Ukerewe   Nyahanga   L.   Magadi   Kibwezi
Lokandu   Bukavu   Butare   I.   Gerta   Mwanza   Natron   5895   Malindi
BURUNDI   Nguqu   Mandera   Moshi   Taveta   Takaungu
Kibombo   Bujumbura   Kibondo   Kahama   Nzega   Arusha   Same   Mombasa
Uvira   Kigoma-Ujiji   Bukene   Singida   L.   Lushoto   Tanga
Kasongo   Fizi   Kasulu   Kaliua   Tabora   Manyara   Korogwe   Pangani   Pemba I.
Kongolo   Uvinza   Handeni
Kabalo   722   Mpanda   Kibwesa   Manyoni   Dodoma   Mpwapwa   Bagamoyo   Zanzibar
Ankoro   Karema   Rungwa   T A N Z A N I A   Zanzibar I.
Moba   Iringa   Dar-es-Salaam
Kamina   Kiambi   Sumbawanga   L.   Kipembawe   Gt Ruaha   Rufiji   Utete   Mafia I.
Mwanza   Rukwa   Mahenge   Mohoro
Mitwaba   Chenya   Tukuyu   Njombe   Kilwa Kivinje
Bukama   L. Upemba   Pweto   L. Mweru   Sumbu   Mbeya   Liwale
Kasenga   Mpulungu   Songea   Lindi
Kawambwa   Kasama   Itigi   Nachingwea   Mtwara
Likasi   ZAMBIA   Luwingu   L. Nyasa   Manda   Masasi   Newala   Cabo   G
Mansa   Chinsali   Livingstonia   Songea   Ruvuma   Delgado
L. Chambeshi   MALAWI   Nkhata Bay   Mbamba Bay   Tunduru   Palma   Moçambique
Bangweulu   da Praia

5   6

CARTOGRAPHY BY PHILIP'S. COPYRIGHT REED INTERNATIONAL BOOKS LTD

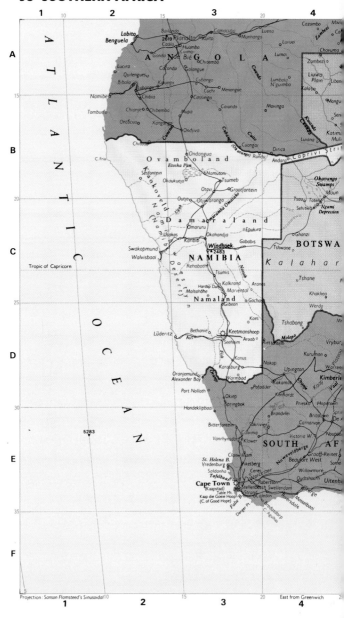

East from Greenwich

INDIAN

OCEAN

Bassas da India
(Réunion)

Île Europa (Réunion)

MADAGASCAR

On same scale as General Map

Îles Glorieuses
(Réunion)

INDIAN

OCEAN

Tropic of Capricorn

CARTOGRAPHY BY PHILIP'S. COPYRIGHT REED INTERNATIONAL BOOKS LTD.

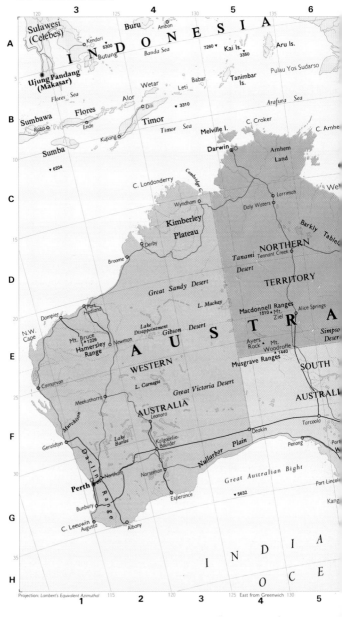

Projection: Lambert's Equivalent Azimuthal   East from Greenwich

1: 26 700 000

100   0   100   200   300   400   500 miles
100   0   200   400   600   800 km

7   145   8   150   9   155   10   160   11

Mount Hagen ○ 4508 ▲ Mt.
                    Wilhelm   ● Lae
PAPUA NEW GUINEA   New Britain   ▲ Mt.   **Bougainville**   **SOLOMON**
                                              Balbi   Choiseul   **ISLANDS**
Fly   Gulf of   Owen Stanley Range   9140   Santa Isabel   B
         Papua   Solomon   New○
                Port ◎   Sea   Georgia   Malaita
                Moresby   D'Entrecasteaux Arch.   Honiara ○ ▲ 3331   10
Torres Strait   **Guadalcanal**
         C. York   Louisiade   **San Cristobal**
Weipa ○ Cape   Archipelago   Rennell   C
        York
        Peninsula
                Cooktown ○   C o r a l   S e a   15
        Mitchell   P   A   C   I   F   I   C
        ○ Normanton   ▲ 1611   Cairns   D
        Forsayth ○   Bartle Frere   Coral
Mount Isa   Townsville   Sea   Chesterfield Is.
        Hughenden   Charters Towers ○   Islands   O   C   E   A   N   20
                                        ● Mackay
                Winton   Rockhampton Territory
QUEENSLAND   Longreach   Tropic of Capricorn E
        Yaraka ○   ● Gladstone
                                        ● Bundaberg   25
                Charleville   Roma ○   Maryborough ○
        Grey Range   Quilpie ○   ● Gympie
        Thargomindah ○   Cunnamulla ○   Toowoomba ● **BRISBANE**   F
                                        ○ Ipswich
                            Dirranbandi   ● Gold
                Bourke ○   Walgett   Coast
                                        ● Lismore
        Flinders Range   Tamworth   ▲ 1615
                            Cobar   Round
        Broken Hill   **NEW SOUTH**   Mt.   ● Taree   Lord Howe   G
                                        ● Dubbo   (Austr.)
        Port Pirie   **WALES** Newcastle   ▼ 734
                Mildura   Orange ○ Bathurst ○
        Murray   **SYDNEY**   30
        ● Adelaide   Wagga Wagga ○ ● **Wollongong**
                Shepparton ○ Goulburn ○ Shellharbour   T a s m a n   S e a   35
                            Mt.   ● **Canberra**
                Albury ○ Kosciusko   CAPITAL TERRITORY
        Horsham ○   **VICTORIA** Australian ○ Bombala
                ● Bendigo 2237 ▲   H
        Ballarat ● **MELBOURNE**   ● C. Howe
Mount Gambier   ● Geelong
        Warrnambool
                King I.   Bass Strait   Furneaux Group   40
                                                        ▼ 5267
        N   Burnie ○ ● Launceston   J
                TASMANIA   1617
                            ▲ Mt.Ossa
                140   ● **Hobart**
                            S.E. Cape   CARTOGRAPHY BY PHILIP'S. COPYRIGHT REED INTERNATIONAL BOOKS LTD.

7   8   9   10   11

East from Greenwich

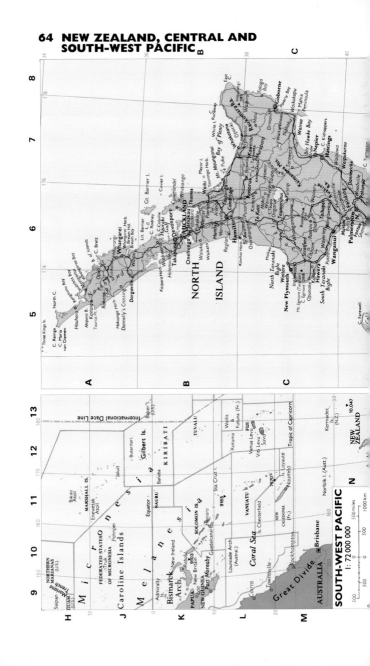

NORTH ISLAND

Three Kings Is.
C. Reinga
C. Maria van Diemen
North C.
North Island

Whangarei

AUCKLAND
Manukau
Hamilton

New Plymouth
Wanganui

Gisborne
Napier
Hastings
Palmerston N.

SOUTH-WEST PACIFIC
1: 72 000 000

NEW ZEALAND 10,047

International Date Line

NORTHERN MARIANAS (U.S.)
Mariana Trench
Guam (U.S.)
Saipan

Micronesia
FEDERATED STATES OF MICRONESIA
Caroline Islands
Truk
Pohnpei

MARSHALL IS.
Bikini Atoll
Enewetak Atoll
Jaluit

Melanesia
Bismarck Arch.
New Ireland
New Britain
Rabaul
Admiralty Is.
PAPUA NEW GUINEA
Port Moresby
Louisiade Arch.

Gilbert Is.
KIRIBATI
Banaba
Butaritari
NAURU
Equator

SOLOMON IS.
Guadalcanal
9103

TUVALU

Rotuma
Wallis Futuna (Fr.)
FIJI
Vanua Levu
Viti Levu
Suva

Tropic of Capricorn

Kermadec Is. (N.Z.)

VANUATU

NEW CALEDONIA (Fr.)
Nouméa
Is. Chesterfield
Is. Loyauté
9165

Norfolk I. (Aust.)

AUSTRALIA
Brisbane
Rockhampton
Coral Sea
Great Divide
Townsville
Cairns

N
500   0   500   1000 km
500 miles

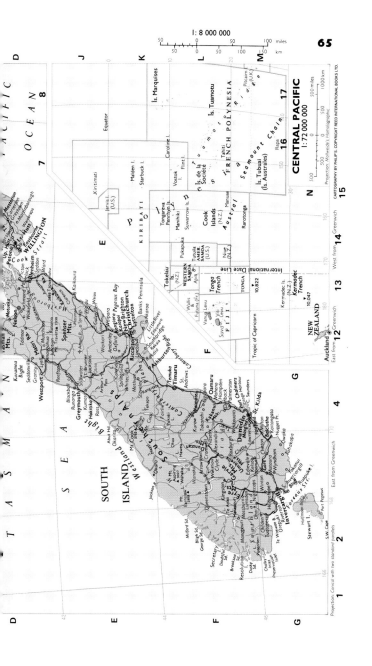

65

1 : 8 000 000

miles
50 0 50 100

km
50 0 50 100 150 200

CENTRAL PACIFIC
1 : 72 000 000

Projection: Mollweide's Homolographic

500   0   500   1000 km
500   0   500   1000 miles

CARTOGRAPHY BY PHILIP'S. COPYRIGHT REED INTERNATIONAL BOOKS LTD.

Projection: Conical with two standard parallels

East from Greenwich

West from Greenwich

East from Greenwich

International Date Line

PACIFIC   OCEAN

TASMAN   SEA

SOUTH
ISLAND

NEW
ZEALAND

FRENCH POLYNESIA

KIRIBATI

WESTERN
SAMOA

TONGA

FIJI

Cook
Islands

Austral
(Is. Australes)

Is. Tubuai

Is. de la
Société

Tahiti

Is. Tuamotu

Is. Marquises

Pitcairn I.
(U.K.)

Rapa

Seamount Chain

Rarotonga

Niue
(N.Z.)

Tutuila
AMER.
SAMOA
(U.S.)

Tokelau
Is.
(N.Z.)

Apia

Manihiki

Penrhyn I.

Tongareva

Suwarrow I.

Pukapuka

Manuae

Wallis
& Futuna (Fr.)

Vanua Levu

Viti Levu
Suva

Kermadec Is.
(N.Z.)
Kermadec
Trench
10,047

Tonga
Trench
10,882

Tropic of Capricorn

Equator

Caroline I.

Vostok

Flint I.

Starbuck I.

Malden I.

Jarvis I.
(U.S.)

Kiritimati

Auckland

WELLINGTON

Christchurch

Dunedin

Invercargill

Timaru

Oamaru

Greymouth

Nelson

Blenheim

Cook Strait

Southern Alps

Canterbury
Bight

Banks Peninsula

Foveaux Str.

Stewart I.

Mt. Cook
3764

S.W. Cape

Port Pegasus

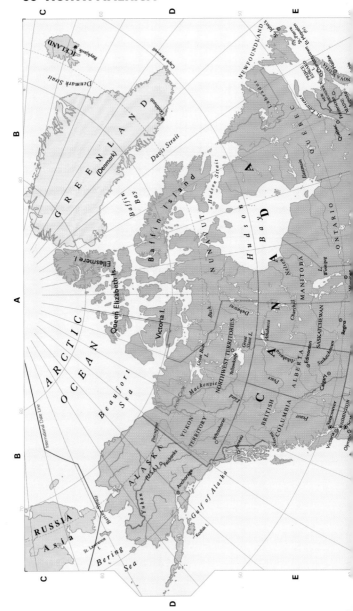

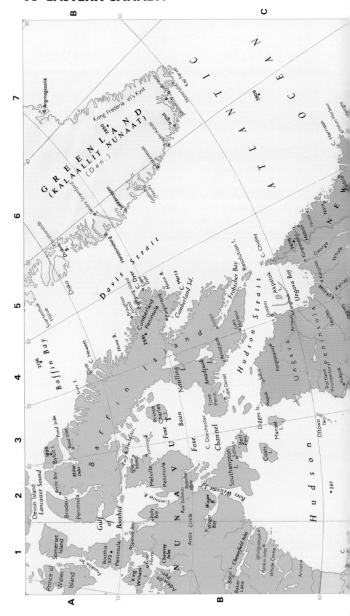

1: 20 000 000

CARTOGRAPHY BY PHILIP'S. COPYRIGHT REED INTERNATIONAL BOOKS LTD.

West from Greenwich

Projection: Bonne

1 : 20 000 000

100 0 100 200 300 400 miles

100 0 100 200 300 400 500 600 km

CARTOGRAPHY BY PHILIP'S. COPYRIGHT REED INTERNATIONAL BOOKS LTD.

ALASKA
1 : 40 000 000

100 0 100 200 300 miles

100 0 100 200 300 400 km

Projection Bonne

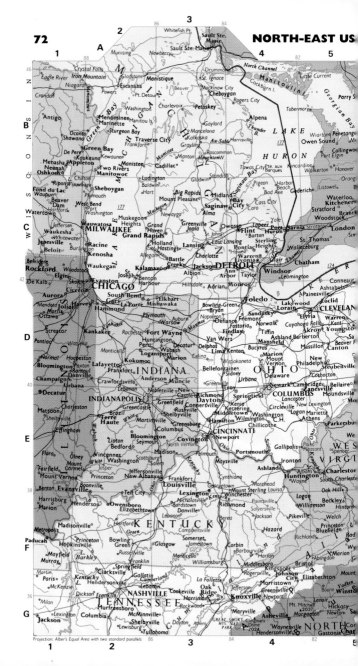

1: 8 000 000

50 0 50 100 miles
50 0 50 100 150 km

6   7   8   9   10

CANADA

Pembroke Fort Coulonge Hawkesbury Ottawa **MONTREAL** Lachine Granby Sherbrooke Coaticook Richardson Mt.

Huntsville Bracebridge Gravenhurst Barry's Bay Eganville Buckingham Hull Renfrew Arnprior Carleton Place Smiths Falls Perth Cornwall St-Jean Beauharnois Cowansville Newport Island Pond

Bancroft Kingston Prescott Brockville Gananoque Ogdensburg Potsdam Massena Malone Plattsburg St. Albans **NEW HAMPSHIRE** Berlin Conway 1917 44

Lindsay Peterborough Belleville Trenton Picton Watertown Lowville Saranac Lakes Gouverneur Champlain Burlington Winooski Montpelier St. Johnsbury Barre White Mts.

LAKE ONTARIO 75 Oswego Fulton Rome Oneida Watertown Adirondack Mts. 1629 Ticonderoga **VERMONT** Rutland Lebanon Concord Rochester Dover Laconia Franklin

TORONTO Niagara Falls Rochester Syracuse Utica Gloversville Amsterdam Schenectady Saratoga Springs Glens Falls Hudson Falls Granville Claremont Keene Manchester Nashua Haverhill Lawrence Lowell Salem Portsmouth Newburyport Ann

Buffalo West Seneca Amherst Batavia Geneva Auburn Cayuga Cortland Norwich Oneonta Albany Troy Greenfield Pittsfield Leominster Fitchburg Worcester **BOSTON** Cambridge Quincy

Dunkirk **NEW YORK** Penn Yan Bath Ithaca Johnson City Catskill Catskill Mts. 1281 Kingston Northampton Chicopee Springfield Hartford Woonsocket Providence Brockton Taunton Fall River New Bedford Cape Cod

Salamanca Hornell Corning Endicott Binghamton Mts. Delaware Hudson Beacon Waterbury New Britain Meriden Warwick Newport Martha's Vineyard

Jamestown Bradford Wellsville Towanda Elmira Sayre Carbondale Poughkeepsie Middletown Danbury New Haven New London

Warren Coudersport 759 Wellsboro Williamsport Scranton Wilkes Barre Hazleton Newburgh Bridgeport Stamford Long Island Riverhead

Kane Ridgway St. Marys Lock Haven Bloomsburg Berwick Nanticoke Sunbury Paterson Jersey City Mount Vernon **NEW YORK**

Brookville Du Bois Clearfield State College Lewistown Pottsville Allentown Bethlehem Easton Newark Elizabeth New Brunswick Long Branch

PENNSYLVANIA Punxsutawney Indiana Altoona 956 Harrisburg Lebanon Reading Trenton Asbury Park

PITTSBURGH Johnstown Carlisle York Lancaster **PHILADELPHIA** Morristown Chester Wilmington Camden **NEW JERSEY**

Uniontown Connellsville Greensburg Chambersburg Hanover Westminster Newark Vineland Atlantic City

Cumberland Keyser Martinsburg Hagerstown Frederick Columbia Towson Bridgeton Millville Ocean City

Romney Winchester **BALTIMORE** **MARYLAND** Dover Cape May Henlopen

Elkins Front Royal Arlington **WASHINGTON D.C.** Annapolis Chesapeake Milford

1482 Luray Culpeper Alexandria Easton **DELAWARE** Seaford Salisbury

Harrisonburg Fredericksburg Orange Lexington Park Cambridge Snow Hill

Staunton Charlottesville Tappahannock Potomac Accomac

Waynesboro Buena Vista Clifton Forge Colonial Heights **VIRGINIA** West Point Williamsburg Elbe Charles Chesapeake Bay

Lynchburg Bedford Farmville **Richmond** Lakeside Petersburg Hampton Newport News Virginia Beach Chesapeake

Roanoke John H. Kerr Reservoir Emporia Franklin Portsmouth Norfolk

Danville Roxboro Oxford Roanoke Rapids Winton Elizabeth City Currituck Sd.

Eden Henderson Weldon Edenton Albemarle Sd. Manteo

Durham Graham Chapel Hill Raleigh Wilson Washington Greenville Williamston Pamlico Sound Hatteras

High Point Lexington Asheboro Sanford Smithfield Goldsboro Kinston New Bern

AROLINA Dunn West from Greenwich

Continuation Eastwards On same scale

CANADA Edmundston Fort Kent Van Buren Grand Falls Eagle Lake Caribou Presque Isle St. John

Eagle L. Chesuncook Mt. Katahdin 1605 Patten Chiputneticook Lakes Houlton

Moosehead Greenville **MAINE** Mattawamkeag Lincoln Millinocket

Richardson Lakes Rangeley Dover Foxcroft Old Town Machias East Quoddy

Berlin Farmington Rumford Skowhegan Waterville Bangor Brewer Ellsworth

Mt. Washington 1917 Augusta Gardiner Belfast Bar Harbor Mt. Desert

Auburn Lewiston Bath Rockland

NEW HAMPSHIRE Westbrook Portland Biddeford Saco Laconia

Dover Rochester Portsmouth Haverhill

Continuation Eastwards On same scale

6   7   10   11

CARTOGRAPHY BY PHILIP'S. COPYRIGHT REED INTERNATIONAL BOOKS LTD.

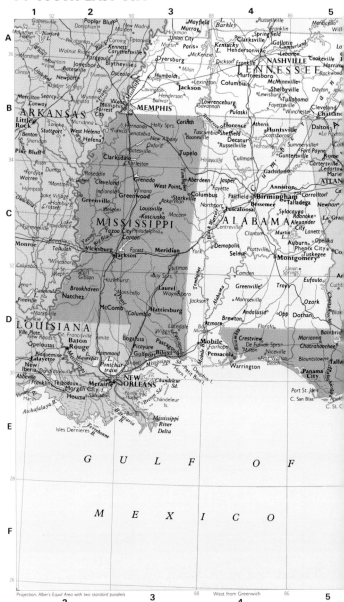

A

B

C

D

E

F

1   2   3   4   5

36

34

32

30

28

26

ARKANSAS

LOUISIANA

MISSISSIPPI

ALABAMA

TENNESSEE

MEMPHIS

NASHVILLE

NEW ORLEANS

Baton Rouge

Birmingham

Montgomery

Jackson

GULF   OF

MEXICO

Projection: Alber's Equal Area with two standard parallels

West from Greenwich

88   86

2   3   4   5

1: 8 000 000

50   0   50   100 miles
50   0   50   100   150 km

6   7   8   9   10

Harlan
Middlesboro
Rogersville Kingsport Bristol Abingdon Galax Martinsville Danville Emporia Currituck Sd.
Jefferson City Morristown Elizabethton Mount Airy Reidsville Eden Roxboro Oxford Roanoke Rapids Winton Elizabeth City
Knoxville Newport Boone Yadkin Greensboro Burlington Durham Henderson Rocky Mount Edenton Monteo
Maryville Mt. Mitchell Lenoir Hickory Statesville Thomasville High Point Graham Chapel Hill Raleigh Wilson Williamston Roanoke I.
SMOKY Clingmans 2037 Morganton Newton Salisbury Lexington Asheboro Smithfield Washington Greenville
Dome Asheville Waynesville NORTH CAROLINA Concord Albemarle Sanford Dunn Goldsboro Kinston New Bern Pamlico Sound
Murphy Hendersonville Brevard Spartanburg Shelby Gastonia Charlotte Southern Pines Fayetteville Neuse Hatteras
grasstown Bald Greenville Gaffney Monroe Pines Clinton Jacksonville Raleigh B.
1458 Easley Rock Hill Lancaster Laurinburg Cape C. Lookout
Toccoa Seneca Union Chester Bennettsville Dillon Lumberton Fear Onslow B.
Anderson Belton Laurens Hartsville Camden Darlington Mullins Whiteville Wilmington
Gainesville Hartwell L. Greenwood Newberry Florence Marion Conway
Elberton Abbeville L. Columbia Sumter Lake City Southport
Athens Clark Murray SOUTH CAROLINA Manning Kingstree C. Fear
Lawrenceville Hill L. Orangeburg Aiken Myrtle Beach
st Point Covington Augusta Marion L. Georgetown
GEORGIA Waynesboro Bamberg Maultrie Summerville North Charleston
Griffin Sparta Milledgeville Millen Walterboro Charleston Mt. Pleasant
Thomaston Macon Swainsboro Ridgeland Hampton Beaufort
Valley Warner Robins Dublin Statesboro Parris I.
Perry Cochran Vidalia Savannah
Cordele Hazlehurst Fitzgerald Baxley Hinesville Ossabaw I.
Sylvester Douglas Jesup St. Catherines I.
Tifton Waycross Sapelo I.
moultrie Adel Brunswick
Cairo Valdosta Okefenokee Folkston Cumberland I. A T L A N T I C
ville Quitman Swamp Fernandina Beach
Monticello Madison Jasper St. Johns
Perry Live Oak Lake Jacksonville Jacksonville Beach
Apalachee City FLORIDA Green Cove Springs
elle B. High Springs Starke St. Augustine
Cross City Palotka Bunnell O C E A N
Gainesville
Ocala Daytona Beach Ormond Beach
Crystal River De Land New Smyrna Beach
Inverness Leesburg Eustis Sanford
Brooksville L. George Titusville
Dade City Winter Park C. Canaveral
Tarpon Springs Kissimmee Orlando Cocoa Merritt Island
Clearwater Lakeland Haines City Melbourne
Largo Winter Haven
St. Petersburg TAMPA Bartow Vero Beach
Tampa Bay Sebring L. Fort Pierce
Bradenton Istokpoga Okeechobee Stuart Grand Cays
Sarasota Arcadia L. Little Abaco I. Gt. Guana Cay
Punta Gorda Okeechobee Pahokee Settlement Pt. Hope Town
La Belle Belle Glade West Palm Beach Grand
Charlotte Harb. Cape Coral Fort Myers Immokalee Boca Raton Delray Beach Freeport Bahama I. Great Abaco I.
Naples Big Cypress Swamp Pompano Beach
Carol City Fort Lauderdale BAHAMAS
EVERGLADES Hialeah Hollywood
NAT. PARK MIAMI Miami Beach
Biscayne B.
Homestead

A

B

C

D

E

F

G

38

36

34

32

30

28

26

84   82   80   78   76

CARTOGRAPHY BY PHILIP'S. COPYRIGHT REED INTERNATIONAL BOOKS LTD.

6   7   8   9

1 2 3 102 4 100 5 98 6

A

Scobey • Plentywood • Crosby • Bowbells Mohall Bottineau • Rolla • Langdon • Cavalier • Emé

Williston • Kenmare • Souris • Towner • Rugby • Cando • Grafton • Park River

48 Wall Point • Missouri • Stanley Minot • Velva • Harvey • New Rockford • Devils Lake Lakota Larimore • Northwood • Grand Forks

Fort Peck L. • Fairview • L. Sakakawea • New Town • Fessenden McClusky • Carrington • Cooperstown Hillsboro

Circle • Sidney • Watford City • Garrison • Manning • Stanton Washburn • N O R T H   D A K O T A • Mooreton

B

Terry • Glendive Wibaux • Beach • Dickinson • Hebron Mandan • Center • Steele • Jamestown • Valley City • Fargo

Miles City • Baker • Heart • Carson • Napoleon • La Moure • Lisbon • Wahp

Yellowstone • Little Missouri • White Butte 1069 Bowman • Mott • Cannonball • Linton • Lake • Ashley • Ellendale Forman

46 Broadus • Ekalaka • Hettinger • Fort Yates Selfridge • McIntosh • Eureka Leola • Britton Sisseton

W Y O M I N G • Buffalo • Lemmon • Grand • Mobridge Selby • Mound City Ipswich • Aberdeen Webster • Mi

Little Missouri • Biron • Timber Lake • Oahe • Redfield • Clark

C

Belle Fourche • Moreau • Dupree Eagle Butte • S O U T H   D A K O T A • Gettysburg • Onida Highmore • Miller • De Smet Huron

Gillette • Belle Fourche • Spearfish Deadwood Lead • Cheyenne • Oahe Pierre Fort Pierre • Wessington Sprs. Woonsocket • Madison

44 Sundance • Sturgis • Rapid City • Philip • Bad • Kadoka • Murdo • Stamford • Chamberlain • Mitchell Alexandria • Salem • Sio Fa

Newcastle • Black Hills 2207 Custer Harney Pk. • Hot Springs • Badlands • White • White River • L. Francis Case • Winner • Armour • Lake Andes Parker

Edgemont • Martin • Pine Ridge • Niobrara • Butte • Yankton

D

Douglas • Lusk Harrison • Chadron • Rushville • Valentine • Bassett • Atkinson • O'Neill Elkhorn • Neligh Wayne • South Si Plainview Norf

Laramie Mountains 3131 • Torrington Wheatland • Hemingford • Alliance Sand Hills 1036 • Mullen • Ainsworth • Burwell • Albion Greeley • St. Paul Central • Madison West

42 Scottsbluff Gering • Bridgeport • Hyannis Thedford • N E B R A S K A • Loup City Fullerton • Colu Schu

Laramie Lodgepole Cr. • Harrisburg • Kimball • Oshkosh • Stapleton • Broken Bow Loup • David City

Cheyenne • Sidney • Ogallala L. McConaughy North Platte • Gothenburg Cozad Lexington • Grand Island York Seward • Aurora

E

Fort Collins Loveland Greeley • Sterling • Julesburg • Grant • Imperial Curtis • Elwood • Kearney • Hastings Geneva

Boulder Longmont • Fort Morgan Akron • Holyoke • Trenton • McCook Beaver City • Holdrege • Red Cloud • Fairbury

Lafayette Golden DENVER Brighton Aurora Englewood • Byers • Wray • Benkelman Republican • Alma • Franklin • Hebron

Lakewood • Castle Rock • Atwood Oberlin • Norton Smith Center Mankato • Belleville • Concordia Republic

F

C O L O R A D O • St. Francis • Colby • Philipsburg Stockton Solomon Osborne Beloit

Pikes Pk. 4300 Colorado Springs • Hugo • Burlington • Goodland Oakley • S. Fork • Hill City • Smoky Hills Saline • Minneapolis Lincoln • Abilene

Fountain • Canon City • Sandy Cr. • Eads • Sharon Springs • Smoky Hill • Hays • Russell • Salina • Man Junctio

Pueblo • Ordway • Tribune • Leoti • Scott City • Dighton • Great Bend Lyons • McPherson

38 Las Animas Lamar • K A N S A S • La Crosse • Ellsworth

1: 8 000 000

50 0 50 100 miles
50 0 50 100 150 km

A

CANADA

Lake of the Woods
Roseau
Warroad
Rainy River
Baudette
Rainy L.
Fort Frances
Atikokan
Thunder Bay
Isle Royale

Thief River Falls
Upper Red L.
Red Lake Falls
Lower Red L.
kston
International Falls
Little Fork
Vermilion L.
Lac la Croix
Grand Marais

LAKE SUPERIOR
Copper Harbor
Keweenaw Pt.
Keweenaw Pen.

Fosston
Bagley
Bemidji
Winnibigoshish L.
Cass L.
Mahnomen
Hibbing
Virginia
Eveleth
Hancock
Houghton
Keweenate B.
L'Anse
604
Ishpeming Marquette
Negaunee

Hawley
head
Detroit Lakes
Perham
Leech L.
Grand Rapids
Walker
Two Harbors
Apostle Is.
Ontonagon
Bessemer
Hurley
Ironwood
Crystal Falls
MICHIGAN

esville
ken
MINNESOTA
Cloquet
Duluth
Superior
Washburn
Ashland
Iron River
Niagara
Powers

Fergus Falls
Wadena
Staples
Brainerd
Mille Lacs
Moose Lake
Hayward
Park Falls
Eagle River
Iron Mountain
Menominee

Alexandria
Little Falls
Mora
Milaca
Grantsburg
Spooner
Phillips
Rhinelander
Crandon
Antigo
Marinette

Morris
St. Cloud
Sauk Rapids
Cambridge
Pine City
Cumberland
Rice Lake
Ladysmith
Medford
Merrill
Menominee

heaton
Willmar
Litchfield
Anoka
St. Croix
Stillwater
Chippewa Falls
Cornell
Wausau
Shawano
Oconto
Sturgeon Bay

Granite Falls
Montevideo
Hutchinson
Glencoe
MINNEAPOLIS
St. PAUL
Hudson
Menomonie
WISCONSIN
Marshfield
Stevens Point
De Pere
Green Bay
Kewaunee

Redwood Falls
New Ulm
Northfield
Hastings
Red Wing
Lake City
Eau Claire
Alma
Wisconsin Rapids
Waupaca
Menasha
Neenah
Appleton
Two Rivers
Manitowoc

ngs
Marshall
St. Peter
Faribault
Owatonna
Winona
Rochester
Black River Falls
Sparta
Montello
Oshkosh
Ripon
Chilton
Sheboygan

Pipestone
Windom
St. James
Waseca
Mankato
Preston
La Crosse
Tomah
Mauston
Waupun
Fond du Lac
Plymouth
LAKE

Worthington
Jackson
Fairmont
Albert Lea
Austin
Viroqua
Reedsburg
Baraboo
Portage
Beaver Dam
West Bend
Port Washington
MICHIGAN

dso
Sibley
ston
Estherville
Northwood
Decorah
Waukon
Richland Center
Prairie du Chien
Lancaster
Wisconsin Dells
Madison
Watertown
Jefferson
Waukesha
Whitewater
MILWAUKEE

ion
Le Mars
Sheldon
Spencer
Emmetsburg
Algona
Mason City
Garner
Charles City
New Hampton
Dodgeville
Darlington
Monroe
Janesville
Beloit
Burlington
Racine
Kenosha

Sioux City
Cherokee
Storm Lake
Webster City
Iowa Falls
Hampton
Waverly
Cedar Falls
Oelwein
Independence
Dubuque
Freeport
Rockford
Belvidere
Elgin
Woodstock
Skokie
Evanston
Waukegan
CHICAGO

nanff
now
Ida Grove
Denison
IOWA
Fort Dodge
Marshalltown
Waterloo
Vinton
Cedar Rapids
Marion
Maquoketa
Clinton
De Kalb
Dixon
Sterling
Aurora
Cicero

Audubon
Carroll
Jefferson
Boone
Ames
Grinnell
Iowa City
Marengo
Tipton
Rock Island
Moline
Davenport
Peru
Ottawa
Morris
Joliet
Harvey

Fremont
maha
Atlantic
Council Bluffs
Greenfield
Winterset
W. Des Moines
Des Moines
Red Rock L.
Newton
Montezuma
Washington
Muscatine
Aledo
Kewanee
Princeton
Streator
Pontiac
Kankakee

tsmouth
incoln
Nebraska City
Glenwood
Red Oak
Corning
Creston
Osceola
Indianola
Knoxville
Oskaloosa
Pella
Fairfield
Mt. Pleasant
Burlington
Monmouth
Galesburg
Peoria
Pekin
Canton
Normal
Bloomington
Rantoul
Paxton
Champaign

rice
Auburn
Shenandoah
Clarinda
Bedford
Leon
Centerville
Bloomfield
Fort Madison
Keokuk
Macomb
Rushville
Lincoln
Decatur

Rockport
Grant City
Bethany
Princeton
Unionville
Milan
Kirksville
Edina
Quincy
Beardstown
Springfield
ILLINOIS
Taylorville
Pana
Shelbyville

awnee
Falls City
Hipwatha
rysville
Holton
Atchison
St. Joseph
Excelsior Spes.
Chillicothe
Brookfield
Palmyra
Macon
Hannibal
Jacksonville
Carlinville
Litchfield
Mattoon
Effingham
Greenville

Topeka
Lawrence
Leavenworth
Kansas City
Independence
Lexington
Marshall
Fayette
Mexico
Columbia
Fulton
Troy
St. Charles
Jerseyville
Alton
St. Louis
Vandalia
Flora
Fairfield

ansas
Olathe
Ottawa
Paolo
Warrensburg
Sedalia
Harrisonville
Boonville
Jefferson City
MISSOURI
Union
ST. LOUIS
Granite City
E. St. Louis
Belleville
Centralia
Mount Vernon
Benton

Council
Emporia
Garnett
Clinton
Butler
Lake of the Ozarks
Sullivan
De Soto
Pinckneyville
Du Quoin

urlington

CARTOGRAPHY BY PHILIP'S. COPYRIGHT REED INTERNATIONAL BOOKS LTD.

B

C

D

E

F

7 8 9 10 11

1 104 2 102 3 100 4 98 5

COLORADO

La Junta
Walsenburg
Sangre de Cristo Mts.
Trinidad
Springfield

Syracuse Garden City Kinsley St. John Hutchinson New
Lakin Arkansas Cimarron Dodge City Pratt Kingman Wichita
Johnson Ulysses Meade Coldwater Greensburg Medicine Lodge Anthony Wellington Arkansas City

K A N S A S

A

Raton
Black Mesa 1516
Boise City Guymon Beaver Buffalo Alva Cherokee Blackwell
Hugoton Elkhart Liberal Ashland

Springer
Truchas Mora Pk. 3993
Clayton Perryton Woodward Fairview Canton Enid Perry Stillwater Guthrie
Stratford Gruver Spearman Booker Lipscomb Arnett Seiling Crescent Watonga
Dalhart Sunray Canadian

Las Vegas
Mosquero
Tucumcari
Canadian Dumas Cheyenne Weatherford Clinton Edmond Chond
Channing Meredith Borger Pampa Elk City Sayre Cordell **Oklahoma City** Shawo
Vega Panhandle Weatherford

Santa Rosa
Amarillo Claude Shamrock Mangum Hobart Chickasha Purcell Sem
Hereford Canyon Clarendon Wellington Hollis Altus Marlow Norman Paul's Valley
Vaughn Ft. Sumner Dimmitt Tulia Memphis Silverton Quail Town Fork Lawton Frederick Waurika Duncan Ardmore

B

N E W
Clovis Farwell Muleshoe Plainview Childress Quanah Paducah Vernon Burkburnett Wichita Falls Henrietta Gainesville
Portales Littlefield Floydada Crowell L. Kemp
Roswell Levelland Llano Abernathy Guthrie Paducah Seymour Bowie Decatur
M E X I C O Estacado Crosbyton Spur Aspermont Haskell Jacksboro Graham Denton **Fort Worth** Irvi
Lubbock Double Mtn Fork Mineral Wells Kingdom L.
Plains Tahoka Post Rotan Anson Breckenridge Albany Weatherford

C

Artesia
L. McMillan Lavington Seagraves Seminole Gail Snyder Sweetwater Abilene Baird Eastland Granbury Stephenville Cleb
Hobbs Andrews Lamesa Colorado Colorado City Cross Plains Gorman Hillsboro
Carlsbad Stanton Big Spring Sterling City Roberta Coleman Comanche Meridian
Loving Red Bluff Jal Robert Lee Ballinger Brownwood Hamilton Gatesville **Wa**

Guadalupe Peak 2667
Kermit Odessa **Midland** Garden City San Angelo Colorado Goldthwaite
Wink Monahans Eden San Saba Killeen Tem
Pecos Crane Rankin Big Lake Mertzon Brady L. Buchanan Lampasas Stillhouse Hollow Lake Belton
Kent McCamey **T E X A S** Menard Mason Llano Burnet Georgetown Camero
Van Horn Mt. Livermore 2555 Fort Stockton Eldorado Edwards Llano Rockd
Davis Mts. Fort Davis Ozona Sonora Junction Fredericksburg Taylor
Marfa Alpine Stockton Plateau **Austin**
Chinati Pk. 2356 Sanderson Plateau Rocksprings Kerrville Johnson City Bastrop

D

Presidio Balcones Es Boerne San Marcos Lockhart
Rio Grande Leakey Medina L. New Braunfels Seguin Gonzales
Chisos Mts. 2388 Del Rio Bracketville **SAN ANTONIO** Guadalu
Ciudad Acuña Uvalde Hondo Floresville
CHIHUAHUA Pearsall Pleasanton Karnes City Cu
Victori

E

Piedras Negras Eagle Pass Crystal City Dilley Goliad Por
Zaragoza Carrizo Sprs. Cotulla Tilden George West Beeville Re
Allende Nueces San Diego Alice Mathis inton
C O A H U I L A Corpus Christi
Nueva Rosita

F

M E X I C O Sabinas Nuevo Laredo **Laredo** Robstown Cor
Sierra Mojada Rio Bravo del Norte Kingsville

Projection: Albers' Equal Area with two standard parallels 2 3 100 West from Greenwich 4 98

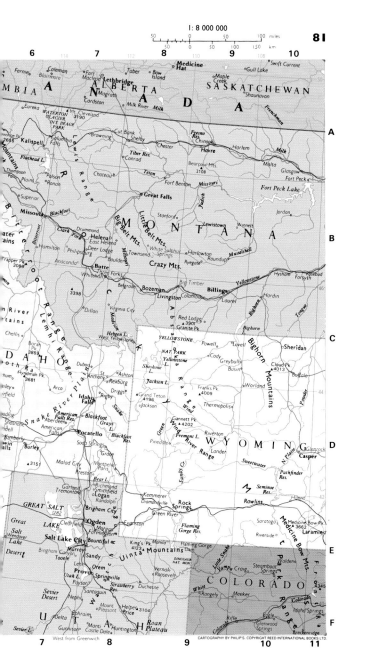

NEVADA

Tonopah
Goldfield
Pioche
Caliente
Pahute Mesa
Beatty
3021
Las Vegas
Lake Mead
Henderson
Paradise
Boulder City
Spring Mts. 3833
Hoover Dam
Davis Dam
Kingman

Oakland
SAN FRANCISCO
Stockton
Sonora
Tuolumne
Bridgeport
Redwood City
Fremont
Sunnyvale
SAN JOSE
Modesto
Turlock
Merced
YOSEMITE NAT. PARK
Mono Lake
Santa Cruz
Watsonville
Gilroy
Los Banos
Madera
Mariposa
4341
White Mts.
Pacific Grove
Monterey
Salinas
Hollister
Chowchilla
Clovis
Fresno
Bishop Mts.
North Palisade 4341
Gonzales
Soledad
Mendota
Selma
Sanger
Reedley
Mt. Whitney
KINGS CANYON NAT. PARK
Independence
Pt. Sur
King City
Coalinga
Hanford
Visalia
Lemoore
Tulare
SEQUOIA NAT. PARK
Owens L.
DEATH VALLEY NAT.
Cambria
Paso Robles
Atascadero
Corcoran
Lindsay
Porterville
Panamint Mts.
3366 MON.
Morro Bay
San Luis Obispo
Earlimart
Delano
Wasco
Shafter
3021
Searles L.
Guadalupe
Arroyo Grande
Taft
Buena Vista
Bakersfield
Ridgecrest
Santa Maria
Lompoc
Pt. A.
Pt. Arguello
Pt. Conception
Santa Barbara
Tehachapi Mts.
2692
Mojave
Santa Lucia Range
Ojai
Ventura
Lancaster
Palmdale
Termo
Barstow
Soda L.
Providence Mts.
Needles
Oxnard
San Fernando
Glendale
Pasadena
Victorville
Bristol L.
Twentynine Palms
Lake Hove
Colorado R. Aqueduct
Parker
LOS ANGELES
Beverly Hills
Garden Grove
Long Beach
Huntington Beach
Santa Ana
Anaheim
Fullerton
San Bernardino
3505
Riverside
Palm Springs
Blythe
Quartzsite
Channel Is.
San Nicolas I.
Santa Catalina
San Clemente
Hemet
Indio
Coachella
Colorado R.
Parker
San Clemente I.
Oceanside
Carlsbad
Vista
Escondido
Salton Sea
Chocolate Mts.
Sonora Desert
Santa Catalina I.
Gulf of
SAN DIEGO
El Cajon
Chula Vista
La Mesa
Westmorland
El Centro
Calipatria
Brawley
Imperial Dam
Tijuana
Tecate
Calexico
All American Canal
Mexicali
San Luis
Yuma
Somerton

BAJA CALIFORNIA

PACIFIC OCEAN

Ensenada
Pta. Sto. Tomas
Santa Tomas
Sierra de Juarez
Rio Colorado
Gran Desierto
Cabo Colonet
Cerro de la Encantada 3078
San Felipe
Bahía de San Jorg
Puerto Peñasco
C. S. Quintin
Golfo de Califo
Pta. Baja
Rosario
Pta. San Antonio
San Luis
I. Angel de la Guarda
Punta Prieta
Canal de Ballenas
I. Cedros
Bahía Sebastián Vizcaíno

HAWAII
1 : 13 300 000

Kauai
Lihue
Niihau
Kauai Channel
Oahu
Honolulu
PACIFIC OCEAN
Kaiwi Channel
Molokai
Lanai
Lahaina
Maui
Haleakala 3055
Hawaiian
Alenuihaha Channel
4205
Mauna Kea
Mauna Loa 4169
Hilo
Islands
Kilauea Crater

20   0   20   40   60   80 miles
20   0   40   80   120 km

Projection: Albers' Equal Area with two standard parallels.

San Diego
Tijuana
Ensenada
Mexicali
Phoenix
Yuma
Tucson
Deming
365B
Wichita Falls
Carlsbad
Abilene
Fort Wor

A
3078
Quintin
Pta.Baja
Nogales
Bisbee
Cananea
Nacozari
Ciudad Juárez
Agua Prieta
El Paso
Villa Ahumada
Pecos
U
N
I
T
E
E
Brown
S. Angelo
Wa
Temp
Austin

Pta. Sta.
Eugenia
Sonora
Ures
Hermosillo
Torres
Galeana
Sta. Maria
Chihuahua
Conchos
San Carlos
2896
Piedras Negras
San Antonio
H

B
Sta. Rosalia
Mulege
Guaymas
Empalme
Ciudad
Obregón
Navojoa
Huatabampo
Fuerte
Madera
Sierra
M
Ciudad
Camargo
Delicias
Jimenez
Nueva Rosita
Sabinas
Eagle Pass
Laredo
Nuevo Laredo
B

B. Ballenas
Pta.S.Juanico
La Purisima
El Fuerte
Los Mochis
Sinaloa
Topolobampo
Guamúchil
3150
Hidalgo del
Parral
Lerdo
Nazas
Monclova
S. Pedro
Gómez Palacio
Falcon Res.
Reynosa
Sabinas
Hidalgo
M
La
S. Fern

Culiacan
Elota
E
Durango
Torreón
Matamoros
Saltillo
Monterrey

C
C. San Lucas
2406
La Paz
La Paz
Elota
Mazatlán
Rosario
M
4054
Catorce
Sombrerete
Concepcion
del Oro
Linares
Monterreios
Ciudad
Montec
Ciudad
Madero

Escuinapa
Cd. Garcia
Fresnillo
Matehuala
Victoria
Charcas
Zacatecas
Tula
3353
Acaponeta
San Luis
Potosí
Panuco
Tamp
C.

D
Is. de
Revillagigedo
(Mex.)
Is. Tres
Marias
Tuxpan
Tepic
R. Grande
Santiago
Guadalajara
Ameca
Zacoalco
Colima Vol.
4339
L. de Chapala
Zamora
Aguascalientes
León
Guanajuato
Celaya
Morelia
Querétaro
Arapuato
MEXICO
Toluca
Cuernavaca
Puebla
Pachuca
Tulancingo
Tlaxcala
Papantla
Tux
C.
Ori

Manzanillo
Colima
Balsas
Iguala
Popocatepetl
5452
3703
Mexcala
Tlaxid
Chilpancingo
Chilapa
Oaxaca
Acapulco
Ayutla
Ometepec
Verde Tehu
Sali

E
P A C I F I C

O C E A N

F
Projection: Bonne

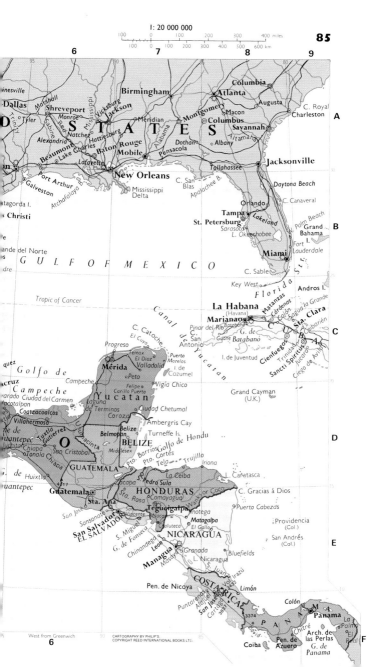

I: 20 000 000

GULF OF MEXICO

Tropic of Cancer

Golfo de Campeche

Golfo de Tehuantepec

La Habana (Havana)
Marianao

Matanzas
Cárdenas

Pinar del Río
San Antonio
Batabanó
G. de Batabanó

Sta. Clara
Cienfuegos
Sancti Spíritus

C. Catoche
El Cuyo
Progreso
Temax
El Díez
Mérida
Peto
Valladolid
Puerto Morelos
I. de Cozumel
Vigía Chico

Felipe Carrillo Puerto
Yucatan
Laguna de Términos
Ciudad del Carmen
Ciudad Chetumal
Corozal
Belize
Ambergris Cay
Turneffe Is.
BELIZE
Middlesex
Pto. Barrios
Pto. Cortés
Golfo de Hondu

Campeche
Coatzacoalcos
Villahermosa
Tuxtla Gutierrez
San Cristobal
Jacinta
GUATEMALA
Chiapa
Guatemala
Sta. Ana
Sta. Rosa
Jacoba
Pedro Sula
La Ceiba
Trujillo
Iriona
HONDURAS
Comayagua
Tegucigalpa
Yuscarán
L. Caratasca

San José
Sonsonate
San Salvador
EL SALVADOR
S. Miguel
G. de Fonseca
Juticalpa
Matagalpa
El Gallo
C. Gracias á Dios
Puerto Cabezas

Chinandega
León
Managua
Granada
L. Nicaragua
Masoya
Bluefields

Providencia (Col.)
San Andrés (Col.)

Grand Cayman (U.K.)

Pen. de Nicoya
COSTA RICA
Puntarenas
Alajuela
San José
Cartago
Irazú
Limón
San Juan

Colón
Panama
Chitré
Pen. de Azuero
Coiba
G. de Panamá
Arch. de las Perlas

UNITED STATES

Dallas
Tyler
Marshall
Shreveport
Monroe
Vicksburg
Jackson
Birmingham
Atlanta
Columbia
Augusta
C. Royal
Charleston
Alexandria
Natchez
Hattiesburg
Meridian
Montgomery
Columbus
Macon
Savannah
Beaumont
Lake Charles
Baton Rouge
Mobile
Dothan
Albany
Pensacola
Tallahassee
Jacksonville
Lafayette
New Orleans
Port Arthur
Galveston
C. San Blas
Apalachee B.
Mississippi Delta
Daytona Beach
Orlando
C. Canaveral
Tampa
Lakeland
St. Petersburg
Sarasota
L. Okeechobee
W. Palm Beach
Grand Bahama
Fort Lauderdale
Miami
C. Sable
Key West

Florida Str.
Andros I.

Canal de Yucatan

I. de Juventud

s Christi
ande del Norte
dre
quez
acruz
arado
acotalpan
te de
uantepec
de Huixtla
uantepec

West from Greenwich

West from Greenwich

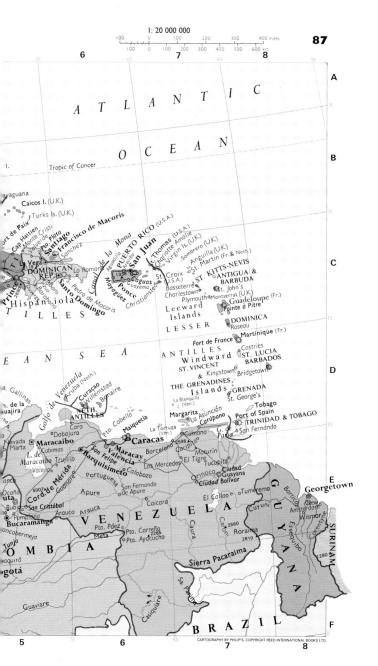

1: 20 000 000

A T L A N T I C

O C E A N

Tropic of Cancer

I.

ayaguana

Caicos I. (U.K.)
Turks Is. (U.K.)

ort de Paix
Cap Haitien
Monte Cristi
Pto. Plata   Francisco de Macoris
Verde   Sánchez
Vega

Prince
Bonao

DOMINICAN
REP.
La Romana
Pedro de Macoris

Santo Domingo

Hispaniola

Canal de la Mona

PUERTO RICO (U.S.A.)
1338   San Juan
Mayagüez   Caguas
Ponce   Guayama
Christiansted

T I L L E S

St. Thomas (U.S.A.)
Charlotte Amalie
Virgin Is. (U.K.)

St. Croix
(U.S.A.)

Sombrero (U.K.)
St. Martin (Fr. & Neth.)

Anguilla (U.K.)

ST. KITTS-NEVIS   ANTIGUA &
Basseterre   BARBUDA
Charlestown   St. John's
Plymouth Montserrat (U.K.)
Guadeloupe (Fr.)
Pointe à Pitre

Leeward
Islands

DOMINICA
Roseau

L E S S E R

Fort de France   Martinique (Fr.)

A N T I L L E S   Castries

Windward   ST. LUCIA
ST. VINCENT   BARBADOS
& Kingstown's   Bridgetown

THE GRENADINES

I s l a n d s   GRENADA
La Blanquilla   St. George's
(Ven.)

Tobago
Port of Spain   TRINIDAD & TOBAGO
Margarita   La Asunción
Carúpano   San Fernando
G. de
Paria

E A N   S E A

a. Gallinas
n. de la
uajira

Golfo de Venezuela

Aruba (Neth.)
Curaçao
Willemstad
Bonaire

NETH.
ANTILLES

Pto. Cabello

Maiquetía

La Tortuga
(Ven.)

Cumaná

Caracas

Barcelona   2596 e
Coripito
Maturín
El Tigre
Tucupita

Nevada
Marta   Maracaibo
L. de Cabimas
Maracaibo Trujillo
Valero

Dabajuro
Coro

San Felipe   Maracay   Valencia
Barquisimeto
Calabozo
Las Mercedes

Orinoco   Ciudad
Guayana
Ciudad Bolívar

Georgetown

 anco

Ocaño
uta
Rubio
Pamplona
Bucaramanga
ancabermeja

Cord. de Mérida
San Cristóbal

Portuguesa
San Fernando
de Apure

El Callao   Tumeremo

Apure   Caicara

V E N E Z U E L A

New
Amsterdam
Wismure

GUYANA

SURINAM

unja

Pto. Páez
Pto. Carreño
Meta   Pto. Ayacucho

2285
Caura   2560
Roraima
2810

Essequibo   280

gotá   O M B I A

Sierra Pacaraima

Guaviare

Sa. Parida

Casiquiare

B R A Z I L

CARTOGRAPHY BY PHILIP'S. COPYRIGHT REED INTERNATIONAL BOOKS LTD.

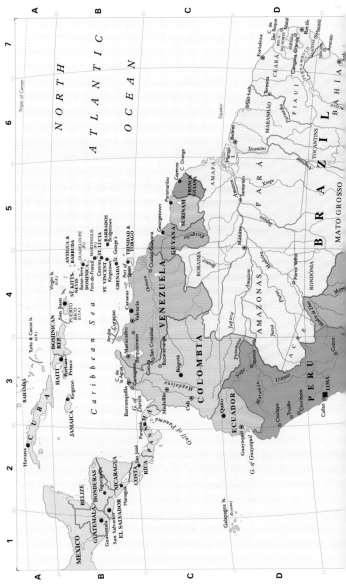

200   0   200   400   600   800 miles
400   0   400   800   1200 km

E   F   G   H

MINAS GERAIS

ESPÍRITO
SANTO

Goiânia

Belo
Horizonte

Juiz
de Fora

Vitória

Campos

Ribeirão
Preto

Ouro
Preto

Tietê

Niterói

RIO DE
JANEIRO

SÃO PAULO

SÃO PAULO

PARANÁ

SANTA CATARINA

Curitiba

Porto Alegre

RIO GRANDE
DO SUL

Pelotas

7

SOUTH

ATLANTIC

OCEAN

6

Paraguai

MATO GROSSO
DO SUL

Paraná

PARAGUAY

Asunción

Pilcomayo

Paraguai

Corrientes

Paraná

URUGUAY

Montevideo

Río de la Plata

Mar del Plata

5

Santa Cruz

Sucre

Cochabamba

Resistencia

Salado

Santa Fe

Rosario

BUENOS AIRES

La Plata

Bahía
Blanca

South Georgia
(U.K.)

FALKLAND IS.
(U.K.)

West Falkland   East Falkland

Stanley

West from Greenwich

Salta

San Miguel
de Tucumán

Córdoba

San Juan

Mendoza

N

T

I

N

A

Jujuy

Arequipa

Iquique

Antofagasta

Negro

Colorado

Viedma

Chubut

Gulf of San Jorge

Comodoro Rivadavia

4

C

H

I

L

E

Viña del Mar

Valparaíso

SANTIAGO

Concepción

Valdivia

Puerto Montt

Gulf of Penas

Magellan's Str.

Tierra del Fuego

Punta Arenas

C. Horn

3

San Félix
(Chile)

San Ambrosio
(Chile)

Arch. de Juan Fernández
(Chile)

Tropic of Capricorn

P   A   C   I   F   I   C

O   C   E   A   N

2

1

■ LIMA   Capital Cities

CARTOGRAPHY BY PHILIP'S
COPYRIGHT REED INTERNATIONAL BOOKS LTD

Projection: Lambert's Azimuthal Equal Area

E   F   G   H

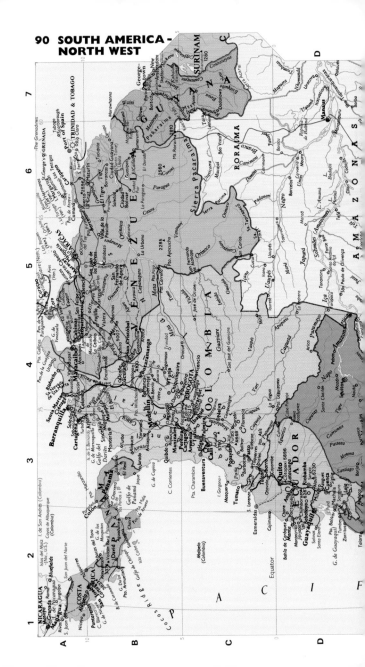

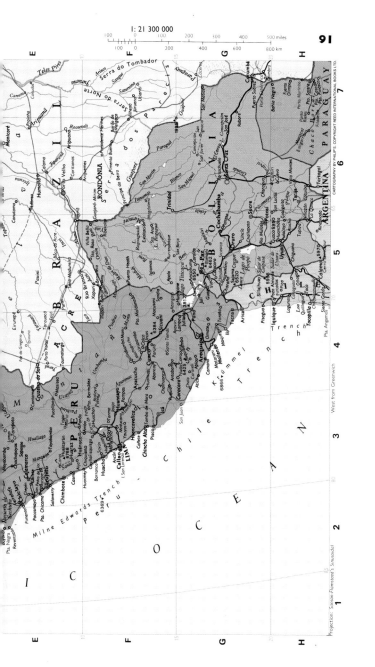

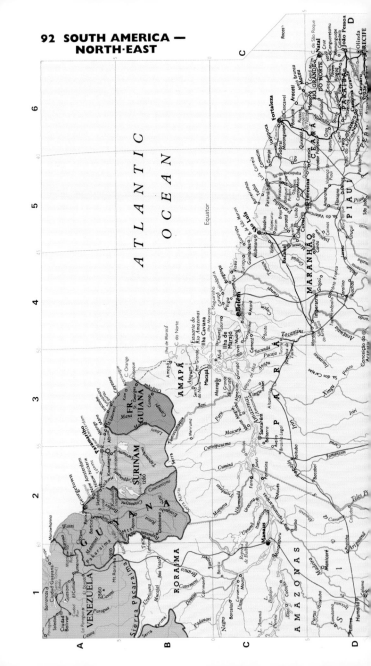

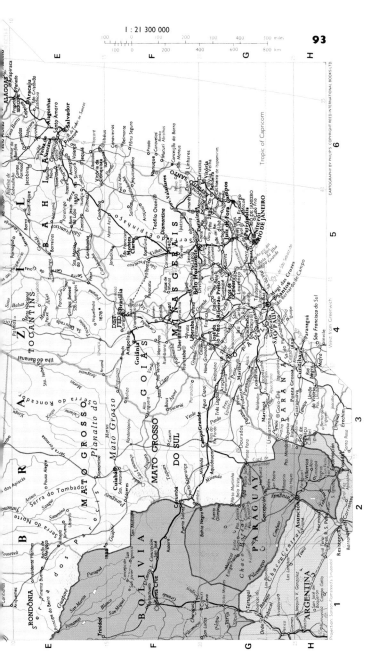

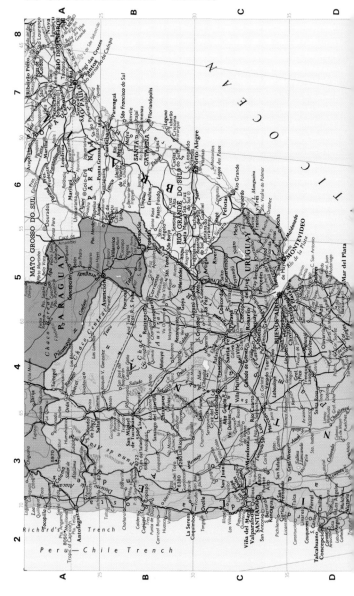

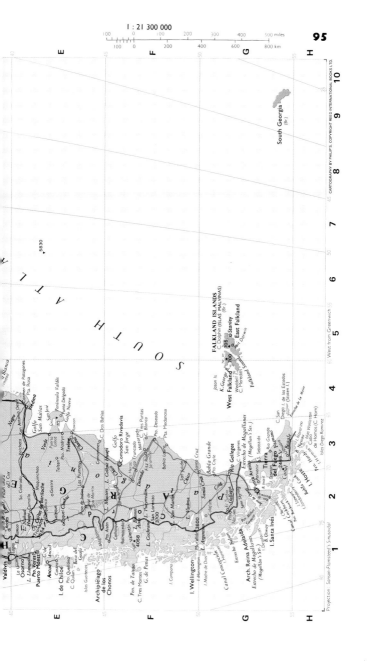

1 : 21 300 000

100   0   100   200   300   400   500 miles
100   0   200   400   600   800 km

E   F   G   H

10
9
South Georgia
(Br.)
8

CARTOGRAPHY BY PHILIP'S. COPYRIGHT REED INTERNATIONAL BOOKS LTD.

7

5830

6

S   O   U   T   H   A   T   L

FALKLAND ISLANDS
(ISLAS MALVINAS)
C. Dolphin
Stanley
West Falkland   East Falkland
C. Meredith   Falkland Sd.

Jason Is.
K. George
Weddell I.

5   West from Greenwich

Valdivia
Osorno
Pto. Varas
Puerto Montt
Ancud
I. de Chiloé
Archipiélago
de los
Chonos

Gulf
San Matías
Península Valdés
Golfo
San José
Golfo
Nuevo

Comodoro Rivadavia
Golfo
San Jorge

Río Gallegos
Estrecho de Magallanes
Tierra
del Fuego
C. San
Diego I. de Estados
(Staten I.)
Cabo
de Hornos (C. Horn)
Isla Diego Ramírez

I. Wellington
Arch. Reina Adelaida
Estrecho de Magallanes
(Magellan's Str.)
I. Santa Inés

Projection Sanson-Flamsteed's Sinusoidal

E   F   G   H

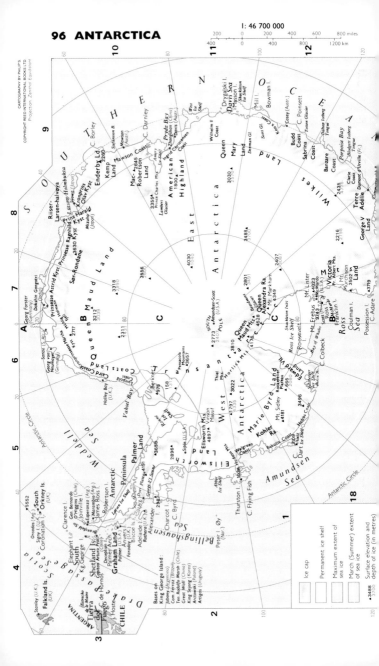

96 ANTARCTICA

Index to Map Pages

The index contains the names of all principal places and features shown on the maps. Physical features composed of a proper name (Erie) and a description (Lake) are positioned alphabetically by the proper name. The description is positioned after the proper name and is usually abbreviated:

Erie, L. **72** **C5**

Where a description forms part of a settlement or administrative name however, it is always written in full and put in its true alphabetical position:

Lake Charles **79** **D7**

Names beginning St. are alphabetized under Saint, but Sankt, Sint, Sant, Santa and San are all spelt in full and are alphabetized accordingly.

The number in bold type which follows each name in the index refers to the number of the map page where that feature or place will be found. This is usually the largest scale at which the place or feature appears.

The letter and figure which are in bold type immediately after the page number give the grid square on the map page, within which the feature is situated.

Rivers carry the symbol → after their names. A solid square ■ follows the name of a country while an open square □ refers to a first order administrative area.

Aachen 14 C4
Aalen 14 D6
Aarau 13 C8
Aare → 13 C8
Ābādān 47 E7
Abakan 30 D7
Abashiri . . . 32 F12
Abbeville . . 12 A4
Abéché 53 F3
Abeokuta . . 55 G5
Aberdeen,
  U.K. 10 C5
Aberdeen,
  S. Dak.,
  U.S.A. . . 76 C5
Aberdeen,
  Wash.,
  U.S.A. . 80 B2
Aberystwyth 11 E4
Abidjan 55 G4
Abilene 78 C4
Abitibi L. . . 69 D3
Abkhazia □ . 25 C5
Abohar 42 D9
Absaroka
  Range . . . 81 C9
Abu Dhabi =
  Abū Ẓāby . 44 E3
Abū Ẓāby . 44 E3
Abuja 55 G6
Abukuma-
  Gawa → . 33 G12
Acapulco . 84 D5
Accra 55 G4
Achill I. 11 E1
Achinsk 30 D7
Acireale . . . 21 F5
Acklins I. . 86 B5
Aconcagua,
  Cerro . 94 C3
Acre □ 91 E4
Ad Dammām 47 F7

Ad Dawhah . 44 E2
Ada 79 B5
Adaja → . . . 18 B3
Adamaoua,
  Massif de l' 53 G1
Adamello,
  Mte. 20 A3
Adam's
  Bridge . 43 Q11
Adams Mt. . 80 B3
Adana 46 C3
Adapazan . . 46 B2
Adare, C. . 96 B15
Adda → . . . 20 B2
Addis Abeba 53 G6
Adelaide . . . 62 B2
Adelaide I. . 96 A3
Adelaide Pen. 70 B10
Adélie, Terre 96 A14
Aden = Al
  'Adan . . . 49 E4
Aden, G. of . 49 E4
Adige → . . . 20 B4
Adirondack
  Mts. . . . 73 C8
Admiralty I. . 71 C6
Admiralty Is. . 64 K9
Ado-Ekiti . . 55 G6
Adoni . . . 43 M10
Adour → . . . 12 E3
Adra 18 D4
Adrano . . . 21 F5
Adrar 54 C4
Adré 53 F3
Adriatic Sea . 20 C5
Ægean Sea . 23 E5
Aerhtai Shan 34 B4
Afghanistan ■
  . . . . . 45 C6
'Afif 47 G5
Afognak I. . 71 C4
Afyonkarahisar
  . . . . . 46 C2

Agadez 55 E6
Agadir 54 B3
Agartala . . . 41 F8
Agde 13 E5
Agen 12 D4
Agra 42 F10
Agri → 21 D6
Ağn Dağı . . 46 C6
Ağn Karakose 46 C5
Agrigento . . 21 F4
Agrinion . . . 23 E3
Aguascalientes
  . . . . . 84 C4
Aguilas . . . 19 D5
Agulhas, C. . 58 E4
Ahaggar . . . 54 D6
Ahmadabad . 43 H8
Ahmadnagar . 43 K9
Ahmadpur . 42 E7
Ahvāz 47 E7
Aigues-
  Mortes . 13 E6
Aiken 75 C7
Air 55 E6
Aisne → . . 13 B5
Aix-en-
  Provence . 13 E6
Aix-les-Bains 13 D6
Aiyion 23 E4
Ajaccio . . . 13 F8
Ajanta Ra. . 43 J9
Ajaria □ . . . 25 E5
Ajmer 42 F9
Ajo, C. de . 18 A4
Akashi . . . 32 B4
Akharnai . . 23 E4
Akhelóós → . 23 E3
Akhisar . . . 23 E6
Akimiski I. . 69 C2
Akita . . . 33 G12
'Akko . . . 46 D3
Aklavik . . . 70 B6

Akola 43 J10
Akpatok I. . 68 B4
Akron 72 D5
Aksaray . . . 46 C3
Akşehir . . . 46 C2
Aktsyabrski . 17 B9
Akure 55 G6
Al 'Adan . . 49 E4
Al Başrah . . 47 E6
Al Ḥijāz . . . 47 F4
Al Ḥudaydah 49 E3
Al Hufūf . . . 47 F7
Al Jawf . . . 47 D4
Al Jazirah . . 46 D5
Al Kūt 47 D6
Al Kuwayt . . 47 E7
Al Lādhiqiyah 46 D3
Al Madīnah . 46 F4
Al Manāmah . 46 E2
Al Mawşil . . 46 C5
Al Mubarraz . 47 F7
Al Qāmishli . 46 C5
Al Qaţīf . . . 47 F7
Al 'Ulā . . . 47 F4
Alabama □ . 74 C4
Alabama → . 74 D4
Alaçam
Alania =
  North
  Ossetia □ . 25 E5
Alanya . . . 46 C2
Alaşehir . . . 23 E7
Alaska □ . . 71 B4
Alaska, G. of 71 C5
Alaska Range 71 B4
Alba 20 B2
Alba-Iulia . . 17 E6

Albacete . . . 19 C5
Albania ■ . . 23 D3
Albany,
  Australia . 60 H2
Albany, Ga.,
  U.S.A. . . . 75 D5
Albany, N.Y.,
  U.S.A. . . 73 C9
Albany, Oreg.,
  U.S.A. . . 80 C2
Albany → . . 69 C2
Albemarle . 75 B7
Alberche → . 18 C3
Albert L. . . 57 D6
Albertville . 13 D7
Albi 12 E5
Ålborg . . . 9 G9
Alborz,
  Reshteh-ye
  Kūhhā-ye . 44 B3
Albuquerque 83 C9
Albury . . . 63 C4
Alcalá de
  Henares . 18 B4
Alcalá la Real 18 D4
Alcamo . . . 21 F4
Alcaniz . . . 19 B5
Alcántara,
  Embalse de 18 C2
Alcantarilla . 19 D5
Alcaraz,
  Sierra de . 19 C4
Alcaudete . 18 D3
Alcázar de
  San Juan . 18 C4
Alchevsk . . 25 D4
Alcira . . . 19 C5
Alcoy . . . 19 C5
Aldabra Is. . 51 G8
Aldan → . . 31 C10
Alderney . . 11 G5
Alençon . . 12 B4

Aleppo

Aleppo = Ḥalab 46 C4
Alès 13 D6
Alessándria . 20 B2
Ålesund 8 F9
Aleutian Is. . 71 C2
Alexander Arch. 71 C6
Alexander I. . 96 A3
Alexandria = El Iskandarîya 52 B4
Alexandria, Canada ... 71 C7
Alexandria, S. Africa . 59 E5
Alexandria, La., U.S.A. 79 D7
Alexandria, Va., U.S.A. 73 C7
Alexandroúpolis 22 D5
Algarve 18 D1
Algeciras .. 18 D3
Algemesí .. 19 C5
Alger 54 A5
Algeria ■ .. 54 C5
Alghero ... 21 D2
Algiers = Alger 54 A5
Algoa B. ... 59 E5
Aliağa 23 E6
Alicante ... 19 C5
Alice Springs 60 E5
Aligarh 42 F11
Alipur Duar . 41 D7
Aliwal North 59 E5
Aljustrel ... 18 D1
Alkmaar 14 B3
All American Canal 82 D5
Allahabad .. 40 E3
Allegheny → 73 D5
Allegheny Plateau .. 73 F5
Allentown .. 73 D8
Alleppey ... 43 Q10
Aller → 14 B5
Allier → ... 13 C5
Alma Ata = Almaty ... 29 E8
Almada 18 C1
Almadén .. 18 C3
Almansa ... 19 C5
Almanzor, Pico del Moro 18 B3
Almanzora → 19 D5
Almaty 29 E8
Almazán .. 19 B4
Almelo 14 B4
Almendralejo 18 C2
Almería ... 19 D4
Alnwick ... 10 D6
Alor 39 F2
Alps 14 E5
Alsace 13 B7
Alsask 71 C9
Alsåsua ... 19 A4
Altai = Aerhtai Shan . 34 B4
Altamura .. 21 D6
Altay 34 B3
Altea 19 C5
Alton 77 F9
Altoona ... 73 D6
Altun Shan . 34 C3
Alwar ... 42 F10
Amadjuak . 68 B3
Amadjuak L. 68 B3
Amagasaki . 32 B4

Amakusa-Shotō ... 32 C2
Amaliás ... 23 F3
Amarillo ... 78 B3
Amaro, Mte. 20 C5
Amasya ... 46 B3
Amasya ... 46 B3
Amazon = Amazonas → 92 C3
Amazonas □ 90 D6
Amazonas → 92 C3
Ambala ... 42 D10
Amberg ... 15 D6
Ambikapur . 40 F4
Amboise ... 12 C4
Ambon 39 E3
Amchitka I. . 71 C1
Ameland .. 14 B3
American Highland . 96 B10
American Samoa ■ . 65 L13
Americus .. 75 C5
Amery 71 C10
Ames 77 D8
Amherst ... 69 D4
Amiata, Mte. 20 C3
Amiens ... 12 B5
Amirante Is. 26 K9
'Ammān ... 47 E3
Amorgós ... 23 F5
Amper → .. 15 D6
Amravati ... 43 J10
Amreli 43 J7
Amritsar ... 42 D9
Amroha ... 42 E11
Amsterdam . 14 B3
Amstetten .. 15 D8
Amudarya → 29 E6
Amundsen Gulf 70 A7
Amundsen Sea .. 96 B1
Amur → ... 31 D12
An Nafūd .. 47 E5
An Najaf ... 47 D6
An Nhon ... 36 B3
Anaconda .. 81 B7
Anadolu ... 46 C2
Anaheim ... 82 D4
Anambas, Kepulauan 37 D3
Anamur ... 46 C3
Anan 32 C4
Anantnag .. 42 C9
Ananyiv ... 17 E9
Anápolis .. 93 F4
Anár 44 D3
Anatolia = Anadolu .. 46 C2
Anchorage .. 71 B5
Ancona ... 20 C4
Andalucía □ 18 D3
Andalusia . 74 D4
Andaman Is. 27 H13
Anderson .. 72 D3
Anderson → 70 B7
Andes, Cord. de los .. 91 G4
Andhra Pradesh □ 43 L11
Andijon ... 29 E8
Andikíthira . 23 G4
Andorra ■ . 19 A6
Andreanof Is. 71 C2
Ándria ... 20 D6
Ándros ... 23 F5
Ándros I. .. 86 B4
Andújar ... 18 C3
Aneto, Pico de 19 A6
Angara → .. 30 D7
Angarsk ... 30 D8

Ånge 8 F11
Ångermanälven → 8 F11
Angers 12 C3
Anglesey ... 11 E4
Angola ■ .. 58 A3
Angoulême . 12 D4
Angoumois . 12 D4
Anguilla ■ . 87 C7
Anhui □ ... 35 C6
Anjou 12 C3
Ankara 46 C3
Ann Arbor .. 72 C4
Annaba ... 54 A6
Annan 11 D5
Annapolis .. 73 E7
Annecy ... 13 D7
Anniston ... 74 C5
Annobón ... 51 G4
Ansbach ... 14 D6
Anshun ... 35 D5
Antakya ... 46 C4
Antalya ... 46 C2
Antalya Körfezi ... 46 C2
Antananarivo 59 H9
Antarctic Pen. 96 A4
Antarctica . 96 C
Antequera .. 18 D3
Antibes ... 13 E7
Anticosti, I. d' 69 D4
Antigua & Barbuda ■ 87 C7
Antofagasta . 94 A2
Antrim ... 11 D3
Antsiranana . 59 G9
Antwerp = Antwerpen 14 C3
Anyang ... 35 C6
Anzhero-Sudzhensk 29 D9
Ánzio 20 D4
Aomori ... 33 F12
Aosta 20 B1
Apalachicola → 74 E5
Aparri 38 A2
Apeldoorn . 14 B3
Apia 65 L13
Appalachian Mts. 73 F5
Appennini .. 20 C4
Appleton ... 72 B1
Aprília 20 D4
Aqmola ... 29 D8
Aqtöbe ... 29 D6
Aquitain, Bassin ... 12 D3
Ar Ramādî .. 46 D5
Ar Riyāḍ ... 47 F6
Ara 40 E5
Arabian Gulf = Gulf, The 44 E2
Arabian Sea 26 H10
Araç 46 B3
Aracaju ... 93 E6
Araçatuba .. 93 G3
Aracena ... 18 D2
Arad 16 E5
Arafura Sea . 39 F4
Aragón □ ... 19 B5
Aragón → .. 92 C3
Arakan Yoma 41 H10
Aral 29 E7
Aral Sea ... 29 E6
Aran I. 10 D2
Aran Is. ... 11 E2
Aranda de Duero ... 18 B4
Aranjuez ... 18 B4
Arapgir ... 46 C4
Arapiraca .. 93 D6

Ararat 62 C3
Ararat, Mt. = Ağri Daği . 46 C6
Arbatax ... 21 E2
Arbîl 46 C6
Arbroath ... 10 C5
Arcachon ... 12 D3
Arcos de la Frontera . 18 D3
Arctic Bay .. 68 A2
Arctic Red River ... 70 B6
Ardabîl ... 46 C7
Ardahan ... 46 B5
Ardenne ... 14 D3
Ardmore ... 78 B5
Arendal ... 9 G9
Arequipa ... 91 G4
Arévalo ... 18 B3
Arezzo ... 20 C3
Arganda ... 18 B4
Argentan ... 12 B3
Argentário, Mte. ... 20 C3
Argentina ■ 94 D3
Argolikós Kólpos ... 23 F4
Árgos 23 F4
Argostólion . 23 E3
Århus 9 G10
Arica 91 G4
Arizona □ .. 83 C7
Arkansas □ . 79 B7
Arkansas → 79 C8
Arkansas City 78 A5
Arkhangelsk 28 C5
Arklow ... 11 E3
Arlanzón → . 18 A3
Arlberg P. .. 14 E6
Arles 13 E6
Arlington, Va., U.S.A. . 73 E7
Arlington, Wash., U.S.A. 80 A2
Arlon 14 D3
Armagh ... 11 D3
Armenia ... 90 C3
Armenia ■ . 25 E5
Armidale ... 63 B5
Armstrong . 69 C2
Arnaud → .. 68 B3
Arnhem ... 14 C3
Arnhem Land 60 C5
Arno → ... 20 C3
Arnsberg ... 14 C5
Arran 10 D4
Arras 13 A5
Arrée, Mts. d' 12 B2
Árta 23 E3
Artois ... 12 A5
Artsyz ... 17 F9
Artvin ... 46 B5
Aru, Kepulauan 39 F4
Aruba ■ ... 87 D6
Arunachal Pradesh □ 41 C10
Arusha ... 57 E7
Arvi 70 B10
Arvayheer . 34 B5
Asahigawa . 32 F12
Asansol ... 40 F6
Ascension I. 51 G2
Aschaffenburg 14 D5
Aschersleben 15 C6
Áscoli Piceno 20 C4
Ash Shām, Bādiyat ... 47 D4
Ash Shāriqah 44 E3
Ashburton .. 65 F4
Ashcroft ... 71 C7
Asheville ... 75 B6
Ashford ... 11 F7

Ashgabat ... 29 F6
Ashikaga ... 32 A6
Ashizuri-Zaki 32 C3
Ashkhabad = Ashgabat . 29 F6
Ashmyany .. 17 A7
Ashqelon ... 47 E3
Ashtabula .. 72 D5
Ashuanipi, L. 69 C4
Asifabad ... 43 K11
Asinara ... 20 D2
Asinara, G. dell' ... 20 D2
Asipovichy . 17 B9
'Asîr □ 48 D3
Asir, Ras ... 49 E5
Asmera ... 53 E6
Assam □ ... 41 D9
Assen 14 B4
Assiniboia . 71 D9
Assiniboine → 71 D10
Assisi 20 C4
Asti 20 B2
Astipálaia .. 23 F6
Astorga ... 18 A2
Astoria ... 80 B2
Astrakhan .. 25 D6
Asturias □ .. 18 A3
Asunción ... 94 B5
Aswân 52 D5
Atacama, Desierto de 94 A3
Atami 32 B6
Atbara ... 53 E5
Atbara → .. 53 E5
'Atbara → .. 53 E5
Athabasca .. 71 C8
Athabasca → 70 C8
Athabasca, L. 70 C8
Athens = Athínai ... 23 F4
Athens, Ala., U.S.A. .. 74 B4
Athens, Ga., U.S.A. .. 75 C6
Athínai ... 23 F4
Athlone ... 11 E3
Áthos 23 D5
Athy 11 E3
Atlanta ... 75 C5
Atlantic City 73 E8
Atlas Mts. = Haut Atlas 54 B3
Attawapiskat → 69 C2
Atyraū ... 29 E6
Aubagne ... 13 E6
Aube → ... 13 B5
Auburn ... 74 C5
Aubusson .. 12 D5
Auch 12 E4
Auckland .. 64 B6
Aude → ... 13 E5
Augsburg .. 14 D6
Augusta, Italy 21 F5
Augusta, Ga., U.S.A. .. 75 C7
Augusta, Maine, U.S.A. . 73 B11
Aunis 12 C3
Aurangabad, Bihar, India 40 E5
Aurangabad, Maharashtra, India 43 K9
Aurich ... 14 B4
Aurillac ... 12 D5
Aurora, Colo., U.S.A. .. 76 F2
Aurora, Ill., U.S.A. .. 72 D1
Austin, Minn., U.S.A. .. 77 D8

Name		
Austin, *Tex., U.S.A.*	78	D5
Australia ■	60	E6
Australian Alps	63	C4
Australian Capital Territory □	63	C4
Austria ■	15	E8
Autun	13	C6
Auvergne	13	D5
Auvergne, Mts. d'	13	D5
Auxerre	13	C5
Avallon	13	C5
Aveiro	18	B1
Avellino	21	D5
Aversa	21	D5
Avezzano	20	C4
Aviemore	10	C5
Avignon	13	E6
Ávila	18	B3
Avilés	18	A3
Avola	21	F5
Avranches	12	B3
Axiós →	23	D4
Ayabe	32	B4
Ayamonte	18	D2
Aydın	23	F6
Ayers Rock	60	E5
Áyios Evstrátios	23	E5
Aylmer, L.	70	B8
Ayr	10	D4
Ayvacık	23	E6
Ayvalık	23	E6
Az Zarqā	46	D4
Azamgarh	40	D4
Azerbaijan ■	25	E6
Azores	50	C1
Azov, Sea of	25	D4
Azuaga	18	C3
Azuero, Pen. de	86	E3
Baba Burnu	23	E6
Babaeski	22	D6
Bābol	44	B3
Babruysk	17	B9
Babuyan Chan.	38	A2
Bacabal	92	C5
Bacău	17	E8
Back →	70	B9
Bacolod	38	B2
Bad Ischl	15	E7
Bad Kissingen	14	C6
Bad Lands	76	D3
Badajoz	18	C2
Badalona	19	B7
Baden	15	D8
Baden-Baden	14	D5
Baden-Württemberg □	14	D5
Badgastein	15	E7
Baena	18	D3
Baeza	18	D4
Baffin B.	68	A4
Baffin I.	68	B3
Bafra	46	B3
Baghdād	46	D6
Bagheria	21	E4
Baguio	38	A2
Bahamas ■	86	A4
Baharampur	40	E7
Bahawalpur	42	E7
Bahía □	93	E5
Bahía Blanca	94	D4
Bahraich	40	D3
Bahrain ■	44	E2
Baia Mare	17	E6
Baie Comeau	69	D4
Baikal, L. = Baykal, Oz.	30	D8
Baird Mts.	71	B3
Baja California	84	A1
Baker, L.	70	B10
Baker Lake	70	B10
Baker Mt.	80	A3
Baker's Dozen Is.	69	C3
Bakersfield	82	C3
Bākhtarān	46	D6
Bakı	25	E6
Bakony Hegyseg	16	E3
Baku = Bakı	25	E6
Balabac Str.	36	C5
Balaguer	19	B6
Balaklava	25	E3
Balaton	16	E3
Baleares, Is.	19	C7
Baleshwar	40	G6
Bali	37	F5
Balıkesir	23	E6
Balıkpapan	37	E5
Balkan Mts. = Stara Planina	22	C4
Ballarat	62	C3
Ballater	10	C5
Ballina	11	D2
Ballinasloe	11	E2
Ballymena	11	D3
Balqash	29	E8
Balqash Köl	29	E8
Balrampur	40	D4
Balsas →	84	D4
Balta	17	D9
Bălți	17	E8
Baltic Sea	9	G11
Baltimore	73	E7
Baluchistan □	42	F4
Balya	23	E6
Bam	44	D4
Bamako	55	F3
Bamberg	14	D6
Bamenda	55	G7
Banda, Kepulauan	39	E3
Banda Aceh	36	C1
Banda Sea	39	F3
Bandar 'Abbās	44	E4
Bandar-e Khomeyni	47	E7
Bandar Seri Begawan	36	D4
Bandırma	23	D7
Bandon	11	F2
Bandundu	56	E3
Bandung	37	F3
Banff, *Canada*	71	C8
Banff, *U.K.*	10	C5
Bangalore	43	N10
Banggai, Kepulauan	39	E2
Banghāzī	52	B3
Bangka, P.	37	E3
Bangka, Selat	37	E3
Bangkok	36	B2
Bangladesh ■	41	E7
Bangor, *Down, U.K.*	11	D4
Bangor, *Gwynedd, U.K.*	11	E4
Bangor, *U.S.A.*	73	B11
Bangui	56	D3
Bangweulu, L.	57	G6
Banja Luka	20	B6
Banjarmasin	37	E4
Banjul	55	F1
Banks I., *Australia*	63	B4
Banks Pen.	65	E5
Bankura	40	F6
Bannu	42	C7
Banská Bystrica	16	D4
Bantry	11	F2
Banyak, Kepulauan	37	D1
Baoding	35	C6
Baoji	35	C5
Baotou	35	B6
Bar	17	D8
Bar-le-Duc	13	B6
Baracaldo	19	A4
Baramula	42	B9
Baran	43	G10
Baranavichy	17	B8
Baranof I.	71	C6
Barbados ■	87	D8
Barbastro	19	A6
Barberton	59	D6
Barcellona Pozzo di Gotto	21	E5
Barcelona	19	B7
Barddhaman	40	F6
Bareilly	42	E11
Barfleur, Pte. de	12	B3
Barhi	40	E5
Bari	20	D6
Bari Doab	42	D8
Baring, C.	70	B8
Barisal	41	F8
Barito →	37	E4
Barkly Tableland	60	D6
Barletta	20	D6
Barmer	42	G7
Barnaul	29	D9
Barnsley	11	E6
Barnstaple	11	F4
Barquisimeto	90	A5
Barra	10	C3
Barrancabermeja	90	B4
Barrancos	18	C2
Barranquilla	90	A4
Barreiro	18	C1
Barrow	71	A4
Barrow-in-Furness	11	D5
Barry	11	F5
Barstow	82	C4
Bartin	46	B3
Bartlesville	79	A6
Barysaw	17	A9
Basarabeasca	17	E9
Basel	13	C7
Bashkortostan □	29	D6
Basilan	38	C2
Basildon	11	F7
Basingstoke	11	F6
Basque Provinces = Pais Vasco □	19	A4
Basra = Al Başrah	47	E6
Bass Str.	61	H8
Bassano	71	C8
Bassano del Grappa	20	B3
Basseterre	87	C7
Basti	40	D4
Bastia	13	E8
Bastogne	14	C3
Bata	56	D1
Batangas	38	B2
Bath	11	F5
Bathurst, *Australia*	63	B4
Bathurst, *Canada*	69	D4
Bathurst, C.	70	A7
Bathurst Inlet	70	B9
Batman	46	C5
Batna	54	A6
Baton Rouge	79	D8
Battambang	36	B2
Battipáglia	21	D5
Battle Creek	72	C3
Battle Harbour	69	C5
Battleford	71	C9
Batu, Kepulauan	37	E1
Batu Pahat	37	D2
Batumi	25	E5
Bauru	93	G4
Bautzen	15	C8
Bavaria = Bayern □	15	D6
Bawean	37	F4
Bay City	72	C4
Bayamo	86	B4
Bayan Har Shan	34	C4
Bayburt	46	B5
Bayern □	15	D6
Bayeux	12	B3
Bayındır	23	E6
Baykal, Oz.	30	D8
Bayonne	12	E3
Bayramiç	23	E6
Bayreuth	15	D6
Bayrūt	46	D3
Baytown	79	E6
Baza	19	D4
Beagle, Canal	95	G3
Beardmore Glacier	96	C14
Béarn	12	E3
Beauce, Plaine de la	12	B4
Beaufort Sea	66	B6
Beaufort West	58	E4
Beaumont	79	D6
Beaune	13	C6
Beauvais	12	B5
Beauval	71	C9
Beaver	71	B5
Beaver →	71	C9
Beawar	42	F9
Béchar	54	B4
Bedford	11	E6
Be'er Sheva	47	E3
Bei'an	35	B7
Beijing	35	C6
Beira	59	B6
Beirut = Bayrūt	46	D3
Beja	18	C2
Béjar	18	B3
Békéscsaba	16	E5
Bela	42	F5
Belarus ■	24	C2
Belcher Is.	69	C3
Belém	92	C4
Belfast	11	D4
Belfort	13	C7
Belgaum	43	M9
Belgium ■	14	C3
Belgorod	24	C4
Belgrade = Beograd	22	B3
Belitung	37	E3
Belize ■	85	D7
Belize City	85	D7
Bell Peninsula	69	B2
Bellary	43	M10
Belle-Ile	12	C2
Belle Isle	69	C5
Belle Isle, Str. of	69	C5
Belleville, *Canada*	69	D3
Belleville, *U.S.A.*	77	F10
Bellingham	80	A2
Bellingshausen Sea	96	A2
Bellinzona	13	C8
Belluno	20	A4
Belmopan	85	D7
Belo Horizonte	93	F5
Beloit	77	D10
Belokorovichi	17	C9
Belonia	41	F8
Belorussia ■ = Belarus ■	24	C2
Beloye More	28	C4
Belukha	29	E9
Bemidji	77	B7
Ben Nevis	10	C4
Benalla	63	C4
Benares = Varanasi	40	E4
Benavente	18	A3
Benbecula	10	C3
Bend	80	C3
Bendigo	63	C3
Benevento	20	D5
Bengal, Bay of	41	J7
Bengbu	35	C6
Benghazi = Banghāzī	52	B3
Bengkulu	37	E2
Beni Suef	52	C5
Benidorm	19	C5
Benin ■	55	G5
Benin, Bight of	55	H5
Benin City	55	G6
Benoni	59	D5
Benton Harbor	72	C2
Benue →	55	G6
Benxi	35	B7
Beograd	22	B3
Beppu	32	C2
Berber	53	E5
Berbera	49	E4
Berbérati	56	D3
Berdyansk	25	D4
Berdychiv	17	D9
Berehove	17	D6
Berestechko	17	C7
Bereza	17	B7
Berezhany	17	D7
Berezniki	28	D6
Berga	19	A6
Bergama	23	E6
Bérgamo	20	B2
Bergen	8	F9
Bergerac	12	D4
Berhala, Selat	37	E2
Bering Sea	71	C1
Bering Strait	71	B3
Berja	19	D4
Berkeley	80	G2
Berkner I.	96	B4
Berlin	15	B7
Bermuda ■	67	F13
Bern	13	C7
Bernburg	15	C6
Bernina, Piz	13	C8
Beroun	16	D2
Berry	12	C5
Bershad	17	D9
Berwick-upon-Tweed	10	D6
Besançon	13	C7
Besni	46	C4
Bessarabiya	17	E9
Bessemer	74	C4
Betanzos	18	A1

Bethel 71 B3
Bethlehem,
  S. Africa .. 59 D5
Bethlehem,
  U.S.A. 73 D8
Béthune 13 A5
Betsiamites . 69 D4
Bettiah 43 D4
Betul 43 J10
Beverley 11 E6
Beverly Hills 82 C3
Beypazarı ... 46 B2
Beyşehir Gölü 46 C2
Béziers 13 E5
Bhagalpur .. 40 E6
Bhandara ... 43 J11
Bhanrer Ra. . 43 H11
Bharatpur .. 42 F10
Bhatpara ... 41 F7
Bhavnagar .. 43 J8
Bhilwara ... 43 G9
Bhima → ... 43 L10
Bhimavaram 40 J3
Bhiwani 42 E10
Bhopal 43 H10
Bhubaneshwar
  .... 40 G5
Bhuj 43 H6
Bhusawal ... 43 J9
Bhutan ■ ... 41 D8
Biała Podlaska 17 B6
Białystok ... 17 B6
Biarritz 12 E3
Biberach ... 14 D5
Biddeford .. 73 C10
Bié, Planalto
  de 58 A3
Biel 13 C7
Bielefeld ... 14 B5
Biella 20 B2
Bielsko-Biała 16 D4
Bien Hoa ... 36 B3
Bienville, L. 69 C3
Big Spring .. 78 C3
Big Trout L. . 69 C2
Biğa 23 D6
Bigadiç 23 E7
Biggar 71 C9
Bighorn → . 81 B10
Bighorn Mts. 81 C10
Bihać 20 B5
Bihar 40 E5
Bihar □ 40 E5
Bijeljina ... 20 B7
Bikaner 42 E8
Bikini Atoll . 64 H11
Bila Tserkva 17 D10
Bilaspur ... 40 F4
Bilbao 19 A4
Bilecik 46 B2
Bilhorod-
  Dnistrovskyy
  .... 25 D3
Billings 81 C9
Biloxi 79 D9
Bina-Etawah 43 G11
Bingham
  Canyon .. 81 E7
Binghamton 73 C8
Bingöl 46 C5
Binjai 37 D1
Bioko 56 D1
Birecik 46 C4
Birmingham,
  U.K. 11 E5
Birmingham,
  U.S.A. ... 74 C4
Birr 11 E3
Biscay, B. of 12 D2
Bishkek 29 E8
Biskra 54 B6
Bismarck .. 76 B4
Bismarck
  Arch. 64 K9

Bissau 55 F1
Bitlis 46 C5
Bitola 22 D3
Bitterfontein 58 E3
Bitterroot
  Range .. 81 B6
Biwa-Ko ... 32 B5
Biysk 29 D9
Bjelovar ... 20 B6
Black Forest
  =
  Schwarzwald
  .... 14 D5
Black Hills .. 76 D3
Black Sea ... 25 E3
Black
  Volta → .. 55 G4
Blackburn .. 11 E5
Blackpool ... 11 E5
Blackwater →
  .... 11 E2
Blagoveshchensk
  .... 31 D10
Blairmore .. 71 D8
Blanc, Mont . 13 D7
Blanca Peak . 83 B10
Blanes 19 B7
Blantyre ... 59 B6
Blenheim ... 65 D5
Bloemfontein 59 D5
Bloemhof ... 59 D5
Blois 12 C4
Bloomington,
  Ill., U.S.A. 77 E10
Bloomington,
  Ind., U.S.A. 72 E2
Blue Mts.,
  Oreg.,
  U.S.A. .. 80 C4
Blue Mts., Pa.,
  U.S.A. .. 73 D7
Blue Nile =
  Nîl el
  Azraq → . 53 E5
Blue Ridge
  Mts. 75 A7
Bo Hai ... 35 C6
Bobo-
  Dioulasso . 55 F4
Bóbr → ... 16 B2
Boca Raton . 75 F7
Bochum ... 14 C4
Boden 8 E12
Bodensee .. 13 C8
Bodø 8 E10
Bodrog → .. 16 D5
Bodrum ... 23 F6
Bogalusa ... 79 D9
Bogotá 90 C4
Bogra 41 E7
Böhmerwald 15 D7
Bohol 38 C2
Bohol Sea .. 38 C2
Boise 80 D5
Boise City .. 78 A3
Bolbec 12 B4
Bolekhiv ... 17 D6
Bolhrad ... 17 F9
Bolivia ■ ... 91 G6
Bologna ... 20 B3
Bolsena, L. di 20 C3
Bolshevik,
  Ostrov ... 30 B8
Bolton 11 E5
Bolu 46 B2
Bolvadin ... 46 C2
Bolzano ... 20 A3
Boma 56 F2
Bombay =
  Mumbai .. 43 K8
Bonavista .. 69 D5
Bonifacio .. 13 F8
Bonn 14 C4

Bonny, Bight
  of 56 D1
Boothia, Gulf
  of 68 A2
Boothia Pen. 70 A10
Borås 9 G10
Bordeaux .. 12 D3
Borger 78 B3
Borkum ... 14 B4
Borneo ... 37 D4
Bornholm .. 9 G11
Boryslav ... 17 D6
Bosa 21 D2
Bosanska
  Gradiška .. 20 B6
Bosna → .. 20 B7
Bosnia-
  Herzegovina ■
  .... 20 B6
Bosporus =
  Karadeniz
  Boğazı .. 22 D7
Boston, U.K. 11 E6
Boston,
  U.S.A. ... 73 C10
Botletle → . 58 C4
Botoşani ... 17 E8
Botswana ■ 58 C4
Bouaké ... 55 G3
Bouar 56 C3
Boulder ... 76 E2
Boulogne-sur-
  Mer 12 A4
Bourbonnais 13 C5
Bourg-en-
  Bresse .. 13 C6
Bourg-St.-
  Maurice .. 13 D7
Bourges ... 12 C5
Bourgogne . 13 C6
Bourke 63 B4
Bournemouth 11 F6
Boyne → .. 11 E3
Boz Dağları . 23 E7
Bozburun ... 23 F7
Bozcaada .. 23 E6
Bozdoğan .. 23 F7
Bozeman .. 81 C8
Bra 20 B1
Brač 20 C6
Bracciano, L.
  di 20 C4
Bräcke ... 8 F11
Bradenton . 75 F6
Bradford ... 11 E6
Braga 18 B1
Bragança .. 18 B2
Brahmapur . 40 H5
Brahmanbaria 41 F8
Brahmani → 40 G6
Brahmaputra →
  .... 41 F7
Bráila ... 17 F8
Branco → .. 90 D6
Brandenburg 15 B7
Brandenburg □
  .... 15 B7
Brandon .. 71 D10
Brandvlei .. 58 E3
Brantford .. 69 D2
Brasília ... 93 F4
Braşov ... 17 F7
Bratislava .. 16 D3
Bratsk ... 30 D8
Braunau ... 15 D7
Braunschweig 14 B6
Brawley ... 82 D5
Bray 11 E3
Bray, Pays de 12 B4
Brazil ■ ... 93 E4
Brazos → .. 79 E6

Brazzaville . 56 E3
Brčko 20 B7
Brecon ... 11 F5
Breda 14 C3
Bredasdorp . 58 E4
Bregenz ... 14 E5
Bremen ... 14 B5
Bremerhaven 14 B5
Bremerton .. 80 B2
Brenner P. .. 15 E6
Bréscia ... 20 B3
Bressanone . 20 A3
Brest, Belarus 17 B6
Brest, France 12 B1
Bretagne ... 12 B2
Briançon ... 13 D7
Bridgeport .. 73 D9
Bridgetown . 87 D8
Bridgewater 69 D4
Bridlington . 11 D6
Brig 13 C7
Brigham City 81 E7
Brighton ... 11 F6
Brindisi ... 21 D6
Brisbane ... 63 A5
Bristol 11 F5
Bristol, U.S.A. 75 A6
Bristol B. .. 71 C3
Bristol
  Channel . 11 F4
Britstown .. 58 E4
Brittany =
  Bretagne 12 B2
Brive-la-
  Gaillarde . 12 D4
Brno 16 D3
Brocken ... 14 C6
Brodeur Pen. 68 A2
Brody 17 C7
Broken Hill . 62 B3
Brooks Ra. . 71 B5
Broughton
  Island .. 68 B4
Brownsville . 78
Brownwood . 78 D4
Bruay-en-
  Artois ... 13 A5
Bruce, Mt. .. 60 E2
Bruck an der
  Mur 15 E8
Brugge ... 14 C2
Brunei ■ ... 36 D4
Brunswick .. 75 D7
Brussel ... 14 C3
Bryan 79 D5
Bryansk ... 24 C3
Bucak 46 C2
Bucaramanga 90 B4
Buchach ... 17 D7
Buchans ... 69 D5
Bucharest =
  Bucureşti . 22 B6
Buckie ... 10 C5
Bucureşti .. 22 B6
Budapest .. 16 E4
Bude 11 F4
Buenaventura 90 C3
Buenos Aires 94 C5
Buffalo ... 73 C6
Bug → ... 16 B5
Buh → 25 D3
Bujumbura . 57 E5
Bukavu ... 57 E5
Bukhoro ... 29 F7
Bukittinggi . 37 E2
Bulandshahr 42 E10
Bulawayo .. 59 C5
Buldan ... 23 E7
Bulgaria ■ .. 22 C5
Bunbury ... 60 G2
Buncrana .. 11 D3
Bundaberg . 63 C5
Bundi 43 G9
Bundoran .. 11 D2

Bungo-Suidō 32 C3
Bûr Sa'îd .. 52 B5
Bûr Sûdân . 53 E6
Buraydah .. 47 F6
Burdur ... 46 C2
Burgas ... 22 C6
Burgersdorp 59 E5
Burgos ... 18 A4
Burgundy =
  Bourgogne 13 C6
Burhaniye . 23 E6
Burkina
  Faso ■ .. 55 F4
Burlington,
  Iowa,
  U.S.A. .. 77 E9
Burlington,
  N.C., U.S.A. 75 A8
Burlington,
  Vt., U.S.A. 73 B9
Burlyu-Tyube 29 E8
Burma ■ ... 41 G11
Burnie ... 62 D4
Burnley ... 11 E5
Burnside → 70 B9
Bursa 23 D7
Buru 39 E3
Burundi ■ .. 57 E6
Bury St.
  Edmunds . 11 E7
Büshehr ... 44 D2
Busto Arsízio 20 B2
Buton 39 E2
Butte 81 B7
Butterworth . 36 C2
Butuan ... 38 C3
Buxtehude . 14 B5
Büyük
  Menderes →
  .... 23 F6
Büyükçekmece
  .... 22 D7
Buzău ... 17 F8
Buzen 32 C2
Byarezina → 17 B10
Bydgoszcz .. 16 B3
Byelorussia =
  Belarus ■ . 24 C2
Bykhaw ... 17 B10
Bylot I. ... 68 A3
Byrranga,
  Gory 30 B8
Bytom ... 16 C4

Cabimas .. 90 A4
Cabinda □ . 56 F2
Cabinet Mts. 81 B6
Cabonga,
  Réservoir . 69 D3
Cabot Str. . 69 D5
Cabra 18 D3
Cabrera ... 19 C7
Cabriel → . 19 C5
Čačak ... 22 C3
Cáceres ... 18 C2
Cádiz 18 D2
Cádiz, G. de . 18 D2
Caen 12 B3
Cagayan de
  Oro 38 C2
Cágliari ... 21 E2
Cágliari, G. di 21 E2
Cahors ... 12 D4
Cahul 17 F9
Caicos Is. .. 87 B5
Cairns ... 61 D8
Cairo = El
  Qâhira .. 52 B5
Cairo 79 A9
Cajamarca . 91 E3
Calabar ... 55 H6
Calábria □ .. 21 E6
Calahorra .. 19 A5

Calais 12 A4
Calamian Group ... 38 B1
Calamocha . 19 B5
Calapan ... 38 B2
Calatayud .. 19 B5
Calbayog .. 38 B2
Calcutta ... 41 F7
Caldas da Rainha .. 18 C1
Caldwell ... 80 D5
Caledon ... 58 E3
Caledon → . 59 E5
Calgary ... 71 C8
Cali 90 C3
Calicut ... 43 P9
California □ 82 B3
California, G. de 84 B2
Callao ... 91 F3
Caltagirone . 21 F5
Caltanissetta 21 F5
Calvi ... 13 E8
Calviá ... 19 C7
Calvinia ... 58 E3
Camagüey .. 86 B4
Camargue .. 13 E6
Cambodia ■ 36 B3
Cambrai ... 13 A5
Cambrian Mts. ... 11 E5
Cambridge, U.K. ... 11 E7
Cambridge, U.S.A. ... 73 C10
Cambridge Bay = Ikaluktutiak 70 B9
Camden, Ark., U.S.A. ... 79 C7
Camden, N.J., U.S.A. ... 73 E8
Cameroon ■ 56 C2
Cameroun, Mt. ... 56 D1
Caminha ... 18 B1
Campânia □ 21 D5
Campbellton 69 D4
Campbelltown 63 B5
Campbeltown 10 D4
Campeche .. 85 D6
Campeche, B. de 85 D6
Campina Grande .. 92 D6
Campinas .. 94 A7
Campo Grande .. 93 G3
Campobasso 20 D5
Campos ... 93 G5
Camrose ... 71 C8
Çan 23 D6
Can Tho .. 36 B3
Canada ■ .. 70 C8
Çanakkale .. 23 D6
Çanakkale Boğazı .. 23 D6
Canarias, Is. 54 C1
Canberra .. 63 C4
Cangas de Narcea .. 18 A2
Canicattì .. 21 F4
Canigou, Mt. 12 E5
Çankırı ... 46 B3
Cannes ... 13 E7
Canora ... 71 C9
Cantabria □ 18 A4
Cantábrica, Cordillera . 18 A3
Cantal, Plomb du 13 D5
Canterbury . 11 F7

Canterbury Plains ... 65 E4
Canton = Guangzhou 35 D6
Canton ... 72 D5
Cape Breton I. 69 D4
Cape Coast . 55 G4
Cape Dorset 68 B3
Cape Dyer .. 68 B4
Cape Girardeau 79 A9
Cape Town . 58 E3
Cape Verde Is. ■ ... 50 E1
Cape York Peninsula . 61 C7
Capraia ... 20 C2
Capri ... 21 D5
Caracas ... 90 A5
Caratinga .. 93 F5
Caravaca .. 19 C5
Carballo ... 18 A1
Carbonara, C. 21 E2
Carbondale . 79 A9
Carbonear .. 69 D5
Carbonia ... 21 E2
Carcassonne 12 E5
Carcross ... 70 B6
Cardiff ... 11 F5
Cardigan B . 11 E4
Cardston ... 71 D8
Caria ... 23 F7
Caribbean Sea ... 86 D5
Cariboo Mts. 71 C7
Carlisle ... 11 D5
Carlow ... 11 E3
Carlsbad ... 78 C1
Carmacks .. 70 B6
Carman ... 71 D10
Carmarthen . 11 F4
Carmaux ... 12 D5
Carmona .. 18 D3
Carnac ... 12 C2
Carnarvon, Australia . 60 E1
Carnarvon, S. Africa . 58 E4
Carnegie, L. 60 F3
Caroline Is. . 64 J10
Carpathians . 16 D5
Carpaţii Meridionali 17 F7
Carpentaria, G. of ... 60 C6
Carpentras . 13 D6
Carpi ... 20 B3
Carrara ... 20 B3
Carrauntoohill 11 E2
Carrick-on-Suir ... 11 E3
Carşamba .. 46 B4
Carson City . 80 F4
Cartagena, Colombia . 90 A3
Cartagena, Spain ... 19 D5
Carthage ... 79 A6
Cartwright . 68 C5
Caruaru ... 92 D6
Carúpano .. 90 A6
Carvoeiro, C. 18 C1
Casablanca . 54 B3
Cascade Ra . 80 B3
Cascais ... 18 C1
Cáscina ... 20 C3
Caserta ... 20 D5
Casiquiare → 90 C5
Caspe ... 19 B5
Casper ... 81 D10
Caspian Sea . 29 E6
Castellammare di Stábia . 21 D5

Castellón de la Plana . 19 C5
Castelo Branco .. 18 C2
Castelsarrasin 12 D4
Castelvetrano 21 F4
Castilla La Mancha □ 18 C4
Castilla y León □ .. 18 A3
Castlebar .. 11 E2
Castleblaney 11 D3
Castlereagh → 63 B4
Castres ... 12 E5
Castries ... 87 D7
Castuera .. 18 C3
Çatalca ... 22 D7
Cataluña □ . 19 B6
Catanduanes 38 B2
Catánia ... 21 F5
Catanzaro .. 21 E6
Catskill Mts. 73 D8
Caucasus Mountains 25 E5
Caux, Pays de 12 B4
Cavan ... 11 D3
Caxias ... 92 C5
Caxias do Sul 94 B6
Cayenne ... 92 A3
Cayman Is. ■ 67 H11
Ceadâr-Lunga 17 E9
Ceanannus Mor ... 11 E3
Cebu ... 38 B2
Cedar L. ... 71 C10
Cedar Rapids 77 E9
Cefalù ... 21 E5
Cegléd ... 16 E4
Celebes = Sulawesi □ 39 E2
Celebes Sea 39 D2
Celje ... 20 A5
Celle ... 14 B6
Central African Rep. ■ ... 56 C4
Central Makran Range ... 42 F4
Ceres ... 58 E3
Cerignola .. 20 D5
Çerkeş ... 46 B3
Çerkezköy .. 22 D6
Cervera ... 19 B6
Cesena ... 20 B4
České Budějovice 16 D2
Ceskomoravská Vrchovina . 16 D2
Çeşme ... 23 E6
Cessnock .. 63 B5
Cetraro ... 21 E5
Ceuta ... 18 E3
Cévennes .. 13 D5
Ceyhan ... 46 C3
Ceylon = Sri Lanka ■ .. 43 R12
Chad ■ ... 53 E2
Chad, L. = Tchad, L. . 53 F1
Chagos Arch. 27 K11
Chakradharpur 40 F5
Chalisgaon .. 43 J9
Chalon-sur-Saône ... 13 C6
Châlons-en-Champagne 13 B6
Chamba ... 42 C10
Chambal → . 42 F11
Chambéry .. 13 D6
Chamonix-Mont Blanc 13 D7

Champagne . 13 B6
Champaign . 72 D1
Champlain, L. 73 B9
Chandigarh . 42 D10
Chandpur .. 41 F8
Chang Jiang → . 35 C7
Changchun . 35 B7
Changde ... 35 D6
Changsha .. 35 D6
Changzhou . 35 C6
Channel Is. . 11 G5
Chantada .. 18 A2
Chanthaburi 36 B2
Chantrey Inlet 70 B10
Chanute ... 79 A6
Chao Phraya → 36 B2
Charente → . 12 D3
Chārīkār .. 42 B6
Chärjew ... 29 F7
Charleroi .. 14 C3
Charles, C. . 73 F8
Charleston, S.C., U.S.A. 75 C8
Charleston, W. Va., U.S.A. ... 72 E5
Charleville . 63 A4
Charleville-Mézières . 13 B6
Charlotte .. 75 B7
Charlotte Amalie ... 87 C7
Charlottesville 73 E6
Charlottetown 69 D4
Charolles .. 13 C6
Charters Towers ... 61 E8
Chartres ... 12 B4
Châteaubriant 12 C3
Châteaulin . 12 B1
Châteauroux 12 C4
Châtellerault 12 C4
Chatham, N.B., Canada ... 69 D4
Chatham, Ont., Canada ... 69 D2
Chatham, U.K. ... 11 F7
Chattahoochee → 74 D5
Chattanooga 74 B5
Chaumont .. 13 B6
Chaves ... 18 B2
Chcheybinsk 29 D7
Cheboksary . 24 B6
Chechnia □ 25 E6
Cheju Do .. 35 C7
Chełm ... 17 C6
Chelmsford . 11 F7
Cheltenham . 11 F5
Chelyabinsk 29 D7
Chemnitz .. 15 C7
Chenab → . 42 D7
Chengdu ... 35 C5
Chennai ... 43 N12
Cher → ... 12 C4
Cherbourg . 12 B3
Cherepovets 24 B4
Cherkasy .. 24 D3
Chernihiv ... 24 C3
Chernivtsi . 17 D7
Chernobyl = Chornobyl 17 C10
Chernovtsy 17 D7
Chervonohrad 17 C7
Cherykaw .. 17 B10
Chesapeake . 73 F7
Chesapeake B. 73 E7

Chester, U.K. 11 E5
Chester, U.S.A.* ... 73 E8
Chesterfield 11 E6
Chesterfield Inlet = Igluligaarjuk 70 B10
Cheviot Hills 10 D5
Cheyenne .. 76 E2
Cheyenne → 76 C4
Chhapra ... 40 E5
Chhatarpur . 43 G11
Chiávari ... 20 B2
Chiavenna . 20 A2
Chiba ... 32 B7
Chibougamau 69 D3
Chicago ... 72 D2
Chichagof I. . 71 C6
Chichibu ... 32 A6
Chickasha . 78 B5
Chiclana de la Frontera . 18 D2
Chiclayo ... 91 E3
Chico ... 80 F3
Chicoutimi . 69 D3
Chidley, C. . 68 B4
Chiemsee .. 15 E7
Chiese → . 20 B3
Chieti ... 20 C5
Chihuahua . 84 B3
Chile ■ ... 94 D2
Chilka L. ... 40 H5
Chillán ... 94 D2
Chiloé, I. de . 95 E2
Chilpancingo 84 D5
Chimborazo . 90 D3
Chimbote .. 91 E3
China ■ ... 35 C5
Chincha Alta 91 F3
Chindwin → 41 G10
Chingola ... 59 A5
Chinon ... 12 C4
Chióggia ... 20 B4
Chipata ... 59 A6
Chişinău ... 17 E9
Chita ... 30 D9
Chitral ... 42 B7
Chittagong . 41 F8
Chiusi ... 20 C3
Chivasso .. 20 B1
Cholet ... 12 C3
Chomutov .. 16 C1
Chŏngjin ... 35 B7
Chongqing . 35 D5
Chŏnju ... 35 C7
Chop ... 17 D6
Chornobyl . 17 C10
Chortkiv ... 17 D7
Chorzów ... 16 C4
Chōshi ... 32 B7
Choybalsan . 35 B6
Christchurch 65 E5
Christiana . 59 D5
Chūgoku-Sanchi . 32 B3
Chula Vista . 82 D4
Chumphon . 36 B1
Chungking = Chongqing 35 D5
Chur ... 13 C8
Churchill ... 70 C10
Churchill →, Man., Canada ... 70 C10
Churchill →, Nfld., Canada ... 69 C4
Churchill, C. 70 C10
Churchill Falls 69 C4
Churchill L. . 71 C9
Churu ... 42 E9
Chushal ... 42 C11
Chuvashia □ 24 B6
Cicero ... 72 D2

Ciechanów . 16 B5
Ciénaga .. 90 A4
Cienfuegos . 86 B3
Cieza 19 C5
Cijara, Pantano de 18 C3
Cilician Gates P. 46 C3
Cimişlia ... 17 E9
Cimone, Mte. 20 B3
Cinca → ... 19 B6
Cincar 20 C6
Cincinnati .. 72 E3
Çine 23 F7
Cinto, Mte. . 13 E8
Circle 71 B5
Cirebon 37 F3
Citlaltépetl .. 84 D5
Città di Castello .. 20 C4
Ciudad Bolívar ... 90 B6
Ciudad Guayana . 90 B6
Ciudad Juárez 84 A3
Ciudad Madero .. 84 C5
Ciudad Obregón .. 84 B3
Ciudad Real . 18 C4
Ciudad Rodrigo .. 18 B2
Ciudad Victoria .. 84 C5
Civitanova Marche ... 20 C4
Civitavécchia 20 C3
Cizre 46 C5
Clanwilliam . 58 E3
Clarksdale .. 79 B8
Clarksville . 74 A4
Clear, C. ... 11 F2
Clearwater . 75 F6
Clearwater Mts. 81 B6
Clermont-Ferrand . 13 D5
Cleveland .. 72 D5
Clinton, Canada ... 71 C7
Clinton, U.S.A. ... 77 E9
Clinton Colden L. . 70 B9
Clones 11 D3
Clonmel 11 E3
Clovis 78 B2
Cluj-Napoca . 17 E8
Clyde → ... 10 D4
Clyde, Firth of 10 D4
Clyde River . 68 A4
Coast Mts. .. 70 C7
Coast Ranges 80 F2
Coats I. 68 B2
Coats Land . 96 B5
Coatzacoalcos 85 D6
Cobalt 69 D3
Cóbh 11 F2
Cobourg ... 69 D3
Coburg 15 C6
Cochabamba 91 G5
Cochin 43 Q10
Cochrane ... 69 D2
Cod, C. 73 C10
Cœur d'Alene 80 B5
Coffeyville .. 79 A6
Coffs Harbour 63 B5
Cognac 12 D3
Coimbatore . 43 P10
Coimbra ... 18 B1
Coín 18 D3
Colac 62 C3
Colchester . 11 F7
Coleman ... 71 D8
Coleraine ... 11 D3

Colesberg .. 59 E5
Colima 84 D4
Coll 10 C3
Colmar 13 B7
Cologne = Köln 14 C4
Colombia ■ . 90 C4
Colombo ... 43 R11
Colón 85 F9
Colonsay ... 10 C3
Colorado □ . 83 A10
Colorado → 82 E5
Colorado Plateau .. 83 B7
Colorado Springs .. 76 F2
Columbia, Mo., U.S.A. 77 F8
Columbia, S.C., U.S.A. 75 B7
Columbia, Tenn., U.S.A. 74 B4
Columbia → 80 B1
Columbia, District of □ 73 E7
Columbia Basin 80 B4
Columbretes, Is. 19 C6
Columbus, Ga., U.S.A. 74 C5
Columbus, Miss., U.S.A. 74 C3
Columbus, Ohio, U.S.A. 72 E4
Colville → . 71 A4
Colwyn Bay . 11 E5
Comácchio . 20 B4
Comilla 41 F8
Comino, C. . 21 D2
Committee B. 68 B2
Como 20 B2
Como, L. di . 20 B2
Comodoro Rivadavia . 95 F3
Comorin, C. 43 Q10
Comoros ■ . 51 H8
Comox 71 D7
Compiègne . 13 B5
Comrat 17 E9
Conakry ... 55 G2
Concarneau . 12 C2
Concepción . 94 D2
Conchos → . 84 B3
Concord, N.C., U.S.A. 75 B7
Concord, N.H., U.S.A. 73 C10
Conegliano . 20 B4
Congo ■ = Zaïre → .. 56 F2
Congo ■ ... 56 E3
Congo, Democratic Republic of the ■ 56 E4
Conn, L. ... 11 D2
Connacht □ . 11 E2
Connecticut □ 73 D9
Connecticut → 73 D9
Connemara . 11 E2
Constance, L. = Bodensee 13 C8
Constanța .. 22 B7
Constantine . 54 A6
Cook, Mt. .. 65 E4
Cook Inlet .. 71 C4
Cook Is. ... 65 L14
Cook Strait . 65 D6
Cootamundra 63 B4

Copenhagen = København 9 G10
Copper Center ... 71 B5
Copper Cliff . 69 D2
Coppermine → Kugluktuk . 70 B8
Coppermine → 70 B8
Coral Harbour = Salliq ... 68 B2
Coral Sea .. 64 L10
Corato 21 D6
Corby 11 E6
Corcubión .. 18 A1
Córdoba, Argentina . 94 C4
Córdoba, Spain 18 D3
Cordova ... 71 B5
Corfu = Kérkira ... 23 E2
Coria 18 C2
Corigliano Cálabro . 21 E6
Cork 11 F2
Çorlu 22 D6
Corner Brook 69 D5
Cornești ... 17 E9
Cornwall .. 69 D3
Coro 90 A5
Coronation Gulf 70 B8
Corpus Christi 78 F5
Corrib, L. ... 11 E2
Corrientes .. 94 B5
Corse 13 E8
Corse, C. .. 13 E8
Corsica = Corse 13 E8
Corsicana .. 79 C5
Corte 13 E8
Çorum 46 B3
Corumbá .. 91 G7
Corvallis ... 80 C2
Cosenza ... 21 E6
Costa Blanca 19 C5
Costa Brava . 19 B7
Costa del Sol 18 D3
Costa Dorada 19 B6
Costa Rica ■ 86 E3
Côte d'Azur . 13 E7
Côte-d'Ivoire ■ = Ivory Coast ■ .. 55 G3
Cotentin 12 B3
Cotonou ... 55 G5
Cotopaxi ... 90 D3
Cotswold Hills 11 F5
Cottbus 15 C8
Council 71 B3
Council Bluffs 77 E7
Coventry ... 11 E6
Covilhã 18 B2
Covington .. 72 E3
Cowra 63 B4
Cox's Bazar . 41 G8
Cradock ... 59 E5
Craigavon ... 11 D3
Crailsheim . 14 D6
Craiova 22 B4
Cranbrook .. 71 D8
Crawley 11 F6
Crazy Mts. .. 81 B8
Crema 20 B2
Cremona ... 20 B2
Cres 20 B5
Crete = Kríti 23 G5
Créteil 12 B5
Creus, C. de . 19 A7
Creuse → .. 12 C4

Crewe 11 E5
Crimean Pen. = Krymskyy Pivostriv .. 25 D3
Crișul Alb → 16 E5
Crișul Negru → . 16 E5
Crna Reka → 22 D3
Croatia ■ ... 20 B6
Cromer 11 E7
Cross Sound 71 C6
Crotone 21 E6
Crowsnest Pass 71 D8
Cruzeiro do Sul 91 E4
Cuba ■ 86 B4
Cubango → . 58 B4
Cúcuta 90 B4
Cuenca, Ecuador .. 90 D3
Cuenca, Spain 19 B4
Cuenca, Serranía de 19 C5
Cuernavaca . 84 D5
Cuevas del Almanzora 19 D5
Cuiabá 93 F2
Culiacán ... 84 C3
Cullera 19 C5
Cumaná ... 90 A6
Cumberland, Canada ... 71 D7
Cumberland, U.S.A. 73 E6
Cumberland Pen. 68 B4
Cumberland Plateau ... 72 F3
Cumberland Sd. 68 B4
Cunene → .. 58 B2
Cúneo 20 B1
Curitiba ... 94 B7
Cuttack 40 G5
Cuxhaven .. 14 B5
Cuzco 91 F4
Cwmbran ... 11 F5
Cyclades = Kikládhes . 23 F5
Cyprus ■ ... 46 D3
Czech Rep. ■ 16 D2
Częstochowa 16 C4

Da Lat 36 B3
Da Nang ... 36 A3
Dacca = Dhaka ... 41 F8
Dachau 15 D6
Dadra and Nagar Haveli □ .. 43 J8
Dadu 42 F5
Dagestan □ . 25 E6
Dagupan ... 38 A2
Dahod 43 H9
Daió-Misaki . 32 B5
Dakar 55 F1
Dakhla 54 D1
Dalaman → . 23 F7
Dalhousie ... 69 D4
Dalian 35 C7
Dallas 79 C5
Dalmacija ... 20 C6
Daloa 55 G3
Dalton 74 B5
Daman 43 J8
Damanhûr .. 54 B5
Damaraland . 58 C3
Damascus = Dimashq . 46 D4
Damāvand .. 44 C3
Damiel 18 C4
Damietta ... 54 B5
Dampier 60 E2
Danbury ... 73 D9
Dandeldhura 40 C3

Dandenong . 63 C4
Dandong ... 35 B7
Danger Pt. .. 58 E3
Dannemora . 9 F11
Dannevirke . 64 D7
Danube = Dunărea → 17 F9
Danville ... 75 A8
Dar es Salaam ... 57 F7
Darbhanga . 40 D5
Dardanelles = Çanakkale Boğazı ... 23 D6
Dargai 42 B7
Dargaville .. 64 A5
Darica 22 D7
Darién, G. del 90 B3
Darjiling ... 40 D7
Darling → .. 62 B3
Darling Ra. . 60 G2
Darlington .. 11 D6
Darmstadt .. 14 D5
Darnley, C. . 96 A10
Darnley B. .. 70 B7
Dartmoor ... 11 F5
Dartmouth .. 69 D4
Darwin 60 C5
Dasht → ... 42 G2
Datça 23 F6
Datong 35 B6
Daugava → . 24 B1
Daugavpils . 24 B2
Daulpur 42 F10
Dauphin ... 71 C9
Dauphiné .. 13 D6
Davao 38 C3
Davao, G. of 38 C3
Davenport .. 77 E9
David 86 E3
Davis Str. .. 68 B5
Davos 13 C8
Davyd Haradok .. 17 B8
Dawson ... 70 B6
Dax 12 E3
Dayton 72 E3
Daytona Beach ... 75 E7
Dead Sea .. 47 E3
Death Valley 82 B4
Debar 22 D3
Debrecen .. 16 E5
Decatur, Ala., U.S.A. 74 B4
Decatur, Ill., U.S.A. 77 F10
Deccan 43 L11
Děčín 16 C2
Dee → 10 C5
Deggendorf . 15 D7
Dehra Dun .. 42 D11
Delano 82 C3
Delaware □ . 73 E8
Delaware → 73 E8
Delhi 42 E10
Delice → ... 46 C3
Delmenhorst 14 B5
Demanda, Sierra de la 18 A4
Demirci 23 E7
Demirköy ... 22 D6
Den Helder . 14 B3
Denia 19 C6
Deniliquin . 63 C3
Denmark ■ . 9 G9
Denmark Str. 66 C17
Denpasar ... 37 F5
Denton 78 C5
Denver 76 F2
Deoghar ... 40 E6
Deolali 43 K8
Deosai Mts. . 42 B9

Dera Ghazi Khan 42 D7
Dera Ismail Khan 42 D7
Derby 11 E6
Derg, L. 11 E2
Des Moines .. 77 E8
Des Moines → 77 E9
Desna → .. 17 C10
Despeñaperros, Paso .. 18 C4
Dessau 15 C7
Detmold 14 C5
Detroit 72 C4
Deutsche Bucht 14 A5
Deventer ... 14 B4
Devonport .. 64 B6
Dewas 43 H10
Dezhneva, Mys .. 31 C16
Dhaka 41 F8
Dhamtari ... 40 G3
Dhanbad ... 40 F6
Dhankuta ... 40 D6
Dhar 43 H9
Dharwad ... 43 M9
Dhaulagiri ... 40 C4
Dhenkanal .. 40 G5
Dhikti Óros .. 23 G5
Dhirfis 23 E4
Dhodhekánisos = ... 23 F6
Dhuburi 41 D7
Dhule 43 J9
Diamantina → 62 A2
Diefenbaker L. 71 C9
Dieppe 12 B4
Digby 69 D4
Digges Is. ... 68 B3
Digne-les-Bains 13 D7
Dijlah, Nahr → . 47 E6
Dijon 13 C6
Dili 39 F3
Dillingham .. 71 C4
Dimashq 46 D4
Dinajpur ... 41 E7
Dinan 12 B2
Dinant 14 C3
Dinar 46 C2
Dinara Planina .. 20 B6
Dinard 12 B2
Dingle 11 E1
Dingwall ... 10 C4
Dinosaur National Monument 81 E9
Dir 42 B7
Disteghil Sar 42 A9
Diu 43 J7
Diyarbakır .. 46 C5
Djerid, Chott 54 B6
Djibouti ■ .. 49 E3
Dnepropetrovsk = ... 25 D5
Dnipro → .. 25 D5
Dniprodzerzhynsk 25 D5
Dnipropetrovsk 25 D5
Dnister → .. 17 E10
Dnistrovskyy Lyman ... 17 E10
Doberai, Jazirah .. 39 E4
Doboj 20 B7

Dobreta-Turnu-Severin ... 22 B4
Dobrich 22 C6
Dobrush 17 B10
Dodecanese = Dhodhekánisos 23 F6
Dodge City . 78 A3
Dodoma 57 F7
Dohazari ... 41 F9
Dolbeau 69 D3
Dole 13 C6
Dolomiti 20 A3
Dolphin and Union Str. 70 B8
Dominica ■ . 87 C7
Dominican Rep. ■ ... 87 C5
Domodóssola 20 A2
Don →, Russia .. 25 D4
Don →, U.K. 10 C5
Don Benito . 18 C3
Donau → 17 F9
Donauwörth 14 D6
Doncaster ... 11 E6
Donegal 11 D2
Donetsk 25 D4
Dongting Hu 35 D6
Donostia = San Sebastián . 19 A5
Dora Báltea → . 20 B2
Dorchester, C. 68 B3
Dordogne → 12 D3
Dordrecht .. 14 C3
Dornbirn 14 E5
Dortmund ... 14 C4
Dos Hermanas 18 D3
Dothan 74 D5
Douai 13 A5
Douala 56 D1
Douarnenez . 12 B1
Doubs → ... 13 C6
Douglas, U.K. 11 D4
Douglas, U.S.A. ... 83 E8
Douro → ... 18 B1
Dover 11 F7
Dover, Str. of 11 F7
Dovrefjell .. 8 F9
Dragichyn .. 17 B7
Draguignan . 13 E7
Drakensberg 59 E5
Dráma 22 D5
Drammen ... 9 G10
Drava → ... 20 B7
Dresden 15 C7
Dreux 12 B4
Drina → 20 B7
Drochia 17 D8
Drogheda ... 11 E3
Drohobych .. 17 D6
Drumheller . 71 C8
Drut → 17 B10
Drygalski I. . 96 A11
Dubăsari ... 17 E9
Dubăsari Vdkhr. 17 E9
Dubawnt → 70 B9
Dubawnt, L. . 70 B9
Dubayy 44 E3
Dubbo 63 B4
Dublin, Ireland ... 11 E3
Dublin, U.S.A. 75 C6
Dubno 17 C7
Dubrovnik .. 20 C7
Dubrovytsya 17 C8

Dudinka 30 C6
Dugi Otok .. 20 B5
Duisburg ... 14 C4
Duluth 77 B8
Dumfries ... 11 D5
Dun Laoghaire . 11 E3
Dunărea → 17 F9
Dunbar 10 D5
Duncan 78 B5
Dundalk 11 D3
Dundee, S. Africa .. 59 D6
Dundee, U.K. 10 C5
Dunedin 65 F4
Dunfermline . 10 C5
Dungarvan .. 11 E3
Dunkerque .. 12 A5
Durance → . 13 E6
Durango, Mexico .. 84 C4
Durango, Spain 19 A4
Durban 59 D6
Düren 14 C4
Durg 40 G3
Durgapur ... 40 F6
Durham, U.K. 11 D6
Durham, U.S.A. 75 B8
Durrësi 22 D2
Dursunbey .. 23 E7
Dushanbe .. 29 F7
Düsseldorf .. 14 C4
Dutch Harbor 71 C3
Duyun 35 D5
Düzce 46 B2
Dvina, Severnaya → 28 C5
Dwarka 43 H6
Dyer, C. 68 B4
Dyersburg .. 79 A9
Dymer 17 C10
Dzerzhinsk .. 24 B5
Dzhankoy ... 25 D3
Dzyarzhynsk 17 B8
Dzyatlava ... 17 B7

East China Sea 35 C7
East Kilbride 10 D4
East London 59 E5
East Orange 73 D8
East St. Louis 77 F9
Eastbourne . 11 F7
Eastern Ghats 43 N11
Eastmain .. 69 C3
Eastmain → 69 C3
Eau Claire .. 77 C9
Eberswalde-Finow ... 15 B7
Ebro → 19 B6
Eceabat 23 D6
Ech Cheliff . 54 A5
Echo Bay ... 70 B8
Echuca 63 C3
Ecija 18 D3
Ecuador ■ .. 90 D3
Eder → 14 C5
Édhessa 23 D4
Edinburg ... 78 F4
Edinburgh .. 10 D5
Edinița 17 D8
Edirne 22 D6
Edmonton .. 71 C8
Edmundston 69 D4
Edremit 23 E6
Edremit Körfezi .. 23 E6
Edson 71 C8
Edward, L. .. 57 E5

Edward VII Land ... 96 C17
Edwards Plateau .. 78 D3
Égadi, Ísole . 21 F4
Eger 16 E5
Egersund .. 9 G9
Eğridir 46 C2
Eğridir Gölü . 46 C2
Egypt ■ 52 C5
Eibar 19 A4
Eifel 14 C4
Eigg 10 C3
Eildon, L. ... 63 C4
Eindhoven .. 14 C3
Eire = Ireland ■ . 11 E3
Eisenach ... 14 C6
Eisenerz ... 15 E8
El Aaiún ... 52 C3
El Centro ... 82 D5
El Dorado, Ark., U.S.A. 79 C7
El Dorado, Kans., U.S.A. 78 A5
El Escorial .. 18 B3
El Faiyûm ... 52 C5
El Fâsher ... 53 F4
El Ferrol ... 18 A1
El Gîza 52 C5
El Iskandarîya 52 B4
El Jadida ... 54 B3
El Khartûm .. 53 E5
El Mahalla el Kubra ... 52 B5
El Mansûra . 52 B5
El Minyâ ... 52 C5
El Obeid 53 F5
El Paso 83 E9
El Prat de Llobregat . 19 B7
El Puerto de Santa María 18 D2
El Qâhira ... 52 B5
El Reno 78 B5
El Salvador ■ 85 E7
El Suweis ... 52 C5
Elâzığ 46 C4
Elba 20 C3
Elbasani 22 D3
Elbe → 14 B5
Elbert, Mt. .. 83 A9
Elbeuf 12 B4
Elbidtan ... 46 C4
Elblag 16 A4
Elbrus 25 E5
Elburz Mts. = Alborz, Reshteh-ye Kühhä-ye . 44 B3
Elche 19 C5
Elde → 15 B6
Eldoret 57 D7
Elephant I. .. 96 A4
Eleuthera .. 86 A4
Elgin, U.K. .. 10 C5
Elgin, U.S.A. 72 C1
Elizabeth, Australia . 62 B2
Elizabeth, U.S.A. .. 73 D8
Elizabeth City 75 A9
Elizabethton 75 A6
Elkhart 72 D3
Elko 80 E6
Ellsworth Land ... 96 B2
Elmshorn ... 14 B5
Eluru 40 J3
Elvas 18 C2
Ely 11 E7

Emämrüd ... 44 B3
Embrun 13 D7
Emden 14 B4
Emerson ... 71 D10
Emet 23 E7
Emmen 14 B4
Empangeni . 59 D6
Ems → 14 B4
Enderby Land 96 A9
Enez 23 D6
Engadin 13 C9
Enggano ... 37 F2
England □ .. 11 E6
Englewood .. 76 F2
English Channel . 11 F5
Enid 78 A5
Enna 21 F5
Ennis 11 E2
Enniskillen .. 11 D3
Enns → 15 D8
Enschede ... 14 B4
Ensenada .. 84 A1
Entebbe 57 D6
Entroncamento 18 C1
Enugu 55 G6
Eólie, Ís. ... 21 E5
Épernay ... 13 B5
Ephesus ... 23 F6
Épinal 13 B7
Equatorial Guinea ■ . 56 D1
Ercyaş Dağı . 46 C3
Erdek 23 D6
Erebus, Mt. . 96 B15
Ereğli, Konya, Turkey ... 46 C3
Ereğli, Zonguldak, Turkey ... 46 B2
Eresma → . 18 B3
Erfurt 15 C6
Ergani 46 C4
Érice 21 E4
Erie 73 C5
Erie, L. 72 C5
Erimanthos .. 23 F4
Erimo-misaki 32 F12
Eritrea ■ ... 49 E2
Erlangen ... 15 D6
Ermenak ... 46 C3
Erne, Lower L. 11 D3
Erode 43 P10
Erzgebirge .. 15 C7
Erzincan ... 46 C4
Erzurum ... 46 C5
Es Sahrâ' Esh Sharqîya . 52 C5
Esbjerg 9 G9
Esch-sur-Alzette ... 13 B6
Eşfahân 44 C2
Eskilstuna .. 9 G11
Eskimo Pt. = Arviat ... 70 B10
Eskişehir ... 46 C2
Esla → 18 B2
Eşme 23 E7
Esmeraldas . 90 C3
Esperance .. 60 G3
Espichel, C. . 18 C1
Espinhaço, Serra do . 93 F5
Essen 14 C4
Esslingen ... 14 D5
Estevan ... 71 D9
Estonia ■ ... 24 B2
Estrêla, Serra da 18 B2
Estremoz ... 18 C2
Étampes ... 12 B5
Etawah 42 F11

Ethiopia

Name	Page	Grid
Ethiopia ■ ..	49	F2
Etna ...	21	F5
Eufaula ...	74	D5
Eugene ...	80	C2
Euphrates = Furāt, Nahr al → .	47	E6
Eureka ...	80	E1
Europa, Picos de ...	18	A3
Evanston ...	72	C2
Evansville ..	72	F2
Everest, Mt. ..	40	C6
Everett ...	80	B2
Everglades National Park ...	75	G2
Évora ...	18	C2
Évreux ...	12	B4
Évry ...	12	B5
Évvoia ...	23	E5
Exeter ...	11	F5
Exmoor ...	11	F5
Exmouth ...	11	F5
Extremadura □ ...	18	C2
Eyre, L. ...	60	F6
Eyre Cr. → .	62	A2
Eyre Pen. ..	62	B2
Ezine ...	23	E6
F.Y.R.O.M. = Macedonia ■ ...	22	D3
Fabriano ..	20	C4
Faenza ...	20	B3
Færøe Is. = Føroyar ...	6	C4
Fair Isle ..	10	B6
Fairbanks ..	71	B5
Fairfield, Ala., U.S.A. ...	74	C4
Fairfield, Calif., U.S.A. ...	80	F2
Fairlie ...	65	F4
Fairweather, Mt. ...	71	C6
Faisalabad ..	42	D8
Faizabad ...	40	D4
Fakfak ...	39	E4
Falaise ...	12	B3
Falconara Marittima ..	20	C4
Falcone, C. ..	20	D2
Fălești ...	17	E8
Falkland Is. □	95	G5
Fall River ..	73	D10
Falmouth ...	11	F4
False B. ...	58	E3
Falun ...	9	F11
Fano ...	20	C4
Farāh ...	42	C3
Fareham ...	11	F6
Farghona ..	29	E8
Fargo ...	76	B6
Faro ...	18	D2
Fársala ...	23	E4
Farvel, Kap .	68	C6
Fasano ...	21	D6
Fastiv ...	17	C9
Fatehgarh ..	42	F11
Fatehpur ...	40	E3
Favara ...	21	F4
Favignana ..	21	F4
Faya-Largeau	53	E2
Fayetteville, Ark., U.S.A.	79	A6
Fayetteville, N.C., U.S.A.	75	B8
Fazilka ...	42	D9
Fdérik ...	54	D2
Feather → .	80	F3
Fécamp ...	12	B4
Fehmarn ..	15	A6
Feilding ...	64	D6
Feira de Santana ..	93	E6
Feldkirch ..	14	E5
Felixstowe ..	11	F7
Feodosiya ..	25	D4
Fermo ...	20	C4
Ferrara ...	20	B3
Ferret, C. ..	12	D3
Fès ...	54	B4
Fetlar ...	10	A6
Feuilles → .	68	C3
Fianarantsoa	59	J9
Ficksburg ..	59	D5
Figeac ...	12	D5
Figueira da Foz ...	18	B1
Figueras ...	19	A7
Fiji ■ ...	64	L12
Filiatrá ...	23	F3
Filyos → .	46	B3
Finike ...	46	C2
Finisterre, C. ..	18	A1
Finland ■ ..	8	F13
Finland, G. of	9	G13
Finlay → .	70	C7
Fiora → .	20	C3
Firenze ...	20	C3
Firozabad ..	42	F11
Firozpur ...	42	D9
Fish → .	58	D3
Fishguard ..	11	F4
Flagstaff ...	83	C7
Flaming Gorge Reservoir .	81	E9
Flandre ...	14	C2
Flathead L. ..	81	B6
Flattery, C. ..	80	A1
Flensburg ..	14	A5
Flers ...	12	B3
Flin Flon ..	71	C9
Flinders → .	61	D7
Flinders Ras. .	62	B2
Flint ...	72	C4
Florence = Firenze ...	20	C3
Florence, Ala., U.S.A. ...	74	B4
Florence, S.C., U.S.A. ...	75	B8
Flores ...	39	F2
Flores Sea ..	39	F2
Floreşti ...	17	E8
Florianópolis	94	B7
Florida □ ..	75	D7
Florida, Straits of .	86	B3
Flórina ...	23	D3
Florø ...	8	F9
Foça ...	23	E6
Focşani ...	17	F8
Fóggia ...	20	D5
Föhr ...	14	A5
Foix ...	12	E4
Foligno ...	20	C4
Folkestone ..	11	F7
Fond du Lac	77	D10
Fondi ...	20	D4
Fonsagrada ..	18	A2
Fontainebleau	13	B5
Fontenay-le-Comte ...	12	C3
Forfar ...	10	C5
Forlì ...	20	B4
Formentera ..	19	C6
Formentor, C. de ...	19	C7
Formia ...	20	D4
Formosa = Taiwan ■ .	35	D7
Føroyar ...	6	C4
Forst ...	15	C8
Fort Albany .	69	C2
Fort Collins .	76	E2
Fort-de-France ...	87	D7
Fort Dodge ..	77	D7
Fort Franklin	70	B7
Fort Good-Hope ...	70	B7
Fort Lauderdale	75	F7
Fort Liard ...	70	B7
Fort Macleod	71	D8
Fort McPherson	70	B6
Fort Myers ..	75	F7
Fort Norman	70	B7
Fort Peck L. .	81	B10
Fort Pierce ..	75	F7
Fort Providence	70	B8
Fort Resolution	70	B8
Fort Sandeman	42	D6
Fort Scott ..	79	A6
Fort Severn .	69	C2
Fort Simpson	70	B7
Fort Smith, Canada ..	70	B8
Fort Smith, U.S.A. ...	79	B6
Fort Walton Beach ...	74	D4
Fort Wayne .	72	D3
Fort William	10	C4
Fort Worth ..	78	C5
Fort Yukon ..	71	B5
Fortaleza ...	92	C6
Foshan ...	35	D6
Fossano ...	20	B1
Fougères ...	12	B3
Foula ...	10	A5
Fournoi ...	23	F6
Foveaux Str.	65	G3
Foxe Basin ..	68	B3
Foxe Chan. ..	68	B2
Foxe Pen. ..	68	B3
Francavilla Fontana ..	21	D6
France ■ ..	13	C5
Franche-Comté ...	13	C6
Francistown	59	C5
Frankfurt, Brandenburg, Germany .	15	B8
Frankfurt, Hessen, Germany .	14	C5
Fränkische Alb ...	15	D6
Franklin B. ..	70	B7
Franklin Mts.	70	B7
Franklin Str.	70	A10
Frankston ...	63	C4
Frantsa Iosifa, Zemlya ...	28	A6
Franz ...	69	D2
Fraser → .	71	D7
Fraser I. ...	63	A5
Fraserburgh	10	C5
Fredericksburg	73	E7
Fredericton ..	69	D4
Fredrikstad ..	9	G10
Freeport ...	77	D10
Freetown ...	55	G2
Fregenal de la Sierra ...	18	C2
Freiburg ...	14	E4
Freising ...	15	D6
Freistadt ...	15	D8
Fréjus ...	13	E7
Fremont	82	B2
French Guiana ■ .	92	B3
French Polynesia ■	65	M16
Fresnillo ...	84	C4
Fresno ...	82	B3
Fribourg ...	13	C7
Friedrichshafen	14	E5
Frobisher B.	68	B4
Frome, L. ..	62	B2
Front Range	81	E11
Frosinone ..	20	D4
Frunze = Bishkek ...	29	E8
Frýdek-Místek	16	D4
Fuengirola ..	18	D3
Fuentes de Oñoro ...	18	B2
Fuji-San ...	32	B6
Fujian □ ...	35	D6
Fujinomiya .	32	B6
Fujisawa ...	32	B6
Fukuchiyama	32	B4
Fukui ...	32	A5
Fukuoka ...	32	C2
Fukushima .	33	G12
Fukuyama ..	32	B3
Fulda ...	14	C5
Fulda → .	14	C5
Fullerton ...	82	D4
Funabashi ..	32	B7
Fundão ...	18	B2
Fundy, B. of	69	D4
Furāt, Nahr al → .	47	E6
Furneaux Group ...	62	D4
Fürstenwalde	15	B8
Fürth ...	14	D6
Fury and Hecla Str.	68	B2
Fushun ...	35	B7
Fuxin ...	35	B7
Fuzhou ...	35	D6
Fyn ...	9	G10
Gabès ...	54	B7
Gabon ■ ...	56	E2
Gaborone ...	59	C5
Gabrovo ...	22	C5
Gadag ...	43	M9
Gadarwara ..	43	H11
Gadsden ...	74	B4
Gagnon ...	69	C4
Gainesville, Fla., U.S.A.	75	E6
Gainesville, Ga., U.S.A.	75	B6
Gainesville, Tex., U.S.A.	78	C5
Gairdner, L. .	62	B2
Galashiels ..	10	D5
Galaţi ...	17	F9
Galatina ...	21	D7
Galdhøpiggen	8	F9
Galesburg ..	77	E9
Galicia □ ..	18	A2
Galilee, Sea of = Yam Kinneret ..	46	D3
Gállego → .	19	B5
Gallípoli ...	21	D6
Gällivare ...	8	E12
Galloway, Mull of ..	11	D4
Galveston ..	79	E6
Galway ...	11	E2
Galway B. ..	11	E2
Gambia ■ ..	55	F1
Gan Jiang →	35	D6
Gäncä ...	25	E6
Gandak → .	40	E5
Gander ...	69	D5
Gandhi Sagar	43	G9
Gandía ...	19	C5
Ganga → .	41	F8
Ganganagar	42	E8
Gangdisê Shan ...	40	B3
Gangtok ...	41	D7
Gansu □ ...	34	C5
Gap ...	13	D7
Garabogazköl Aylagy ...	29	E6
Garda, L. di .	20	B3
Garden City .	78	A3
Garden Grove	82	D4
Gardēz ...	42	C6
Gargano, Mte.	20	D5
Garigliano →	20	D5
Garland ...	81	E7
Garmisch-Partenkirchen	14	E6
Garonne → .	12	D3
Garry, L. ...	70	B9
Gary ...	72	D2
Garzê ...	34	C5
Gascogne ..	12	E4
Gascogne, G. de ...	12	D2
Gaspé ...	69	D4
Gaspé, C. de	69	D4
Gaspé, Pén. .	69	D4
Gastonia ...	75	B7
Gata, C. de .	19	D4
Gata, Sierra de ...	18	B2
Gateshead ..	11	D6
Gauhati ...	41	D8
Gävdhos ...	23	G5
Gävle ...	8	F11
Gawilgarh Hills ...	43	J10
Gaya ...	40	E5
Gaza ...	47	E3
Gaziantep ..	46	C4
Gdańsk ...	16	A4
Gdańska, Zatoka ...	16	A4
Gdynia ...	16	A4
Gebe ...	39	D3
Gebze ...	22	D7
Gediz → .	23	E6
Gedser ...	9	H10
Geelong ...	63	C3
Geesthacht ..	14	B6
Gejiu ...	34	D5
Gela ...	21	F5
Gelibolu ...	23	D6
Gelsenkirchen	14	C4
Gemerek ...	46	C4
Gemlik ...	23	D7
Geneva, L. = Léman, L. .	13	C7
Genève ...	13	C7
Genil → .	18	D3
Gennargentu, Mti. del ...	21	D2
Génova ...	20	B2
Génova, G. di	20	C2
Gent ...	14	C2
George ...	58	E4
George → .	68	C4
George Town	36	C2
George V Land ...	96	A14
Georgetown	90	B7
Georgia □ ..	75	C6
Georgia ■ ..	25	E5
Georgian B. .	69	D2
Gera ...	15	C7
Geraldton ..	60	F1
Gerede ...	46	B3
Germany ■ .	14	C6

Germiston 59 D5
Gerona 19 B7
Getafe 18 B4
Gettysburg . . . 73 E7
Ghaghara → . . 40 E5
Ghana ■ 55 G4
Ghanzi 58 C4
Ghazâl, Bahr
el → . . . 57 C6
Ghaziabad . . . 42 E10
Ghazipur 40 E4
Ghazni 42 C6
Ghent = Gent 14 C2
Giarre 21 F5
Gibraltar ■ . 18 D3
Gibraltar, Str.
of 18 E3
Gibson Desert 60 E4
Giessen 14 C5
Gifu 32 B5
Giglio 20 C3
Gijón 18 A3
Gila → 82 D5
Gilgit 42 B9
Gióna, Óros . 23 E4
Giridih 40 E6
Gironde → . . 12 D3
Girvan 10 D4
Gisborne . . . 64 C8
Gjoa Haven . 70 B10
Glace Bay . . 69 D5
Gladstone . . 61 E5
Glasgow . . . 10 D4
Glen Canyon
National
Recreation
Area . . . 83 B7
Glendale . . . 82 C3
Glenrothes . . 10 C5
Glens Falls . . 73 C9
Gliwice 16 C4
Głogów 16 C3
Glomma → . 9 G10
Gloucester . . 11 F5
Glusk 17 B9
Gmünd 15 D8
Gmunden . . . 15 E7
Gniezno 16 B3
Go Cong . . . 36 B3
Goa 43 M8
Goa □ 43 M8
Gobabis 58 C3
Gobi 35 B6
Godavari → . 40 J4
Godhra 43 H8
Gods → . . . 71 C10
Gods L. 71 C10
Godthåb . . . 68 B5
Goiânia 93 F4
Gökçeada . . . 23 D5
Gold Coast . 63 A5
Golden Gate 80 G2
Goldsboro . . 75 B9
Golfo Aranci 20 D3
Golspie 10 C5
Gomel =
Homyel . 17 B10
Gómez
Palacio . . 84 B4
Gonâbâd . . . 44 C4
Gonda 40 D3
Gonder 53 F6
Gönen 23 D6
Good Hope,
C. of . . . 58 E3
Goondiwindi 63 A5
Göppingen . 14 D5
Gorakhpur . . 40 D4
Goražde . . . 20 C7
Gorízia 20 B4
Gorkiy =
Nizhniy
Novgorod 24 B5

Görlitz 15 C8
Gorontalo . . 39 D2
Gorzów
Wielkopolski
. . . . 16 B2
Gosford 63 B5
Goslar 14 C6
Gospič 20 B5
Göteborg . . 9 G10
Gotha 14 C6
Gothenburg
= Göteborg 9 G10
Gotland . . . 9 G11
Göttingen . . 14 C5
Gouda 14 B3
Gouin, Rés. . 69 D3
Goulburn . . . 63 B4
Governador
Valadares . 93 F5
Gozo 21 F5
Graaff-Reinet 58 E4
Gračac 20 B5
Grado 18 A2
Grafton 63 A5
Graham Bell,
Os. 28 A7
Graham Land 96 A3
Grahamstown 59 E5
Grampian
Mts. . . . 10 C4
Gran Canaria 54 C1
Gran Chaco . 94 B4
Gran Paradiso 20 B1
Granada ■ . . 18 D4
Granby 69 D3
Grand
Bahama I. 86 A4
Grand
Canyon . . 83 B6
Grand
Cayman . . 86 C3
Grand Coulee
Dam 80 B4
Grand Forks,
Canada . 71 D8
Grand Forks,
U.S.A. . . 76 B6
Grand Island 76 E5
Grand Rapids,
Canada . 71 C10
Grand Rapids,
U.S.A. . . 72 C3
Grand St-
Bernard,
Col du . . 13 D7
Grand Teton 81 D8
Grande,
Rio → . . 79 F5
Grande
Baleine, R.
de la → . 69 C3
Grande de
Santiago →
. . . . 84 C3
Granite City . 77 F9
Granollers . . 19 B7
Grantham . . 11 E6
Granville . . . 12 B3
Gras, L. de . 70 B8
Grasse 13 E7
Graulhet . . . 12 E4
's-
Gravenhage 14 B3
Gravesend . . 11 F7
Graz 15 E8
Great Abaco I. 86 A4
Great
Australian
Bight . . . 60 G4
Great Barrier
Reef 61 D8
Great Basin . 80 F5

Great
Bear → . . 70 B7
Great Bear L. 70 B7
Great
Dividing Ra. 61 E8
Great Falls . . 81 B8
Great Inagua
I. 86 B5
Great Karoo . 58 E4
Great
Ouse → . 11 E7
Great Salt L. 81 E7
Great Salt
Lake Desert 81 E7
Great Sandy
Desert . . 60 E3
Great Slave L. 70 B8
Great Smoky
Mts. Nat.
Pk. 75 B6
Great Victoria
Desert . . 60 F4
Great
Yarmouth . 11 E7
Greater
Antilles . . 86 C5
Gredos,
Sierra de . 18 B3
Greece ■ . . . 23 E4
Greeley 76 E2
Green → . . . 83 A8
Green Bay . . 72 B2
Greenland ■ 66 C9
Greenock . . . 10 D4
Greensboro . 75 A8
Greenville,
Ala., U.S.A. 74 D4
Greenville,
Miss.,
U.S.A. . . 79 C8
Greenville,
N.C., U.S.A. 75 B9
Greenville,
S.C., U.S.A. 75 B6
Greenwood,
Miss.,
U.S.A. . . 79 C8
Greenwood,
S.C., U.S.A. 75 B6
Greifswald . . 15 A7
Greiz 15 C7
Grenada ■ . . 87 D7
Grenoble . . . 13 D6
Grey Ra. . . . 63 A3
Greymouth . . 65 E4
Greytown . . 59 D6
Griffin 75 C5
Griffith 63 B4
Grimsby . . . 11 E6
Gris-Nez, C. . 12 A4
Groningen . . 14 B4
Gross
Glockner . 15 E7
Grosser Arber 15 D7
Grosseto . . . 20 C3
Groznyy . . . 25 E6
Grudziądz . . 16 B4
Guadalajara,
Mexico . . 84 C4
Guadalajara,
Spain . . . 18 B4
Guadalete → 18 D2
Guadalquivir →
. . . . 18 D2
Guadalupe,
Sierra de . 18 C3
Guadarrama,
Sierra de . 18 B4
Guadeloupe ■
. . . . 87 C7
Guadiana → 18 D2
Guadix 18 D4
Guam ■ . . . 64 H9
Guangdong □ 35 D6

Guangxi
Zhuangzu
Zizhiqu □ . 35 D5
Guangzhou . 35 D6
Guantánamo 86 B4
Guaporé → . 91 F5
Guarda 18 B2
Guatemala . 85 E6
Guatemala ■ 85 D6
Guaviare → . 90 C5
Guayaquil . . 90 D3
Guaymas . . . 84 B2
Guecho 19 A4
Guelph 69 D2
Guéret 12 C4
Guernica . . . 19 A4
Guernsey . . . 11 G5
Guidónia-
Montecélio 20 C4
Guildford . . . 11 F6
Guilin 35 D6
Guimarães . . 18 B1
Guinea ■ . . . 55 F2
Guinea, Gulf
of 51 F3
Guinea-
Bissau ■ . 55 F1
Guingamp . . 12 B2
Guiyang . . . 35 D5
Guizhou □ . . 35 D5
Gujarat □ . . 43 H7
Gujranwala . 42 C9
Gujrat 42 C9
Gulbarga . . . 43 L10
Gulf, The . . 44 E2
Gülük 23 F6
Gümüşhane . 46 B4
Guna 43 G10
Guntur 40 J3
Gurgaon . . . 42 E10
Gurkha 40 D5
Güstrow . . . 15 B7
Gütersloh . . 14 C5
Guthrie 78 B5
Guyana ■ . . 90 B7
Guyenne . . . 12 D4
Gwädar 42 G3
Gwalior 42 F11
Gweru 59 B5
Gympie 63 A5
Györ 16 E3
Gypsumville 71 C10
Gyumri 25 E5

Haldwani . . 42 E11
Halifax,
Canada . 69 D4
Halifax, U.K. 11 E6
Hall Beach . 68 B2
Halle 15 C6
Halmahera . 39 D3
Halmstad . . 9 G10
Hamada . . . 32 B3
Hamadān . . 46 D7
Hamäh 46 D4
Hamamatsu . 32 B5
Hamar 8 F10
Hamburg . . . 14 B5
Hameln 14 B5
Hamersley
Ra. 60 E2
Hamilton,
Canada . 69 D3
Hamilton,
N.Z. . . . 64 B6
Hamilton,
U.K. . . . 10 D4
Hamm 14 C4
Hammerfest . 8 D12
Hammond . . 72 D2
Hampton . . . 73 F7
Han Pijesak . 20 B7
Hanamaki . . 33 G12
Hanau 14 C5
Hancock . . . 77 C7
Hangzhou . . 35 C7
Hanna 71 C8
Hannibal . . . 77 F9
Hannover . . 14 B5
Hanoi 35 D5
Hantsavichy 17 B8
Haora 40 F7
Haparanda . 8 E12
Happy Valley-
Goose Bay 69 C4
Hapur 42 E10
Harare 59 B6
Harbin 35 B7
Harbour
Grace . . . 69 D5
Hardangerfjorden
. . . . 8 F9
Hari → . . . 37 E2
Haridwar . . 42 E11
Haringhata →
. . . . 41 G7
Harlingen . . 78 F5
Harlow 11 F7
Harney Basin 80 D4
Härnösand . 8 F11
Harris 10 C3
Harrisburg . 73 D7
Harrison, C. 68 C5
Harrison Bay 71 A4
Harrogate . . 11 D6
Hartford . . . 73 D9
Hartlepool . . 11 D6
Harvey 72 D2
Harwich . . . 11 F7
Haryana □ . . 42 E10
Haryn → . . 17 B8
Harz 14 C6
Hasa 47 F7
Hastings, N.Z. 64 C7
Hastings, U.K. 11 F7
Hastings,
U.S.A. . . 76 E5
Hathras . . . 42 F11
Hatteras, C. . 75 B10
Hattiesburg . 79 D9
Haugesund . 9 G9
Hauraki G. . 64 B6
Haut Atlas . 54 B3
Havana = La
Habana . 86 B3
Havant 11 F6
Havel → . . 15 B7

Haverfordwest

Haverfordwest
.... 11 F4
Havlíčkův
  Brod 16 D2
Havre 81 A9
Havza 46 B3
Hawaii □ .. 82 J12
Hawaiian Is. 82 H12
Hawera ... 64 C6
Hawick 10 D5
Hawke B. .. 64 C7
Hay River .. 70 B8
Hayrabolu .. 22 D6
Haysyn 17 D9
Hayvoron .. 17 D9
Hazaribag .. 40 F5
Hearst 69 D2
Hebei □ ... 35 C6
Hebron 68 C4
Hechuan ... 35 C5
Heerlen ... 13 A6
Hefa 46 D3
Hefei 35 C6
Hegang ... 35 B8
Heidelberg . 14 D5
Heilbron ... 59 D5
Heilbronn .. 14 D5
Heilongjiang □
.... 35 B7
Hekimhan .. 46 C4
Helena, Ark.,
  U.S.A. 79 B8
Helena,
  Mont.,
  U.S.A. 81 B7
Helgoland .. 14 A4
Hellín 19 C5
Helmand → 42 D2
Helmsdale . 10 B5
Helsingborg . 9 G10
Helsinki ... 9 F13
Hemel
  Hempstead 11 F6
Henan □ ... 35 C6
Henares → . 18 B4
Henderson . 75 A8
Hengyang .. 35 D6
Henrietta
  Maria, C. . 69 C2
Henzada ... 41 J10
Herät 42 B3
Hereford .. 11 E5
Herford ... 14 B5
Hermosillo . 84 B2
Hernád → . 16 E5
Heron Bay . 69 D2
's-
Hertogenbosch
.... 14 C3
Hessen □ .. 14 C5
Hewett, C. . 68 A4
Hexham ... 11 D5
Hibbing ... 77 B8
Hickory ... 75 B7
Hida-
  Sammyaku 32 A5
Higashiōsaka 32 B4
High Point . 75 B8
High River . 71 C8
High
  Wycombe 11 F6
Hiiumaa ... 24 B1
Hikone 32 B5
Hildesheim . 14 B5
Hilo 82 J13
Hilversum .. 14 B3
Himachal
  Pradesh □ 40 C10
Himalaya ... 40 D5
Himeji 32 B4
Himi 32 A5
Ḥimş 46 D4
Hindu Kush . 42 B7

Hingoli 43 K10
Hinojosa del
  Duque .. 18 C3
Hiratsuka .. 32 B6
Hirosaki ... 33 F12
Hiroshima .. 32 B3
Hisar 42 E9
Hispaniola . 87 C5
Hita 32 C2
Hitachi 32 A7
Hjälmaren . 9 G11
Hlyboka ... 17 D7
Hoare B. .. 68 B4
Hobart 62 D4
Hodgson .. 71 C10
Hódmezővásárhely
.... 16 E5
Hodonín ... 16 D3
Hoek van
  Holland .. 14 B3
Hof 15 C6
Hōfu 32 B2
Hohe Rhön . 14 C5
Hohhot 35 B6
Hokitika ... 65 E4
Hokkaidō □ . 32 F12
Holguín ... 86 B4
Holman
  Island ... 70 A8
Holy Cross . 71 B4
Holyhead .. 11 E4
Home B. .. 68 B4
Homer 71 C4
Homyel ... 17 B10
Hondeklipbaai 58 E3
Honduras ■ 85 E7
Honduras, G.
  de 85 D7
Honfleur ... 12 B4
Hong Kong . 35 D6
Honiara ... 64 K10
Honolulu .. 82 H12
Honshū ... 32 G11
Hood, Mt. . 80 C3
Hoorn 14 B3
Hoover Dam 82 B5
Hope, Pt. . 71 B3
Hopedale .. 68 C4
Hopetown . 58 D4
Hoquiam .. 80 B2
Horlivka ... 25 D4
Hormuz, Str.
  of 44 E4
Horn 15 D8
Horn, Cape =
  Hornos, C.
  de 95 H3
Hornavan .. 8 E11
Hornos, C. de 95 H3
Hornsby ... 63 B5
Horodenka . 17 D7
Horodok,
  Khmelnytskyy,
  Ukraine .. 17 D8
Horodok,
  Lviv,
  Ukraine .. 17 D6
Horokhiv ... 17 C7
Horsham .. 62 C3
Horton → . 70 B7
Hospitalet de
  Llobregat . 19 B7
Hot Springs . 79 B7
Hotan 34 C2
Houlton ... 73 A12
Houma 79 E8
Houston ... 79 E6
Hövsgöl Nuur 34 A5
Howrah =
  Haora ... 40 F7
Höxter 14 C5
Hoy 10 B5
Høyanger ... 8 F9

Hoyerswerda 15 C8
Hradec
  Králové .. 16 C2
Hrodna 17 B6
Hrodzyanka . 17 B9
Hron → ... 16 E4
Hrymayliv .. 17 D8
Hsisha
  Chuntao .. 36 A4
Huainan ... 35 C6
Huambo ... 58 A3
Huancayo .. 91 F3
Huang He → 35 C6
Huangshi .. 35 C6
Huánuco .. 91 E3
Hubei □ ... 35 C6
Huddersfield 11 E6
Hudson → . 73 D8
Hudson Bay 68 B2
Hudson Str. . 68 B4
Hue 36 A3
Huelva 18 D2
Huesca 19 A5
Hughenden . 61 E7
Hughli → .. 40 G7
Hull =
  Kingston
  upon Hull . 11 E6
Hull 69 D3
Humber → . 11 E6
Humboldt → 71 C9
Humboldt → 80 F4
Hume, L. .. 63 C4
Húnaflói ... 8 D3
Hungary ■ . 16 E4
Hŭngnam .. 35 C7
Hunsrück .. 14 D4
Huntington . 72 E4
Huntington
  Beach .. 82 D3
Huntly 10 C5
Huntsville . 74 B4
Huron, L. .. 72 B4
Hutchinson . 78 A5
Hvar 20 C6
Hwang Ho =
  Huang
  He → ... 35 C6
Hyderabad,
  India 43 L11
Hyderabad,
  Pakistan .. 42 G6
Hyères 13 E7
Hyères, Is. d' 13 E7

Ialomiţa → . 22 B6
Iaşi 17 E8
Ibadan 55 G5
Ibagué 90 C3
Ibiza 19 C6
Icá 91 F3
Iceland ■ .. 8 D4
Ichihara ... 32 B7
Ichikawa .. 32 B6
Ichinomiya . 32 B5
Idaho □ ... 81 C6
Idaho Falls . 81 D7
Idar-Oberstein 14 D4
Idhi Óros .. 23 G5
Idhra 23 F4
Ielarépetra . 23 G5
Iesi 20 C4
Ife 55 G5
Igarka 28 C9
Iglésias ... 21 E2
Igloolik ... 68 B2
Iguaçu, Cat.
  del 94 B6
Igualada ... 19 B6

Iida 32 B5
Iisalmi 8 F13
Iizuka 32 C2
IJsselmeer . 14 B3
Ikaluktutiak . 70 B9
Ikaría 23 F6
Iki 32 C1
Île-de-France 12 B5
Ilhéus 93 E6
Ili → 29 E8
Iller → 14 D5
Iloilo 38 B2
Ilorin 55 G5
Imabari ... 32 B3
Imari 32 C1
Imola 20 B3
Imperatriz . 92 D4
Impéria ... 20 C2
Imperial Dam 82 D5
Imphal 41 E9
Ina 32 B5
Inarijärvi .. 8 E13
Inca 19 C7
İnce-Burnu . 46 B3
Inchon 35 C7
Incirliova .. 23 F6
Incomáti → 59 D6
Indalsälven →
.... 8 F11
Independence,
  Kans.,
  U.S.A. 79 A6
Independence,
  Mo., U.S.A. 77 F7
India ■ ... 43 J10
Indian → .. 75 F7
Indian
  Harbour .. 68 C5
Indian Head . 71 C9
Indiana □ .. 72 D2
Indianapolis 72 E2
Indigirka → 31 B12
Indonesia ■ 37 E4
Indore 43 H9
Indre → ... 12 C4
Indus → ... 43 G5
Inebolu ... 46 B3
Ingolstadt .. 15 D6
Ingraj Bazar . 40 E7
Inhulec 25 D3
Inn → 15 D7
Inner
  Hebrides . 10 C3
Inner
  Mongolia =
  Nei
  Monggol
  Zizhiqu □ . 35 B6
Innisfail ... 71 C8
Innsbruck .. 15 E6
Inowrocław . 16 B4
Insein 41 J11
Interlaken . 13 C7
International
  Falls 77 A8
Inukjuak .. 68 C3
Inuvik 70 B6
Invercargill . 65 G3
Inverell ... 63 A5
Invergordon 10 C4
Inverness .. 10 C4
Inverurie .. 10 C5
Ioánnina ... 23 E3
Ionian Sea . 21 F6
Iónioi Nísoi . 23 E3
Íos 23 F5
Iowa □ ... 77 D8
Iowa City .. 77 E9
Ipoh 36 D2
Ipsala 22 D6
Ipswich ... 11 E7
Iqaluit 68 B4
Iquique ... 91 H4
Iquitos 90 D4
Iráklion ... 23 G5

Iran ■ 44 C3
Iran, Gunung-
  Gunung . 37 D4
Irapuato ... 84 C4
Iraq ■ 46 D5
Ireland ■ .. 11 E3
Irian Jaya □ 39 E5
Iringa 57 F7
Irish Sea .. 11 E4
Irkutsk 30 D8
Ironwood .. 77 B9
Irpin 17 C10
Irrawaddy → 41 K10
Irtysh → ... 28 C7
Irún 19 A5
Irunea =
  Pamplona . 19 A5
Irvine 10 D4
Isar → 15 D7
Íschia 21 D4
Ise 32 B5
Ise-Wan ... 32 B5
Isère → ... 13 D6
Isérnia 20 D5
Ishikari-Wan 32 F12
Ishim → ... 29 D8
Ishinomaki . 33 G12
İskenderun . 46 C4
Islamabad . 42 C8
Island L. ... 71 C10
Islay 10 D3
Isle → 12 D3
Isle of
  Wight □ .. 11 F6
Ismâ'ilîya .. 47 E3
Isparta 46 C2
Íspica 21 F5
Israel ■ ... 46 E3
Issoire 13 D5
İstanbul ... 22 D7
Istiaía 23 E4
Istra 20 B4
Istranca
  Dağları .. 22 D6
Istres 13 E6
Itabuna ... 93 E6
Itaipú,
  Reprêsa de 94 B6
Italy ■ 20 C4
Itháki 23 E3
Ito 32 B6
Itzehoe ... 14 B5
Ivanava ... 17 B7
Ivano-
  Frankivsk . 17 D7
Ivanovo ... 24 B5
Ivatsevichy . 17 B7
Ivory Coast ■ 55 G3
Ivrea 20 B1
Ivujivik ... 68 B3
Iwaki 33 G12
Iwakuni ... 32 B3
Iwata 33 H11
Iwate-San . 33 G12
Iwo 55 G5
Izhevsk ... 28 D6
Izmayil ... 17 F9
İzmir 23 E6
İzmit 25 E2
İznik Gölü . 23 D7
Izumi-sano . 32 B4
Izumo 32 B3
Izyaslav ... 17 C8

Jabalpur 43 H11
Jablanica ... 22 D3
Jablonec ... 16 C2
Jaca 19 A5
Jackson,
  Mich.,
  U.S.A. ... 72 C3
Jackson,
  Miss.,
  U.S.A. ... 79 C8

Jackson, Tenn., U.S.A. 74 B3
Jacksonville, Fla., U.S.A. 75 D7
Jacksonville, Ill., U.S.A. .. 77 F9
Jacksonville, N.C., U.S.A. 75 B9
Jacobabad .. 42 E5
Jaén 18 D4
Jaffna 43 Q12
Jahrom 44 D3
Jaipur 42 F9
Jakarta 37 F3
Jalalabad ... 42 B7
Jalgaon 43 J9
Jalna 43 K9
Jalón → 19 B5
Jalpaiguri .. 41 D7
Jamaica ■ .. 86 C4
Jamalpur, Bangla. 41 E7
Jamalpur, India 40 E6
Jambi 37 E2
James → 76 D6
James B. ... 69 C2
Jamestown, N. Dak., U.S.A. 76 B5
Jamestown, N.Y., U.S.A. 73 C8
Jammu 42 C9
Jammu & Kashmir □ 42 B10
Jamnagar ... 43 H7
Jamshedpur 40 F6
Janesville .. 77 D10
Jaora 43 H9
Japan ■ 33 G11
Japan, Sea of 33 G11
Japurá → ... 90 D5
Jarama → ... 18 B4
Jäsk 44 C4
Jasper 74 C4
Játiva 19 C5
Jaunpur 40 E4
Java = Jawa 37 F3
Java Sea ... 37 F3
Jawa 37 F3
Jean Marie River ... 70 B7
Jedburgh ... 10 D5
Jedda = Jiddah 47 G4
Jefferson City 77 F8
Jelenia Góra 16 C2
Jelgava 24 B1
Jena 15 C6
Jequié 93 E5
Jerez de la Frontera .. 18 D2
Jerez de los Caballeros 18 C2
Jersey 11 G5
Jersey City . 73 D8
Jerusalem .. 47 E3
Jessore 41 F7
Jhang Maghiana 42 D8
Jhansi 43 G11
Jhelum 42 C8
Jhelum → ... 42 D8
Jiamusi 35 B8
Ji'an 35 D6
Jiangsu □ .. 35 C6
Jiangxi □ ... 35 D6
Jiddah 47 G4
Jihlava 16 D2
Jihlava → .. 16 D1
Jilin 35 B7
Jima 53 G6
Jinan 35 C6

Jindrichuv Hradec ... 16 D2
Jinja 57 D6
Jinzhou 35 B7
Jixi 35 B8
João Pessoa 92 D7
Jodhpur 42 F8
Johannesburg 59 D5
Johnson City 75 A6
Johnstown . 73 D6
Johor Baharu 37 D2
Joliet 72 D1
Joliette 69 D3
Jolo 38 C2
Jonesboro .. 79 B8
Jönköping .. 9 G10
Jonquière .. 69 D3
Joplin 79 A6
Jordan ■ ... 47 E4
Jos 55 G6
Juan de Fuca Str. 80 A1
Juan Fernández, Arch. de . 89 G3
Juàzeiro do Norte 92 D6
Júcar → 19 C5
Juiz de Fora 93 G5
Juliaca 91 G4
Jullundur ... 42 D9
Jumilla 19 C5
Junagadh ... 43 J7
Juneau 71 C6
Jungfrau ... 13 C7
Junggar Pendi ... 34 B3
Jura 10 D8
Jura, Mts. du 13 C7
Juruá → 90 D5
Jutland = Jylland .. 9 G9
Jylland 9 G9
Jyväskylä .. 8 F13

K2 .... 42 B10
Kabardino Balkaria □ 25 E5
Kábul 42 B6
Kabwe 59 A5
Kachchh, Gulf of 43 H6
Kachchh, Rann of . 43 G6
Kachin □ ... 41 D11
Kaçkar 46 B5
Kadirli 46 C3
Kaduna 55 F6
Kaesŏng ... 35 C7
Kafirevs, Ákra 23 E5
Kağızman .. 46 B5
Kagoshima . 33 D2
Kagoshima-Wan ... 33 D2
Kahoolawe . 82 H12
Kahramanmaraş 46 C4
Kai, Kepulauan 39 F4
Kaifeng 35 C6
Kaiserslautern 14 D4
Kaitaia 64 A5
Kajaani 8 F13
Kakamas ... 58 D4
Kakhovka .. 25 D3
Kakhovka Vdskh. ... 25 D3
Kakinada ... 40 J4
Kalaallit Nunaat = Greenland ■ 66 C9
Kalahari ... 58 C4

Kalámai 23 F4
Kalamazoo . 72 C3
Kalan 46 C4
Kalce 20 B5
Kale 23 F7
Kalemie 57 F5
Kalgoorlie-Boulder .. 60 G3
Kalimantan . 37 E4
Kálimnos ... 23 F6
Kaliningrad . 24 C1
Kalinkavichy 17 B9
Kalispell ... 81 A6
Kalisz 16 C4
Kalmar 9 G11
Kalmykia □ . 25 D6
Kaluga 24 C4
Kalush 17 D7
Kama → 29 D6
Kamaishi ... 33 G12
Kamchatka, P-ov. 31 D13
Kamenjak, Rt. 20 B4
Kamensk Uralskiy . 29 D7
Kamin-Kashyrskyy 17 C7
Kamina 57 F5
Kamloops ... 71 C7
Kampala ... 57 D6
Kampen 14 B3
Kampuchea = Cambodia ■ 36 B3
Kamsack ... 71 C9
Kamyanets-Podilskyy . 17 D8
Kamyanka-Buzka ... 17 C7
Kanaaupscow 69 C3
Kananga ... 56 F4
Kanazawa .. 32 A5
Kanchenjunga 40 D7
Kanchipuram 43 N11
Kandy 43 R12
Kangaroo I. . 62 C2
Kangean, Kepulauan 37 F4
Kangiqsualujjuaq 68 C4
Kangiqsujuaq 68 B3
Kangirsuk .. 68 C4
Kaniapiskau → 68 C4
Kaniapiskau L. 69 C4
Kanin, Poluostrov 28 C5
Kankakee .. 72 D2
Kankan 55 F3
Kannapolis . 75 B7
Kano 55 F6
Kanoya 33 D2
Kanpur 40 E3
Kansas □ ... 76 F5
Kansas City, Kans., U.S.A. ... 77 F7
Kansas City, Mo., U.S.A. 77 F7
Kansk 30 D7
Kanuma ... 32 A6
Kanye 59 C5
Kaolack ... 55 F1
Kapan 25 F6
Kapfenberg . 15 E8
Kaposvár .. 16 E3
Kapuas → .. 37 E3
Kapuas Hulu, Pegunungan 37 D4
Kara Kum .. 29 F6
Kara Sea ... 28 B8
Karabiğa ... 23 D6

Karabük 46 B3
Karaburun . 23 E6
Karacabey . 23 D7
Karacasu .. 23 F7
Karachi 43 G5
Karadeniz Boğazı ... 22 D7
Karaganda = Qaraghandy 29 E8
Karakalpakstan □ 29 E6
Karakoram Ra. 42 B10
Karaman ... 46 C3
Karasburg .. 58 D3
Karbalā 47 D6
Kardhitsa .. 23 E3
Karelia □ ... 28 C4
Karimata, Kepulauan 37 E3
Karimunjawa, Kepulauan 37 F4
Karkinitska Zatoka ... 25 D3
Karlovac ... 20 B5
Karlovy Vary 16 C1
Karlskrona . 9 G11
Karlsruhe .. 14 D5
Karlstad ... 9 G10
Karnal 42 E10
Karnataka □ 43 N10
Kärnten □ .. 15 E7
Kárpathos .. 23 G6
Kars 46 B5
Karsakpay . 29 E7
Karviná 16 D4
Kasai → 56 E3
Kasba L. ... 70 B9
Käshän 44 C2
Kashi 34 C2
Kásos 23 G6
Kassalâ 53 E6
Kassel 14 C5
Kastamonu . 46 B3
Kasur 42 D9
Katanga = Shaba □ . 57 F4
Katerini 23 D4
Katha 41 E11
Katihar 40 E6
Katmandu .. 40 D5
Katoomba .. 63 B5
Katowice ... 16 C4
Katsina ... 55 F6
Kattegat ... 9 G10
Kauai 82 G11
Kaunas 24 C1
Kavála 23 D5
Kawagoe .. 32 B6
Kawaguchi . 32 B6
Kawardha .. 40 G3
Kawasaki .. 32 B6
Kawthule □ . 41 H11
Kayes 55 F2
Kayseri 46 C3
Kazakstan ■ 29 E7
Kazan 24 B6
Kāzerūn ... 44 D2
Kéa 23 F5
Kebnekaise . 8 E11
Kecskemét . 16 E4
Kediri 37 F4
Keetmanshoop 58 D3
Kefallinía .. 23 E3
Keighley ... 11 E6
Keith Arm .. 70 B7
Kelang 37 D2
Kelowna ... 71 D8
Kemah 46 C4
Kemerovo .. 29 D9
Kemi 8 E12
Kemijoki → . 8 E12
Kemp Land . 96 A9

Kempten ... 14 E6
Kendari ... 39 E2
Kenhardt .. 58 D4
Kenitra 54 B3
Kennewick . 80 B4
Kenogami → 69 C2
Kenosha ... 72 D2
Kent Pen. .. 70 B9
Kentucky □ . 72 F3
Kentville ... 69 D4
Kenya ■ ... 57 D7
Kenya, Mt. . 57 E7
Kerala □ ... 43 P10
Kerch 25 D4
Kerinci 37 E2
Kérkira 23 E2
Kermadec Trench ... 65 N13
Kermān ... 44 D4
Kerme Körfezi 23 F6
Kerrobert .. 71 C9
Keşan 22 D6
Ketchikan .. 71 C6
Keweenaw B. 69 D2
Key West .. 86 B3
Khabarovsk . 31 E11
Khairpur ... 42 F6
Khalkís 23 E4
Khambat, G. of 43 J8
Khandwa .. 43 J10
Khanewal .. 42 D7
Khaniá 23 G5
Khanion, Kólpos ... 23 G4
Kharagpur . 40 F6
Khargon ... 43 J9
Kharkiv 24 D4
Kharta 22 D7
Khartoum = El Khartûm 53 E5
Khaskovo .. 22 D5
Khatanga .. 30 B8
Khemelnik . 17 D8
Kherson ... 25 D3
Khios 23 E6
Khmelnytskyy 17 D8
Khodoriv .. 17 D7
Khóra Sfakíon 23 G5
Khorramshahr 47 E7
Khotyn 17 D8
Khouribga .. 54 B3
Khoyniki .. 17 C9
Khulna 41 F7
Khulna □ ... 41 F7
Khushab ... 42 C8
Khust 17 D6
Khuzdar ... 42 F5
Kicking Horse Pass 71 C8
Kiel 14 A6
Kiel Canal = Nord-Ostsee-Kanal → . 14 A5
Kielce 16 C5
Kieler Bucht . 14 A6
Kiev = Kyyiv 17 C10
Kigali 57 E6
Kigoma-Ujiji 57 E5
Kii-Suidō .. 32 C4
Kikládhes .. 23 F5
Kikwit 56 E3
Kilimanjaro . 57 E7
Kilis 46 C4
Kiliya 17 F9
Kilkenny ... 11 E3
Kilkis 23 D4
Killarney ... 11 E2
Killeen 78 D5
Kilmarnock . 10 D4
Kilrush 11 E2
Kimberley .. 58 D4

Kimberley Plateau

Kimberley
  Plateau ... 60 D4
Kindu ... 57 E5
King George
  I. 96 A4
King George
  Is. 69 C2
King William
  I. 70 B10
King
  William's
  Town ... 59 E5
Kings Canyon
  National
  Park 82 B3
King's Lynn . 11 E7
Kingsport ... 75 A6
Kingston,
  Canada ... 69 D3
Kingston,
  Jamaica . 86 C4
Kingston
  upon Hull . 11 E6
Kingstown . 87 D7
Kingsville ... 78 F5
Kınık 23 E6
Kinsale 11 F2
Kinshasa ... 56 E3
Kinston 75 B9
Kiparissía .. 23 F3
Kiparissiakós
  Kólpos .. 23 F3
Kirghizstan =
  Kyrgyzstan ■
  .... 29 E8
Kiribati ■ .. 64 K12
Kırıkkale ... 46 C3
Kirkcaldy ... 10 C5
Kirkcudbright 11 D4
Kirkenes 8 E14
Kirkland Lake 69 D2
Kırklareli ... 22 D6
Kirkūk 46 D6
Kirkwall 10 B5
Kirov 28 D5
Kirovohrad . 25 D3
Kırşehir 46 C3
Kirthar Range 42 F5
Kiruna 8 E12
Kiryū 32 A6
Kisangani ... 57 D5
Kishanganj . 40 D7
Kishinev =
  Chişinău .. 17 E9
Kishiwada .. 32 B4
Kiska I. 71 C1
Kiso-
  Sammyaku 32 B5
Kisumu 57 E6
Kitakami-
  Gawa → . 33 G12
Kitakyūshū . 32 C2
Kitchener ... 69 D2
Kithira 23 F4
Kíthnos 23 F5
Kitwe 59 A5
Kivertsi 17 C7
Kivu, L. 57 E5
Kızıl Irmak → 25 E4
Kladno 16 C2
Klagenfurt .. 15 E8
Klaipėda ... 24 B1
Klamath Falls 80 D3
Klamath Mts. 80 E2
Klarälven → . 9 G10
Klatovy 16 D1
Klawer 58 E2
Klerksdorp . 59 D5
Klondike ... 70 B6
Kluane L. ... 70 B6
Klyetsk 17 B8
Knossós 23 G5
Knoxville ... 75 B6
Kobarid 20 A4

Kōbe 32 B4
København . 9 G10
Koblenz ... 14 C4
Kobroor,
  Kepulauan 39 F4
Kobryn 17 B7
Kočani 22 D4
Koch Bihar . 41 D7
Kochi 32 C3
Kodiak 71 C4
Kodiak I. ... 71 C4
Koforidua .. 55 G4
Kōfu 32 B6
Koh-i-Bābā . 42 B5
Kohat 42 C7
Kokand =
  Qo'qon .. 29 E7
Kokchetav .. 29 D7
Kokomo ... 72 D2
Kokoneau . 39 D7
Kokoda 96 C7
Koksoak → . 68 C4
Kokstad ... 59 E5
Kolar 43 N11
Kolguyev,
  Ostrov ... 28 C5
Kolhapur ... 43 L9
Kolín 16 C2
Köln 14 C4
Kolomna ... 24 B4
Kolomyya .. 17 D7
Kolskiy
  Poluostrov 28 C4
Kolwezi ... 57 G5
Kolyma → . 31 C13
Komatsu ... 32 A5
Komi □ 28 C6
Kommunizma,
  Pik 29 F8
Komotiní ... 22 D5
Kompong
  Cham ... 36 B3
Kompong
  Chhnang . 36 B2
Kompong
  Som 36 B2
Komsomolets,
  Ostrov ... 30 A7
Konin 16 B4
Konjic 20 C6
Konotop ... 24 C3
Konstanz ... 14 E5
Konya 46 C3
Konya Ovası 46 C3
Kootenay L. . 71 D8
Koper 20 B4
Kopychyntsi 17 D7
Korab 22 D3
Korça 23 D3
Korčula 20 C6
Korea,
  North ■ .. 35 C7
Korea,
  South ■ .. 35 C7
Korea Strait . 35 C7
Korets 17 C8
Korinthiakós
  Kólpos .. 23 E4
Kórinthos .. 23 F4
Koriyama .. 33 G12
Körös → ... 16 E5
Korosten ... 17 C9
Korostyshev 17 C9
Kortrijk 14 C2
Kos 23 F6
Košice 16 D5
Kosovo □ .. 22 C3
Kôstî 53 F5
Kostopil ... 17 C8
Kostroma .. 24 B5
Koszalin ... 16 A3

Kotuy → ... 30 B8
Kotzebue ... 71 B3
Kounradskiy 29 E8
Kovel 17 C7
Köyceğiz ... 23 F7
Koyuk 71 B3
Koyukuk → 71 B4
Kozan 46 C3
Kozáni 23 D3
Kozyatyn ... 17 D9
Kra, Kho Khot 36 B1
Kragujevac . 22 B3
Krajina 20 B6
Krakatau =
  Rakata,
  Pulau 37 F3
Kraków 16 C4
Kramatorsk . 25 D4
Kranj 20 A5
Krasnodar .. 25 D4
Krasnoperekopsk
  .... 25 D3
Krasnoturinsk 28 D7
Krasnovodsk 29 E6
Krasnoyarsk 30 D7
Krasnyy Luch 25 D4
Kratie 36 B3
Krefeld 14 C4
Kremen 20 B5
Kremenchuk 24 D3
Kremenchuksk
  Vdskh. .. 24 D3
Kremenets .. 17 C7
Krems 15 D8
Krishna → . 40 K3
Krishnanagar 41 F7
Kristiansand 9 G9
Kristiansund 8 F9
Kriti 23 G5
Krivoy Rog =
  Kryvyy Rih 25 D3
Krk 20 B5
Kroonstad .. 59 D5
Krosno 16 D5
Krugersdorp 59 D5
Krupki 17 A9
Kruševac ... 22 C3
Krychaw ... 17 B10
Krymskyy
  Pivostriv .. 25 D3
Kryvyy Rih . 25 D3
Kuala Lumpur 37 D2
Kuala
  Terengganu 36 C2
Kualakapuas 37 E4
Kuantan ... 37 D2
Kucing 37 D4
Kudat 36 C5
Kufstein ... 15 E7
Kugluktuk .. 70 B8
Kujū-San .. 32 C2
Kula 23 E7
Kumagaya .. 32 A6
Kumamoto . 32 C2
Kumanovo .. 22 C3
Kumasi 55 G4
Kumbakonam 43 P11
Kunlun Shan 34 C3
Kunming ... 34 D5
Kuopio 8 F13
Kupa → 20 B6
Kupyansk ... 28 C4
Kür → 25 E6
Kurashiki .. 32 B3
Kurayoshi .. 32 B3
Kure 32 B3
Kurgan 29 D7
Kurilskiye
  Ostrova .. 31 E12
Kurnool 43 L11
Kurri Kurri . 63 B5
Kursk 24 C4
Kuruman ... 58 D4
Kurume 32 C2

Kus Gölü ... 23 D6
Kuşadası ... 23 F6
Kushiro ... 32 F12
Kushtia 41 F7
Kuskokwim →
  .... 71 B3
Kuskokwim B. 71 C3
Kütahya ... 46 C2
Kutaisi 25 E5
Kuujjuaq ... 68 C4
Kuwait = Al
  Kuwayt .. 47 E7
Kuwait ■ ... 47 E6
Kuwana ... 32 B5
Kuybyshev =
  Samara .. 24 C7
Kuzey
  Anadolu
  Dağları .. 46 B3
Kvarner ... 20 B5
Kvarnerič .. 20 B5
Kwangju ... 35 C7
Kyō-ga-Saki . 32 B4
Kyōto 32 B4
Kyrgyzstan ■ 29 E8
Kyūshū 32 C2
Kyūshū-
  Sanchi ... 32 C2
Kyyiv 17 C10
Kyyivske
  Vdskh. .. 17 C10
Kyzyl Kum . 29 E7

La Albufera . 19 C5
La Alcarria . 19 B4
La Chaux de
  Fonds ... 13 C7
La Coruña .. 18 A1
La Crosse .. 77 D9
La Estrada . 18 A1
La Grange .. 74 C5
La Habana . 86 B3
La Línea de la
  Concepción 18 D3
La Mancha . 19 C4
La Palma del
  Condado . 18 D2
La Paz 91 G5
La Plata 94 D5
La Rioja □ .. 19 A4
La Robla ... 18 A3
La Roche-sur-
  Yon 12 C3
La Rochelle . 12 C3
La Roda 19 C4
La Seyne-sur-
  Mer 13 E6
La Spézia .. 20 B2
La Tuque ... 69 D3
Labé 55 F2
Labrador,
  Coast of □ . 68 C4
Labuk, Telok 36 C5
Lac La Biche 71 C8
Lac la Martre 70 B8
Lacanau ... 12 D3
Lachine 69 D3
Lachlan → .. 63 B3
Lackawanna 73 C6
Lacombe ... 71 C8
Ladakh Ra. . 42 B10
Ladozhskoye
  Ozero ... 28 C4
Ladysmith,
  Canada .. 71 D7
Ladysmith,
  S. Africa . 59 D5
Lae 61 B8
Lafayette ... 79 D7
Lagos,
  Nigeria .. 55 G5
Lagos,
  Portugal . 18 D1

Lahn → 14 C4
Lahore 42 D9
Lahti 8 F13
Lairg 10 B4
Lake Charles 79 D7
Lake City ... 75 D6
Lake Harbour 68 B4
Lake Worth . 75 F7
Lakeland ... 75 E7
Lakewood .. 72 D5
Lakonikós
  Kólpos ... 23 F4
Lakshadweep
  Is. 26 H11
Lalín 18 A1
Lamego 18 B2
Lamia 23 E4
Lamon Bay . 38 B2
Lanai I. 82 H12
Lancaster,
  U.K. 11 D5
Lancaster,
  U.S.A. .. 73 D7
Lancaster Sd. 68 A2
Lanciano ... 20 C5
Landeck ... 14 E6
Landes 12 D3
Landsberg .. 14 D6
Land's End . 11 F4
Landshut ... 15 D7
Langres 13 C6
Langres,
  Plateau de 13 C6
Languedoc . 13 E5
Lannion ... 12 B2
Lansing 72 C3
Lanusei 21 E2
Lanzhou ... 35 C5
Laoag 38 A2
Laois □ 11 D3
Laos ■ 36 A3
Lappland ... 8 E12
Lapseki 23 D6
Laptev Sea . 30 B10
L'Áquila ... 20 C4
Laramie 76 E2
Laredo 78 F4
Lárisa 23 E4
Larne 11 D4
Larvik 9 G10
Las Cruces . 83 D9
Las Palmas . 54 C1
Las Vegas .. 82 B5
Lashio 41 F11
Lassen Pk. .. 80 E3
Lastovo 20 C6
Latina 20 D4
Latvia ■ 24 B1
Lauchhammer 15 C7
Launceston . 62 D4
Laurel 79 D9
Lauria 21 D5
Laurium ... 69 D2
Lausanne .. 13 C7
Laut 36 D3
Laut Kecil,
  Kepulauan 37 E5
Laval 12 B3
Lávrion ... 23 F5
Lawrence ... 77 F7
Lawton 78 B4
Laylá 47 G6
Lazio □ 20 C4
Le Creusot .. 13 C6
Le Havre ... 12 B4
Le Mans ... 12 C4
Le Mont-St.-
  Michel ... 12 B3
Le Puy-en-
  Velay ... 13 D5
Le Touquet-
  Paris-Plage 12 A4
Le Tréport .. 12 A4
Le Verdon-
  sur-Mer .. 12 D3

Leavenworth .. 77 F7
Lebanon ■ .. 46 D3
Lebrija 18 D2
Lecce 23 D2
Lecco 20 B2
Lech → 14 D6
Leduc 71 C8
Leeds 11 E6
Leer 14 B4
Leeton 63 B4
Leeuwarden .. 14 B3
Leeuwin, C. . 60 G2
Leeward Is. .. 87 C7
Leganés 18 B4
Legnago 20 B3
Legnica 16 C3
Leh 42 B10
Leicester 11 E6
Leiden 14 B3
Leie → 14 C2
Leine → 14 B5
Leipzig 15 C7
Leiria 18 C1
Leitrim 11 D2
Lékva Ori ... 23 G5
Léman, L. ... 13 C7
Lemhi Ra. ... 81 C7
Lena → 30 B10
Leningrad =
  St.
  Peterburg . 24 B3
Leninsk-
  Kuznetskiy 29 D9
Lens 13 A5
Lentini 21 F5
Leoben 15 E8
Leokovac 22 B3
León, Mexico 84 C4
León, Spain . 18 A3
León,
  Montañas
  de 18 A2
Leova 17 E9
Lérida 19 B6
Lerwick 10 A6
Les Sables-
  d'Olonne . 12 C3
Leskovac ... 22 C3
Lesotho ■ .. 59 D5
Lésvos 23 E6
Leszno 16 C3
Lethbridge .. 71 D8
Leti,
  Kepulauan 39 F3
Letterkenny . 11 D3
Leuven 14 C3
Levádhia ... 23 E4
Lévis 69 D3
Levkás 23 E3
Levkôsia =
  Nicosia ... 46 D3
Lewis 10 B3
Lewisporte .. 69 D5
Lewiston,
  Idaho,
  U.S.A. ... 80 B5
Lewiston,
  Maine,
  U.S.A. ... 73 B10
Lexington,
  Ky., U.S.A. 72 E3
Lexington,
  N.C., U.S.A. 75 B7
Leyte 38 B7
Lhasa 34 D4
Liaoning □ .. 35 B7
Liaoyuan ... 35 B7
Liard → 70 B7
Liberal 78 A3
Liberec 16 C2
Liberia ■ ... 56 D3
Lībīya, Sahrâ' 52 C4
Libourne ... 12 D3
Libreville ... 56 D1

Libya ■ 52 C2
Licata 21 F4
Lichinga 59 A7
Lichtenburg . 59 D5
Lida 17 B7
Lodi, Italy .. 20 B2
Lodi, U.S.A. 80 F3
Łódź 16 C4
Lofoten 8 E10
Logan 81 E8
Logan, Mt. . 70 B5
Logroño 19 A4
Lohardaga .. 40 F5
Loir → 12 C3
Loire → 12 C2
Loja 18 D3
Lombárdia □ 20 B2
Lomblen ... 39 F2
Lombok 37 F5
Lomé 55 G5
Lomond, L. . 10 C4
Lomza 16 B6
London 11 F6
Londonderry 11 D3
Londrina ... 94 A6
Long Beach . 82 D3
Long I.,
  Bahamas . 86 B4
Long I.,
  U.S.A. ... 73 D9
Long Xuyen 36 B3
Longford ... 11 E3
Longlac ... 69 D2
Longview,
  Tex., U.S.A. 79 C6
Longview,
  Wash.,
  U.S.A. ... 80 B2
Lons-le-
  Saunier .. 13 C6
Lop Nur ... 34 B4
Lora del Rio . 18 D3
Lorain 72 D4
Loralai 42 D6
Lorca 19 D5
Lorient 12 C2
Lorraine ... 13 B7
Los Alamos . 83 C9
Los Angeles,
  Chile 94 D2
Los Angeles,
  U.S.A. ... 82 C3
Los Mochis . 84 B3
Lošinj 20 B5
Lot → 12 D4
Louis
  Trichardt . 59 C5
Louis XIV,
  Pte. 69 C3
Louisiana □ . 79 D8
Louisville .. 72 E3
Loulé 18 D1
Lourdes ... 12 E3
Louth 11 E6
Lowell 73 C10
Lower Hutt . 65 D5
Lowestoft .. 11 E7
Loyew 17 C10
Luanda ... 56 F2
Luanshya .. 59 A5
Luarca 18 A2
Lubbock ... 78 C3
Lübeck 15 B6
Lublin 17 C6
Lubumbashi 59 A5
Lucca 20 C3
Lucena 18 D3
Luckenwalde 15 B7
Lucknow .. 40 D3
Lüderitz ... 58 D3
Ludhiana .. 42 D9
Ludwigsburg 14 D5
Ludwigshafen 14 D5
Lufkin 79 D6
Lugano 13 C8

Lobatse 59 D5
Lobito 58 A2
Locarno ... 13 C8
Loches 12 C4
Lodi, Italy .. 20 B2

Lugo, Italy .. 20 B3
Lugo, Spain . 18 A2
Luhansk ... 25 D4
Lule älv → . 8 E12
Luleå 8 E12
Lüleburgaz . 22 D6
Lüneburg .. 14 B6
Lüneburger
  Heide ... 14 B6
Lunéville .. 13 B7
Luni → 43 G7
Luninyets .. 17 B8
Luoyang ... 35 C6
Lurgan ... 11 D3
Lusaka ... 59 B5
Luta = Dalian 35 C7
Luton 11 F6
Lutsk 17 C7
Luxembourg 13 B7
Luxembourg ■
  .... 14 D4
Luzern 13 C8
Luzhou ... 35 D5
Luzon 38 A2
Lviv 17 D7
Lyakhavichy 17 B8
Lyakhovskiye,
  Ostrova .. 31 B12
Lydenburg . 59 D6
Lydia 23 E7
Lyepyel ... 24 C2
Lynchburg . 73 F6
Lynn Lake . 71 C9
Lyon 13 D6
Lyonnais ... 13 D6
Lysychansk . 25 D4
Lyuboml ... 17 C7

Madison .. 77 D10
Madiun ... 37 F4
Madras =
  Chennai . 43 N12
Madre,
  Laguna . 78 F5
Madre, Sierra 38 A2
Madrid ... 18 B4
Madurai .. 43 Q11
Maebashi .. 32 A6
Maestrazgo,
  Mts. del . 19 B5
Mafikeng .. 59 D5
Mafra 18 C1
Magadan .. 31 D13
Magallanes,
  Estrecho de 95 G2
Magdalena →
  .... 90 A4
Magdeburg . 15 B6
Magelang . 37 F4
Maggiore, L. 20 B2
Magnitogorsk 29 D6
Mahakam → 37 E5
Mahalapye . 59 C5
Mahanadi → 40 G6
Maharashtra □
  .... 43 J9
Mahesana .. 43 H8
Mahilyow .. 17 B10
Mahón ... 19 C8
Maidstone . 11 F7
Maiduguri .. 53 F1
Majīdī 41 F8
Maikala Ra. 40 G3
Main → ... 14 D5
Maine 12 C3
Mainland,
  Orkney,
  U.K. 10 B5
Mainland,
  Shet., U.K. 10 A6
Mainz 14 C5
Maitland .. 63 B5
Maizuru ... 32 B4
Majorca =
  Mallorca . 19 C7
Makasar,
  Selat ... 39 E1
Makedhonía □
  .... 23 D4
Makgadikgadi
  Salt Pans 59 C5
Makhachkala 25 E6
Makiyivka .. 25 D4
Makkah ... 47 G4
Makran Coast
  Range ... 42 G4
Makurazaki 33 D2
Malabar
  Coast ... 43 P9
Malacca, Str.
  of 36 D1
Maladzyechna 17 A8
Málaga 18 D3
Malang ... 37 F4
Malanje ... 56 F3
Mälaren .. 9 G11
Malaryta .. 17 C7
Malatya ... 46 C4
Malawi ■ .. 59 A6
Malawi, L. . 59 A6
Malaysia ■ . 36 D4
Malazgirt .. 46 C5
Maldives ■ . 26 J11
Maléa, Ákra 23 F4
Malegaon .. 43 J9
Mali ■ 55 E4
Malin Hd. .. 10 D3
Malkara ... 22 D6
Mallaig ... 10 C4
Mallorca .. 19 C7
Mallow ... 11 E2
Malmö 9 G10

Malta ■ 21 G5
Maluku 39 E3
Malyn 17 C9
Mamahatun . 46 C5
Man, I. of .. 11 D4
Manacor .. 19 C7
Manado .. 39 D2
Managua .. 85 E7
Manaus .. 90 D7
Manchester, U.K. ... 11 E5
Manchester, U.S.A. .. 73 C10
Mandal .. 9 G9
Mandalay .. 41 F11
Mandi .. 42 D10
Mandla .. 40 F3
Mandsaur .. 43 G9
Mandvi .. 43 H6
Manfredónia 20 D5
Mangalore .. 43 N9
Manggar .. 37 E3
Mangole .. 39 E3
Manicouagan → 69 D4
Manila .. 38 B2
Manila B. .. 38 B2
Manipur □ .. 41 E9
Manisa .. 23 E6
Manitoba □ .. 71 C10
Manitoba, L. .. 71 C10
Manitowoc .. 72 B2
Manizales .. 90 B3
Manly .. 63 B5
Mannar .. 43 Q11
Mannar, G. of 43 Q11
Mannheim .. 14 D5
Manokwari .. 39 E4
Manosque .. 13 E6
Manresa .. 19 B6
Mansel I. .. 68 B2
Mansfield, U.K. ... 11 E6
Mansfield, U.S.A. .. 72 D4
Mantes-la-Jolie .. 12 B4
Mántova .. 20 B3
Manzai .. 42 C7
Manzanares .. 18 C4
Manzhouli .. 35 B6
Maoming .. 35 D6
Mapam Yumco .. 40 B3
Maputo .. 59 D6
Mar del Plata 94 D5
Mar Menor .. 19 D5
Marabá .. 92 D4
Maracaibo .. 90 A4
Maracaibo, L. de .. 90 B4
Maracay .. 90 A5
Marajó, I. de 92 C4
Marañón → .. 90 D4
Marbella .. 18 D3
Marburg .. 14 C5
Marche .. 12 C4
Marchena .. 18 D3
Mardan .. 42 B8
Mardin .. 46 C5
Margarita, I. de .. 90 A6
Margate .. 11 F7
Mari El □ .. 24 B6
Maribor .. 20 A5
Marie Byrd Land 96 B18
Marie-Galante 87 C7
Mariental .. 58 C3
Marília .. 93 G3
Marín .. 18 A1
Marion .. 79 A9
Maritimes, Alpes .. 13 D7

Mariupol ... 25 D4
Markham, Mt. 96 C15
Marmara .. 23 D6
Marmara Denizi 22 D7
Marmaris .. 23 F7
Marmolada, Mte. .. 20 A3
Marne → .. 12 B5
Maroua .. 53 F1
Marquette .. 69 D2
Marquises, Is. 65 K17
Marrakech .. 54 B3
Marsala .. 21 F4
Marseille .. 13 E6
Marshall .. 79 C6
Marwar .. 42 G8
Maryborough 62 C5
Maryland □ .. 73 E7
Masan .. 35 C7
Maseru .. 59 D5
Mashhad .. 44 B4
Mashike .. 32 F12
Mask, L. .. 11 E2
Mason City .. 77 D8
Masqat .. 45 F4
Massa .. 20 B3
Massachusetts □ 73 C9
Massena .. 73 B8
Massif Central 13 D5
Masterton .. 65 D6
Masty .. 17 B7
Masuda .. 32 B2
Masvingo .. 59 C6
Matadi .. 56 F2
Matagami, L. 69 D3
Matamoros .. 84 B4
Matane .. 69 D4
Mataró .. 19 B7
Mathura .. 42 F10
Mato Grosso □ .. 93 C3
Mato Grosso, Planalto do 93 F3
Matosinhos .. 18 B1
Matsue .. 32 B3
Matsumoto .. 32 A6
Matsusaka .. 32 B5
Matsuyama .. 32 C3
Mattagami → 69 C2
Matterhorn .. 13 D7
Maturín .. 90 B6
Maubeuge .. 13 A5
Maudin Sun 41 K10
Maui 82 H12
Maumere .. 39 F2
Maun .. 58 B4
Mauritania ■ 55 D2
Mauritius ■ .. 51 H9
Mawlaik .. 41 F10
Mayenne → .. 12 C3
Mayo, L. .. 70 B6
Mayo .. 70 B6
Mazar-e Sharif .. 45 B6
Mazara del Vallo .. 21 F4
Mazarrón .. 19 D5
Mazatlán .. 84 C3

Mazurski, Pojezierze . 16 B5
Mazyr ... 17 C9
Mbabane .. 59 D6
Mbandaka .. 56 D3
Mbanza Ngungu .. 56 F2
Mbeya .. 57 F6
Mbini □ .. 56 D2
Mbuji-Mayi .. 56 F4
Mead, L. .. 82 B5
Meaux .. 13 B5
Mecca = Makkah .. 47 G4
Mechelen .. 14 C3
Mecklenburg 15 B6
Mecklenburger Bucht .. 15 A6
Medan .. 37 D1
Medellín .. 90 B3
Medford .. 80 B2
Medicine Bow Ra. ... 81 E10
Medicine Hat 71 C8
Medina = Al Madīnah .. 47 F4
Medina del Campo .. 18 B3
Medina-Sidonia .. 18 D3
Mediterranean Sea .. 50 C5
Médoc .. 12 D3
Meekatharra 60 F2
Meerut .. 42 E10
Mégara .. 23 F4
Meghalaya □ 41 E8
Mei Xian .. 35 D6
Meissen .. 15 C7
Mekhtar .. 42 D6
Meknès .. 54 B3
Mekong → .. 36 C3
Melaka .. 37 D2
Melanesia .. 64 K10
Melbourne, Australia .. 63 C3
Melbourne, U.S.A. .. 75 E7
Mélèzes → .. 68 C3
Melfort .. 71 C9
Melitopol .. 25 D4
Melk .. 15 D8
Melun .. 13 B5
Melville .. 71 C9
Melville I. .. 60 C5
Melville Pen. 68 B2
Memmingen .. 14 E6
Memphis, Tenn., U.S.A. .. 74 B3
Memphis, Tex., U.S.A. 78 B3
Mende .. 13 D5
Mendocino, C. .. 80 E1
Mendoza .. 94 C3
Menemen .. 23 E6
Menen .. 23 E6
Menindee .. 62 B3
Menominee .. 72 B2
Menorca .. 19 C7
Mentawai, Kepulauan 37 E1
Menton .. 13 E7
Meppel .. 14 B4
Merabéllou, G. .. 23 G5
Merano .. 20 A3
Merced .. 82 B2
Mercy C. .. 68 B4
Mérida, Mexico .. 85 C7
Mérida, Spain 18 C2
Mérida, Venezuela 90 B4

Mérida, Cord. de 87 E5
Meriden .. 74 D3
Merseburg .. 15 C6
Mersin .. 46 C3
Merthyr Tydfil 11 F5
Mértola .. 18 D2
Mesa 83 D7
Mesolóngion 23 E3
Mesopotamia = Al Jazirah .. 46 D5
Messina, Italy 21 E5
Messina, S. Africa .. 59 C6
Messina, Str. di ... 21 E5
Messíni .. 23 F4
Messiniakós Kólpos .. 23 F4
Metairie .. 79 E8
Metlakatla .. 71 C6
Metz .. 13 B7
Meuse → .. 13 A6
Mexicali .. 84 A1
México .. 84 D5
Mexico ■ .. 84 C4
Mexico, G. of 85 B7
Meymaneh .. 42 B4
Mézène .. 13 D6
Mhow .. 43 H9
Miami .. 75 G7
Miami Beach 75 G7
Mianwali .. 42 C7
Michigan □ .. 72 C3
Michigan, L. 72 C2
Michipicoten 69 D2
Micronesia, Federated States of ■ 64 J10
Middelburg 58 E5
Middlesbrough .. 11 D6
Midi, Canal du → .. 12 E4
Midland .. 78 D3
Midyat .. 46 C5
Mieres .. 18 A3
Mihara .. 32 B3
Mikonos .. 23 F5
Mikura-Jima .. 32 C6
Milano .. 20 B2
Milås .. 23 F6
Milazzo .. 21 E5
Mildura .. 62 B3
Miletus .. 23 F6
Milford Haven 11 F4
Millau .. 13 D5
Millinocket .. 73 B11
Milne Inlet .. 68 A2
Milos .. 23 F5
Milton Keynes 11 E6
Milwaukee .. 72 C2
Minamata .. 32 C2
Minas Gerais □ .. 93 F4
Mindanao .. 38 C2
Minden .. 14 B5
Mindoro .. 38 B2
Mindoro Str. .. 38 B2
Mingan .. 69 C4
Minho □ .. 18 B1
Minneapolis 77 C8
Minnedosa .. 71 C10
Minnesota □ 77 B7
Minorca = Menorca .. 19 C7
Minot .. 76 A4
Minsk .. 24 C2
Minto .. 71 B5
Mira .. 20 B4
Miranda de Ebro .. 19 A4

Miranda do Douro .. 18 B2
Mirpur Khas 42 G6
Mirzapur .. 40 E4
Miskolc .. 16 D5
Misool .. 39 E4
Misrātah .. 52 B2
Misriç .. 46 C5
Missinaibi → 69 C2
Mississippi □ 79 C9
Mississippi → 79 E9
Mississippi River Delta 79 E9
Missoula .. 81 B6
Missouri □ .. 77 F8
Missouri → .. 77 F9
Mistassini L. 69 C3
Mitchell .. 76 D5
Mitchell → .. 61 D7
Mitilíni .. 23 E6
Mito .. 32 A7
Mitumba, Chaîne des 57 F5
Miyake-Jima 32 B6
Miyako .. 33 G12
Miyakonojō 32 D2
Miyazaki .. 32 D2
Mizoram □ .. 41 F9
Mjøsa .. 8 F10
Mladá Boleslav .. 16 C2
Mljet .. 20 C6
Mmabatho .. 59 D5
Mobile .. 74 D3
Mochudi .. 59 C5
Modane .. 13 D7
Módena .. 20 B3
Modesto .. 82 B2
Módica .. 21 F5
Moe 63 C4
Mogadishu = Muqdisho 49 G4
Mogami → .. 33 G12
Mohyliv-Podilskyy 17 D8
Moisie .. 69 C4
Moisie → .. 69 C4
Mojave Desert .. 82 C4
Moldavia ■ = Moldova ■ 17 E9
Molde .. 8 F9
Moldova ■ .. 17 E9
Molepolole .. 59 C5
Molfetta .. 20 D6
Moline .. 77 E9
Mollendo .. 91 G4
Molokai .. 82 H12
Molopo → .. 58 D4
Molucca Sea 39 E2
Moluccas = Maluku .. 39 E3
Mombasa .. 57 E7
Mona, Canal de la .. 87 C6
Mónaco ■ .. 13 E7
Monahans .. 78 D2
Monavyo, Sierra del .. 19 B5
Mönchengladbach ... 14 C4
Monclova .. 84 B4
Mondego → .. 18 B1
Mondoví .. 20 B1
Monforte de Lemos .. 18 A2
Mongólia ■ .. 35 B5
Mongu .. 58 B4
Monópoli .. 21 D6
Monroe, La., U.S.A. .. 79 C7

Monroe, N.C., U.S.A.	75 B7	Mostaganem	54 A5	Muscatine .. 77 E9

Monroe, N.C., U.S.A. 75 B7
Monrovia .. 55 G2
Mons 14 C2
Mont-de-Marsan .. 12 E3
Montalbán .. 19 B5
Montana □ .. 81 B9
Montargis .. 13 C5
Montauban . 12 D4
Montbéliard 13 C7
Montceau-les-Mines .. 13 C6
Monte-Carlo 20 C1
Monte Santu, C. di ... 21 D2
Montecristo . 20 C3
Montego Bay 86 C4
Montélimar . 13 D6
Montenegro □ 22 C2
Monterey .. 82 B2
Monteria .. 90 B3
Monterrey .. 84 B4
Montes Claros 93 F5
Montesilvano Marina .. 20 C5
Montevideo . 94 C5
Montgomery 74 C4
Montijo ... 18 C2
Montilla .. 18 D3
Montluçon .. 13 C5
Montmorillon 12 C4
Montoro .. 18 C3
Montpellier . 13 E5
Montréal .. 69 D3
Montreux .. 13 C7
Montrose, U.K. .. 10 C5
Montrose, U.S.A. .. 83 A9
Montserrat ■ 87 C7
Monza 20 B2
Monzón ... 19 B6
Moonie → .. 63 A4
Moose Jaw . 71 C9
Moosomin .. 71 C9
Moosonee .. 69 C2
Mopti 55 F4
Mora 8 F10
Moradabad . 42 E11
Morava →, Serbia, Yug. 22 B3
Morava →, Slovak Rep. 16 D3
Moray Firth . 10 C5
Morden ... 71 D10
Mordvinia □ 24 C5
Morelia .. 84 D4
Morella .. 19 B5
Morena, Sierra .. 18 C3
Morgan City 79 E8
Morioka .. 33 G12
Morlaix ... 12 B2
Moro G. .. 38 C2
Morocco ■ . 54 B4
Morogoro .. 57 F7
Morón de la Frontera . 18 D3
Morotai ... 39 D3
Morristown . 75 A6
Morvan ... 13 C6
Morwell ... 63 C4
Moscow = Moskva .. 24 B4
Moscow, U.S.A. .. 80 B5
Mosel → .. 13 A7
Moshi 57 E7
Moskva ... 24 B4
Mosselbaai . 58 E4
Mossoró .. 92 D6
Most 16 C1

Mostaganem 54 A5
Mostar 20 C6
Mostyska .. 17 D6
Mosul = Al Mawṣil .. 46 C5
Motihari ... 40 D5
Motril 18 D4
Moúdhros .. 23 E5
Moulins ... 13 C5
Moulmein .. 41 J11
Mount Gambier . 62 C3
Mount Isa . 61 E6
Mount Lofty Ra. .. 62 B2
Mount McKinley National Park .. 71 B4
Mount Vernon .. 73 D9
Mountain View .. 82 B1
Moura 18 C2
Mozambique ■ 59 B7
Mozambique Chan. .. 59 H8
Mu Us Shamo .. 35 C5
Muar 37 D2
Mudanjiang . 35 B7
Mudanya .. 23 D7
Mudgee ... 63 B4
Mufulira ... 59 A5
Muğla 23 F7
Mühlhausen 14 C6
Mukacheve . 17 D6
Muktsar ... 42 D9
Mukur 42 C5
Mula 19 C5
Mulde → .. 15 C7
Mulgrave .. 69 D4
Mulhacén .. 18 D4
Mulhouse .. 13 C7
Muli 10 C4
Muller, Pegunungan 37 D4
Mullingar .. 11 E3
Multan ... 42 D7
Mumbai ... 43 K8
Muna 39 F2
München .. 15 D6
Muncie ... 72 D3
Münden ... 14 C5
Munger ... 40 E6
Munich = München . 15 D6
Münster ... 14 C4
Munster □ .. 11 E2
Muqdisho .. 49 G4
Muratlı ... 22 D6
Murchison → 60 F1
Murcia ... 19 C5
Murcia □ .. 19 D5
Mureș → .. 16 E5
Murfreesboro 74 B4
Müritz-see . 15 B7
Murmansk .. 24 A4
Muroran ... 32 F12
Muroto-Misaki .. 32 C4
Murray → . 62 C2
Murrumbidgee → 62 B3
Murwara .. 40 F3
Murwillumbah 63 A5
Mürzzuschlag 15 E8
Muş 46 C5
Mūsa, G. .. 47 E3
Muscat = Masqaṭ .. 45 F4

Muscatine .. 77 E9
Musgrave Ras. 60 F5
Musi → ... 37 E2
Muskogee .. 79 B6
Mustafakemalpaşa 23 D7
Mustang ... 40 C4
Muswellbrook 63 B5
Mut 46 C3
Mutare ... 59 B6
Muzaffarnagar 42 E10
Muzaffarpur 40 D5
Mwanza ... 57 E6
Mweru, L. .. 57 F5
My Tho ... 36 B3
Myanmar = Burma ■ . 41 G11
Mycenæ ... 23 F4
Myingyan .. 41 G10
Myitkyina .. 41 E11
Mykolayiv .. 25 D3
Mymensingh 41 E8
Mysia 23 E6
Mysore ... 43 N10
Naab → ... 15 D7
Naberezhnyye Chelny ... 29 D6
Nābulus ... 46 D3
Nacogdoches 79 D6
Nadiad ... 43 H8
Nadvirna .. 17 D7
Nagaland □ . 41 E10
Nagano ... 32 A6
Nagaoka .. 33 G11
Nagasaki .. 32 C1
Nagaur ... 42 F8
Nagercoil .. 43 Q10
Nagoya ... 32 B5
Nagpur ... 43 J11
Nahanni Butte 70 B7
Nain 68 C4
Nairn 10 C5
Nairobi ... 57 E7
Najd 47 F5
Najibabad .. 42 E11
Nakamura .. 32 C3
Nakhodka .. 31 E11
Nakhon Ratchasima 36 B2
Nakhon Si Thammarat 36 C2
Nakina ... 69 C2
Nakuru ... 57 E7
Nalchik ... 25 E5
Nam Co ... 34 C4
Namaland .. 58 C3
Namangan .. 29 E8
Namibe ... 58 B2
Namibia ■ . 58 C3
Namibwoestyn 58 C2
Namlea ... 39 E3
Nampa 80 D5
Nampula .. 59 B7
Namur 14 C3
Nanaimo .. 71 D7
Nanao 32 A5
Nanchang .. 35 D6
Nanchong .. 35 C5
Nancy 13 B7
Nanda Devi . 42 D11
Nanded ... 43 K10
Nandurbar .. 43 J9
Nanga Parbat 42 B9
Nanjing ... 35 C6
Nanning .. 35 D5
Nanping ... 35 D6
Nantes ... 12 C3
Nao, C. de la 19 C6
Naoetsu ... 32 A6

Napa 80 F2
Napier 64 C7
Naples = Napoli .. 21 D5
Narayanganj 41 F8
Narbonne .. 13 E5
Nardò 23 D2
Narmada → 43 J8
Narrandera . 63 B4
Narromine .. 63 B4
Narva 24 B2
Narvik 8 E11
Naser, Buheirat en 52 D5
Nashville .. 74 A4
Nasik 43 K8
Nasirabad .. 42 F9
Nassau ... 86 A4
Nata 59 C5
Natal 92 D6
Natashquan . 69 C4
Natashquan → 69 C4
Natchez ... 79 D8
Nathdwara . 43 G8
Natuna Besar, Kepulauan 37 D3
Natuna Selatan, Kepulauan 37 D3
Nauru ■ ... 64 K11
Navahrudak . 17 B7
Navalmoral de la Mata 18 C3
Navan = An Uaimh .. 11 E3
Návpaktos .. 23 E3
Návplion .. 23 F4
Navsari ... 43 J8
Nawabshah . 42 F6
Naxçıvan □ . 25 F6
Náxos 23 F5
Nazilli ... 23 F7
Ndjamena .. 53 F1
Ndola 59 A5
Neagh, Lough 11 D3
Near Is. ... 71 C1
Neath 11 F5
Nebraska □ . 76 E5
Nébrodi, Monti .. 21 F5
Neckar → .. 14 D5
Neepawa .. 71 C10
Negro →, Argentina . 95 E4
Negro →, Brazil .. 90 D6
Negros ... 38 C2
Nei Monggol Zizhiqu □ . 35 B6
Neijiang .. 35 D5
Neiva 90 C3
Nellore ... 43 M11
Nelson ... 71 D8
Nelson, N.Z. 65 D5
Nelson → .. 71 C10
Nelspruit .. 59 D6
Neman → . 24 B1
Nemuro ... 32 F13
Nemuro-Kaikyō . 32 F13
Nenagh ... 11 E2
Nenana ... 71 B5
Nepal ■ ... 40 D5
Neretva → . 20 C6
Ness, L. ... 10 C4
Nesterov ... 17 C6
Netherlands ■ 14 B3
Netherlands Antilles ■ . 87 D6
Nettilling L. . 68 B3

Neubrandenburg 15 B7
Neuchâtel . 13 C7
Neuchâtel, Lac de . 13 C7
Neumünster 14 A5
Neunkirchen 14 D4
Neuquén .. 94 D3
Neuruppin . 15 B7
Neustrelitz . 15 B7
Nevada □ .. 80 F5
Nevada, Sierra, Spain .. 18 D4
Nevada, Sierra, U.S.A. .. 80 F3
Nevers ... 13 C5
Nevşehir .. 46 C3
New Amsterdam 90 B7
New Bedford 73 D10
New Bern .. 75 B9
New Brighton 65 E5
New Britain, Papua N. G. 64 K10
New Britain, U.S.A. .. 73 D9
New Brunswick □ 69 D4
New Caledonia ■ 64 M11
New Glasgow 69 D4
New Guinea 64
New Hampshire □ 73 C10
New Haven . 73 D9
New Jersey □ 73 E9
New London 73 D9
New Mexico □ . 83 C9
New Orleans 79 E8
Newport □, U.K. .. 64 C6
New South Wales □ .. 63 B4
New Westminster 71 D7
New York □ . 73 C8
New York City 73 D9
New Zealand ■ 64 D7
Newark ... 73 D8
Newburgh .. 73 D8
Newbury .. 11 F6
Newcastle, Australia .. 63 B5
Newcastle, S. Africa .. 59 D5
Newcastle-upon-Tyne 11 D6
Newfoundland □ 69 C5
Newman ... 60 E2
Newport, Gwent, U.K. 11 F5
Newport, I. of W., U.K. ... 11 F6
Newport, U.S.A. .. 73 D10
Newport News .. 73 F7
Newquay .. 11 F4
Newry 11 D3
Nha Trang . 36 B3
Niagara Falls, Canada .. 69 D3
Niagara Falls, U.S.A. .. 73 C6
Niamey ... 55 F5

Nias

Nias	37	D1
Nicaragua ■	85	E7
Nicaragua, L. de	85	E7
Nicastro	21	E6
Nice	13	E7
Nichinan	33	D2
Nicobar Is.	27	J13
Nicosia	46	D3
Nicoya, Pen. de	85	E7
Niedersachsen □	14	B5
Nienburg	14	B5
Niğde	46	C3
Niger ■	55	G6
Niger →	55	G6
Nigeria ■	55	G6
Nii-Jima	32	B6
Niigata	33	G11
Niihama	32	C3
Niihau	82	
Nijmegen	14	C3
Nikopol	25	D3
Nîl, Nahr en →	52	B5
Nîl el Abyad →	53	E5
Nîl el Azraq →	53	E5
Nile = Nîl, Nahr en →	52	B5
Nimach	43	G9
Nîmes	13	E6
Ningbo	35	D7
Ningxia Huizu Zizhiqu □	35	C5
Niobrara →	76	D5
Niort	12	C3
Nipawin	71	C9
Nipigon, L.	69	D2
Niš	22	C3
Nishinomiya	32	B4
Niterói	93	G5
Nitra	16	D4
Nitra →	16	E4
Niue	65	L14
Nivernais	13	C5
Nizamabad	43	K11
Nizhniy Novgorod	24	B5
Nizhniy Tagil	29	D6
Nizhyn	24	C3
Nizip	46	C4
Nizké Tatry	16	D4
Nkongsamba	56	D1
Noatak	71	B3
Nobeoka	32	C2
Nocera Inferiore	21	D5
Nogales, Mexico	84	A2
Nogales, U.S.A.	83	E7
Nōgata	32	C2
Noire, Mts.	12	B2
Noirmoutier, I. de	12	C2
Nokomis	71	C9
Nome	71	B3
Noranda	69	D3
Nord-Ostsee-Kanal →	14	A5
Nordegg	71	C8
Norderney	14	B4
Norderstedt	14	B5
Nordfriesische Inseln	14	A5
Nordhausen	14	C6
Nordkapp	8	D13
Nordrhein-Westfalen □	14	C4
Nordvik	30	B9
Norfolk	73	F7
Norfolk I.	64	M11
Norilsk	30	C6
Norman	78	B5
Norman Wells	70	B7
Normandie	12	B4
Norrköping	9	G11
Norrland	8	F11
Norseman	60	G3
North Battleford	71	C9
North Bay	69	D3
North Bend	80	D1
North Carolina □	75	B7
North Channel, Canada	69	D2
North Channel, U.K.	11	D4
North Dakota □	76	B4
North I.	64	B5
North Minch	10	B4
North Ossetia □	25	E5
North Platte	76	E4
North Platte →	76	E4
North Saskatchewan →	71	C8
North Sea	10	D8
North Thompson →	71	C7
North Uist	10	C3
North West Frontier □	42	B8
North West Highlands	10	C4
North West River	69	C4
North West Territories □	70	B8
Northampton	11	E6
Northern Ireland □	11	D3
Northern Marianas ■	64	H9
Northern Territory □	60	D5
Northland □	64	A5
Northumberland Str.	69	D4
Norton Sd.	71	B3
Norway ■	8	F10
Norway House	71	C10
Norwegian Sea	6	B5
Norwich	11	E7
Nossob →	58	D4
Noto-Hanto	33	G11
Notre Dame B.	69	D5
Nottaway →	69	C3
Nottingham	11	E6
Nouâdhibou	54	D1
Nouakchott	55	E1
Nouméa	64	M11
Noupoort	58	E4
Nova Iguaçu	93	G5
Nova Scotia □	69	D4
Novara	20	B2
Novaya Zemlya	28	B6
Novgorod	24	B3
Novhorod-Siverskyy	24	C3
Novi Lígure	20	B2
Novi Sad	22	B2
Novo Mesto	20	B5
Novocherkassk	25	D5
Novohrad-Volynskyy	17	C8
Novokuznetsk	29	D9
Novomoskovsk	24	C4
Novorossiysk	25	E4
Novoselytsya	17	D8
Novoshakhtinsk	25	D4
Novosibirsk	29	D9
Novosibirskiye Ostrova	31	B12
Novotroitsk	29	D6
Novovolynsk	17	C7
Novska	20	B6
Nowy Sącz	16	D5
Noyon	13	B5
Nūbiya, Es Sahrâ En	52	D5
Nuelltin L.	70	B10
Nuevo Laredo	84	B5
Nulato	71	B4
Nullarbor Plain	60	G4
Numazu	32	B6
Nunavut □	68	B2
Nuneaton	11	E6
Nunivak I.	71	B3
Núoro	21	D2
Nuremberg = Nürnberg	15	D6
Nürnberg	15	D6
Nutak	68	C4
Nuuk = Godthåb	68	B5
Nuweveldberge	58	E4
Nyasa, L. = Malawi, L.	59	A6
Nyasvizh	17	B8
Nyíregyháza	17	E5
Nylstroom	59	C5
Nysa	16	C3
Nysa →	16	B2
Ōgaki	32	B5
Ogbomosho	55	G5
Ogden	81	E8
Ogdensburg	73	B8
Oglio →	20	B3
Ohio □	72	D4
Ohio →	72	F1
Ohre →	16	C2
Ohrid	22	D3
Ohridsko Jezero	23	D3
Oise →	12	B5
Ōita	32	C2
Ojos del Salado, Cerro	94	B3
Okahandja	58	C3
Okanogan →	80	A4
Okara	42	D8
Okavango Swamps	58	B4
Okaya	32	A6
Okayama	32	B3
Okazaki	32	B5
Okeechobee, L.	75	F7
Okefenokee Swamp	75	D6
Okhotsk, Sea of	31	D12
Oki-Shotō	32	A3
Okiep	58	D3
Okinawa-Jima	35	D7
Oklahoma □	78	B5
Oklahoma City	78	B5
Okmulgee	79	B6
Oktyabrskoy Revolyutsii, Os.	30	B7
Okushiri-Tō	32	F11
Öland	9	G11
Ólbia	20	D2
Old Crow	70	B6
Oldenburg	14	B5
Oldham	11	E5
Olekminsk	31	C10
Oleksandriya	17	C8
Olenek →	30	B10
Oléron, I. d'	12	D3
Olevsk	17	C8
Olhão	18	D2
Ólimbos, Óros	23	D4
Olinda	92	D7
Olivenza	18	C2
Olomouc	16	D3
Olot	19	A7
Olsztyn	16	B5
Olt □	22	C5
Olt →	22	C5
Oltu	46	B5
Olympia, Greece	23	F3
Olympia, U.S.A.	80	B2
Olympic Mts.	80	B2
Omagh	11	D3
Omaha	77	E7
Oman ■	48	C6
Oman, G. of	45	E4
Omaruru	58	C2
Ombai, Selat	39	F2
Ombrone →	20	C3
Omdurmân	53	E5
Ōmiya	32	B6
Omsk	29	D8
Ōmura	32	C1
Ōmuta	32	C2
Onda	19	C5
Ondo	55	G5
Onega →	28	C4
Onehunga	64	B6
Onezhskaya Guba	28	C4
Onezhskoye Ozero	28	C4
Onitsha	55	G6
Onoda	32	B2
Ontario □	69	D2
Ontario, L.	73	C7
Oostende	14	C2
Opava	16	D3
Opole	16	C3
Oradea	17	E5
Orai	42	G11
Oral	24	C7
Oran	54	A4
Orange, Australia	63	B4
Orange, France	13	D6
Orange, U.S.A.	79	D7
Orangeburg	75	C7
Oranienburg	15	B7
Oranje →	58	D3
Oranjemund	58	D2
Orbetello	20	C3
Ordu	46	B4
Örebro	9	G11
Oregon □	80	C3
Orekhovo-Zuyevo	24	B4
Orel	24	C4
Ören	23	F6
Orenburg	29	D6
Orense	18	A2
Orgaz	18	C4
Orhaneli	23	E7
Orhangazi	23	D7
Orhei	17	E9
Orihuela	19	C5
Orinoco →	90	B6
Orissa □	40	G5
Oristano	21	E2
Oristano, G. di	21	E2
Orizaba	84	D5
Orkney Is.	10	B5
Orlando	75	E7
Orléanais	12	C5
Orléans	12	C4
Ormara	42	G4
Ormoc	38	B2
Ornsköldsvik	8	F11
Orsha	24	C3
Orsk	29	D6
Ortaca	23	F7
Ortegal, C.	18	A2
Orthez	12	E3
Ortigueira	18	A2
Ortles	20	A3
Orümiyeh, Daryācheh-ye	46	C6
Oruro	91	G5
Orvieto	20	C4
Ōsaka	32	B4
Osh	29	E8
Oshawa	69	D3
Oshkosh	76	E3
Oshogbo	55	G5
Osijek	20	B7
Oskarshamn	9	G11
Oskemen	29	E9
Oslo	9	G10
Oslofjorden	9	G10
Osmaniye	46	C4
Osnabrück	14	B5
Osorno	95	E2
Óssa, Óros	23	E4
Ostend = Oostende	14	C2
Öster	17	C10
Österdalälven	8	F10
Östersund	8	F10
Ostfriesische Inseln	14	B4

Ostrava 16 D4
Ostroh 17 C8
Ostrołęka ... 16 B5
Ostrów
 Wielkopolski
 .... 16 C3
Ostrowiec-
 Świętokrzyski
 .... 16 C5
Ostuni 21 D6
Ōsumi-Kaikyō 33 D2
Osuna 18 D3
Oswego 73 D7
Otago □ ... 65 F3
Ōtake 32 B3
Otaru 32 F12
Otjiwarongo 58 C2
Otranto 23 D2
Otranto, C. d' 23 D2
Otranto, Str.
 of 23 D2
Ōtsu 32 B4
Ottawa 69 D3
Ottawa Is. .. 68 C2
Ottumwa ... 77 E8
Ouachita Mts. 79 B6
Ouagadougou 55 F4
Oubangi → .. 56 E3
Oudtshoorn . 58 E4
Ouessant, I. d' 12 B1
Oujda 54 B4
Oulu 8 E13
Oulujärvi .. 8 E13
Oulujoki → .. 8 E13
Outer
 Hebrides .. 10 C3
Outjo 58 C3
Oviedo 18 A3
Ovruch 17 C9
Owase 32 B4
Owen Sound 69 D2
Owo 55 G6
Owyhee → .. 80 D5
Oxford 11 F6
Oxnard 82 C3
Oxus =
 Amudarya →
 .... 29 E6
Oyama 32 A6
Oyo 55 G5
Ozamiz 38 C2
Ozark Plateau 79 A8

Paarl 58 E3
Pab Hills .. 42 F5
Pabna 41 E7
Pacaraima,
 Sierra .. 90 C6
Pachuca ... 84 C5
Padang ... 37 E2
Paderborn .. 14 C5
Padloping
 Island .. 68 B4
Pádova 20 B3
Paducah ... 72 F1
Pag 20 B5
Pagastikós
 Kólpos .. 23 E4
Painted
 Desert .. 83 C7
País Vasco □ 19 A4
Paisley 10 D4
Pajares,
 Puerto de . 18 A3
Pakistan ■ .. 42 E7
Pakse 36 A3
Palagruža .. 20 C7
Palanpur .. 43 G8
Palapye 59 C5
Palawan ... 36 C5
Palembang . 37 E2
Palencia 18 A3
Palermo ... 21 E4

Palestine ... 79 D6
Palghat ... 43 P10
Pali 42 G8
Palioúrion,
 Ákra ... 23 E4
Palk Strait .. 43 Q11
Palm Springs 82 D4
Palma, B. de 19 C7
Palma de
 Mallorca .. 19 C7
Pálmas, G. di 21 E2
Palmer ... 71 B5
Palmer Land 96 B3
Palmerston
 North ... 64 D6
Palmi 21 E5
Palmira 90 C3
Palos, C. de . 19 D5
Palu 46 C5
Pamiers ... 12 E4
Pamirs 29 F8
Pamlico Sd. . 75 B10
Pampa 78 B3
Pampas 94 D3
Pamplona .. 19 A5
Panaji 43 M8
Panamá 85 F9
Panama ■ .. 86 E4
Panamá, G.
 de 86 E4
Panama City 79 D5
Panay 38 B2
Pančevo ... 22 B3
Panevežys .. 24 B1
Pangkalpinang
 .... 37 E3
Pangnirtung 68 B4
Pantar 39 F2
Pantelleria .. 21 F3
Papua New
 Guinea ■ . 61 B8
Pará □ 92 C3
Paracel Is. =
 Hsisha
 Chuntao . 36 A4
Paraguay ■ .. 94 A4
Paraguay → .. 94 B5
Paramaribo . 92 A2
Paraná 94 C4
Paraná → .. 94 C5
Parbhani .. 43 K10
Parchim ... 15 B6
Pardubice .. 16 C2
Parecis, Serra
 dos 91 F7
Parepare .. 39 E1
Párga 23 E3
Paris, France 13 B5
Paris, U.S.A. 79 C6
Park Range . 81 F10
Parkersburg 72 F5
Parkes 63 B4
Parla 18 B4
Parma 20 B4
Parnaíba → 92 C5
Parnassós .. 23 E4
Parnu 24 B1
Páros 23 F5
Parramatta . 63 B5
Parry Sound 69 D3
Partinico .. 21 E4
Pasadena,
 Calif.,
 U.S.A. .. 82 C3
Pasadena,
 Tex., U.S.A. 79 E6
Pascagoula . 79 D9
Pasco 80 B4
Pašman 20 C5
Pasni 42 G3
Passau 15 D7
Passero, C. . 21 F5
Pasto 90 C3
Patagonia .. 95 F3

Patan, India . 43 H8
Patan, Nepal . 40 D5
Paternò ... 21 F5
Paterson ... 73 D8
Pathankot .. 42 C9
Patiala 42 D10
Pátmos ... 23 F6
Patna 40 E5
Patos, L. dos 94 C5
Pátrai 23 E3
Pátraikós
 Kólpos .. 23 E3
Patuakhali .. 41 F8
Pau 12 E3
Pavia 20 B2
Pavlodar .. 29 D8
Pavlohrad .. 25 D4
Pawtucket .. 73 D10
Paxoi 23 E3
Pazar 46 B5
Pazardzhik .. 22 C5
Peace → ... 70 C8
Pechenizhyn 17 D7
Pechora → .. 28 C6
Pecos → ... 78 E3
Pécs 16 E4
Peel → 70 B6
Pegasus Bay 65 E5
Pegu 41 J11
Pegu Yoma . 41 H10
Peine 14 B6
Pekalongan . 37 F3
Pekanbaru .. 37 D2
Pekin 77 E10
Peking =
 Beijing .. 35 C6
Pelagie, Is. .. 21 G4
Peleng 39 E2
Peljesac ... 20 C6
Pelly → ... 70 B6
Pelly Bay .. 68 B2
Pelly L. ... 70 B9
Pelopónnisos □
 .... 23 F4
Peloro, C. .. 21 E5
Pelotas 94 C5
Pelvoux,
 Massif du . 13 D7
Pematangsiantar
 .... 37 D1
Pemba I. ... 57 F7
Pembroke,
 Canada .. 69 D3
Pembroke,
 U.K. 11 F4
Peñarroya-
 Pueblonuevo
 .... 18 C3
Peñas, C. de 18 A3
Pend Oreille
 L. 80 A5
Pendleton .. 80 C4
Peniche ... 18 C1
Peninsular
 Malaysia □ 37 D2
Penmarch,
 Pte. de .. 12 C1
Pennines .. 11 D5
Pennsylvania □
 .... 73 D7
Penrith ... 63 B5
Pensacola .. 74 D4
Pensacola
 Mts. 96 C4
Penticton .. 71 D8
Pentland Firth 10 B5
Penza 24 C6
Penzance .. 11 F4
Peoria 77 E10
Perche,
 Collines du 12 B4
Perdido, Mte. 19 A6
Pereira 90 C3

Pereyaslav-
 Khmelnytskyy
 .... 24 C3
Péribonca → 69 D3
Périgueux .. 12 D4
Perm 29 D6
Pernambuco =
 Recife .. 92 D7
Pernik 22 C4
Perpignan .. 13 E5
Pershotravensk
 .... 17 C8
Persian Gulf
 = Gulf, The 44 E2
Perth,
 Australia . 60 G2
Perth, U.K. . 10 C5
Perth Amboy 73 D8
Peru 90 C3
Perúgia ... 20 C4
Pervomaysk 25 D3
Pésaro 20 C4
Pescara ... 20 C5
Peshawar .. 42 B7
Peterborough,
 Canada .. 69 D3
Peterborough,
 U.K. 11 E6
Peterhead .. 10 C6
Petersburg,
 Alaska,
 U.S.A. .. 71 C6
Petersburg,
 Va., U.S.A. 73 F7
Petitsikapau,
 L. 69 C4
Petropavl .. 29 D7
Petropavlovsk-
 Kamchatskiy
 .... 31 D13
Petrópolis .. 93 G5
Petrozavodsk 28 C4
Pforzheim .. 14 D5
Phalodi ... 42 F8
Phan Rang . 36 B3
Phanh Bho
 Ho Chi
 Minh 36 B3
Philadelphia 73 E8
Philippines ■ 38 B2
Phitsanulok . 36 A2
Phnom Penh 36 B2
Phoenix ... 83 D6
Phuket 36 C1
Pianosa ... 20 C3
Piatra Neamţ 17 E8
Piave → ... 20 B4
Picardie ... 13 B5
Pictou 69 D4
Piedras
 Negras .. 84 B4
Piemonte □ . 20 B2
Piet Retief .. 59 D6
Pietermaritzburg
 .... 59 D6
Pietersburg . 59 C5
Piketberg .. 58 E3
Pilcomayo → 94 B5
Pilibhit ... 42 E11
Pilica → ... 16 C5
Pilos 23 F3
Pinang 36 C2
Pinarhisar .. 22 D6
Pindos Óros 23 E3
Pine Bluff .. 79 B7
Pine Point .. 70 B8
Pinerolo ... 20 B1
Pinetown .. 59 D6
Pingxiang .. 35 D5
Pinhel 18 B2
Piniós → ... 23 E4
Pinnes, Ákra 23 D5
Pinsk 17 B8
Piombino .. 20 C3
Piotrków
 Trybunalski 16 C4

Piraiévs ... 23 F4
Pirgos 23 F3
Pirmasens .. 14 D4
Pisa 20 C3
Pisciotta .. 21 D5
Pisek 16 D2
Pistóia ... 20 C3
Pisuerga → 18 B3
Pitcairn I. .. 65 M17
Piteå 8 E12
Pitesti 22 B5
Pittsburg .. 79 A6
Pittsburgh .. 73 D5
Piura 90 E2
Placentia .. 69 D5
Placentia B. . 69 D5
Plainview .. 78 B3
Pláka, Ákra 23 G6
Plasencia .. 18 B2
Plata, Río de
 la 94 C5
Platani → .. 21 F4
Platte → ... 77 F7
Plauen 15 C7
Plenty, B. of 64 B7
Pleven 22 C5
Plock 16 B4
Plöckenstein 15 D7
Ploiesti ... 22 B6
Plovdiv ... 22 C5
Plymouth .. 11 F4
Plzeň 16 D1
Po → 20 B4
Pocatello .. 81 D7
Podgorica .. 22 C2
Podilska
 Vysochyna 17 D8
Podolsk ... 24 B4
Pofadder .. 58 D3
Pointe-à-Pitre 87 C7
Pointe Noire 56 E2
Poitiers ... 12 C4
Poitou 12 C3
Poland ■ .. 16 B5
Polatsk ... 24 B2
Polillo Is. .. 38 B2
Poliyiros .. 23 D4
Polonne ... 17 C8
Poltava ... 24 D3
Polynesia .. 65 L15
Pombal ... 18 C1
Poméziia .. 20 D4
Ponca City .. 78 A5
Ponce 87 C6
Pond Inlet .. 68 A3
Pondicherry 43 P11
Ponferrada .. 18 A2
Ponta Grossa 94 B6
Pontarlier .. 13 C7
Pontchartrain
 L. 79 D8
Pontevedra . 18 A1
Pontiac ... 72 C4
Pontianak .. 37 E3
Pontivy ... 12 B2
Pontoise .. 12 B5
Ponziane,
 Ísole .. 21 D4
Poole 11 F6
Poona =
 Pune 43 K8
Poopó, L. de 91 G5
Popayán ... 90 C3
Poplar Bluff . 79 A8
Popocatépetl,
 Volcán .. 84 D5
Porbandar .. 43 J6
Porcupine → 71 B5
Pordenone .. 20 B4
Pori 8 F12
Porkkala .. 9 G12
Poroshiri-
 Dake 32 F12

Robertson ..	58	E3
Robson, Mt. .	71	C8
Roca, C. da .	18	C1
Rochefort ..	12	D3
Rochester, Minn., U.S.A.	77	C8
Rochester, N.Y., U.S.A.	73	C7
Rock Hill ..	75	B7
Rock Island .	77	E9
Rock Springs	81	E9
Rockford ..	77	D10
Rockhampton	61	E9
Rocky Mount	75	B9
Rocky Mts. .	70	C7
Rodez	13	D5
Ródhos ...	23	F7
Roes Welcome Sd.	68	B2
Rogatyn ...	17	D7
Rohtak ...	42	E10
Roma, Australia .	63	A4
Roma, *Italy* .	20	D4
Romania ■ .	22	B5
Romans-sur- Isère	13	D6
Rome	74	B4
Romorantin- Lanthenay	12	C4
Ronda	18	D3
Rondônia □ .	91	F6
Ronge, L. la .	71	C9
Ronne Ice Shelf	96	B16
Roodepoort .	59	D5
Roosevelt I. .	96	B16
Roquetas de Mar	19	D4
Roraima □ .	90	C6
Roraima, Mt.	90	B6
Rosario ...	94	C4
Rosas, G. de	19	A7
Roscommon	11	E2
Roseau, *Domin.* ...	87	C7
Roseau, U.S.A. ...	77	A7
Roseburg ..	80	D2
Rosenheim .	15	E7
Rosetown ..	71	C9
Roseville ..	80	F3
Rosignano Marittimo .	20	C4
Ross Ice Shelf	96	C16
Ross Sea ..	96	B15
Rossano Cálabro ..	21	E6
Rossland ..	71	D8
Rosslare ..	11	E3
Rosthern ..	71	C9
Rostock ...	15	A7
Rostov ...	25	D4
Roswell ...	79	D1
Rotherham .	11	E6
Rotondo Mte.	18	B2
Rotorua ...	64	C7
Rotorua, L. .	64	C7
Rotterdam .	14	C3
Rottweil ...	14	D4
Roubaix ...	13	A5
Rouen	12	B4
Roussillon .	13	E5
Rouyn	69	D3
Rovaniemi .	8	E13
Rovereto ..	20	B3
Rovigo ...	20	B3
Rovinj ...	20	B4
Royal Leamington Spa	11	E6
Royan	12	D3
Rozdilna ...	17	E10
Rozhyshche .	17	C7
Ruahine Ra. .	64	C7
Rub' al Khali	48	D4
Rugby	11	E6
Rügen	15	A7
Ruhr → ...	14	C4
Rumania = Romania ■ .	22	B5
Rumoi ...	32	F12
Rupat	37	D2
Rupert → . .	69	C3
Ruse	22	C5
Rustavi ...	25	E6
Rustenburg .	59	D5
Ruteng ...	39	F2
Ruwenzori .	57	D5
Rwanda ■ .	57	E6
Ryazan	24	C4
Rybinsk ...	24	B4
Rybinskoye Vdkhr.	24	B4
Ryūkyū-rettō	35	D7
Rzeszów ...	16	C5

S

Saale → ...	15	C6
Saalfeld ...	15	C6
Saar → ...	13	B7
Saarbrücken	14	D4
Saaremaa ..	24	B1
Sabadell ..	19	B7
Sabah □ ...	36	C5
Sabhah ...	52	C1
Sable, C., *Canada* .	69	D4
Sable, C., U.S.A. ...	86	A3
Sable I. ...	69	D5
Sachsen □ .	15	C7
Sachsen- Anhalt □ .	15	C7
Sacramento .	80	F3
Sacramento →	80	F3
Sacramento Mts.	83	D10
Sado	33	G11
Safi	54	B3
Saga	32	C2
Sagar	43	M9
Saginaw ..	72	C4
Saguenay →	69	D3
Sagunto ...	19	C5
Sahagún ...	18	A3
Sahara ...	54	D4
Saharanpur .	42	E10
Saharien, Atlas	54	B4
Sahiwal ...	42	D8
Sa'īdābād ..	44	D3
Saidpur ...	41	E7
Saigon = Phanh Bho Ho Chi Minh	36	B3
Saijō	32	C3
Saiki	32	C2
St. Andrews	10	C5
St-Augustin- Saguenay .	69	C4
St. Augustine	75	E7
St. Austell .	11	F4
St. Boniface	71	D10
St-Brieuc .	12	B2
St. Catharines	69	D3
St-Chamond	13	D6
St. Christopher- Nevis = St. Kitts- Nevis ■ .	87	C7
St. Cloud ...	77	C7
St.-Denis ...	12	B5
St.-Dizier ...	13	B6
St. Elias, Mt.	70	B5
St.-Étienne .	13	D6
St.-Flour ...	13	D5
St. Francis, C.	58	E4
St.-Gaudens	12	A4
St. George's	87	D7
St. George's Channel .	11	F3
St. Helena ■	51	H3
St. Helena B.	58	E3
St. Helier ..	11	G5
St-Hyacinthe	69	D3
St. John ...	69	D4
St. John's, *Antigua* ..	87	C7
St. John's, *Canada* .	69	D5
St. Johns →	75	D7
St. Joseph ..	77	F7
St. Joseph, L.	69	C1
St. Kilda ...	10	C2
St. Kitts- Nevis ■ .	87	C7
St. Lawrence →	69	D4
St. Lawrence, Gulf of ..	69	D4
St. Lawrence I.	71	B2
St. Leonard .	69	D4
St-Lô	12	B3
St-Louis ...	55	E1
St. Louis ...	77	F9
St. Lucia ■ .	87	D7
St. Lucia, L.	59	D6
St.-Malo ...	12	B2
St.-Mathieu, Pte.	12	B1
St.-Nazaire ..	12	C2
St.-Omer ...	12	A5
St. Paul	77	C8
St. Peter Port	11	G5
St. Petersburg	24	B3
St. Petersburg	75	F6
St.-Pierre et Miquelon □	69	D5
St.-Quentin .	13	B5
St.-Tropez .	13	E7
St. Vincent & the Grenadines ■	87	D7
Saintes ...	12	D3
Saintonge ..	12	D3
Sakai	32	B4
Sakakawea, L.	76	B4
Sakarya → .	25	E3
Sakata ...	33	G11
Sakhalin ...	31	D12
Sala	9	G11
Sala Consilina	21	D5
Salado → .	94	C4
Salamanca .	18	B3
Salamis ...	23	F4
Salayar ...	39	F2
Saldanha ..	58	E3
Sale	63	C4
Salekhard ..	28	C7
Salem, *India*	43	P11
Salem, U.S.A.	80	D2
Salerno ...	21	D5
Salihli	23	E7
Salihorsk ..	17	B8
Salina, *Italy* .	21	E5
Salina, U.S.A.	76	F6
Salinas ...	82	B2
Salisbury, *U.K.*	11	F6
Salisbury, U.S.A. ...	75	B7
Salliq	68	B2
Salluit ...	68	B3
Salmon → .	80	C5
Salmon River Mts.	81	C6
Salon-de- Provence .	13	E6
Salso → ...	21	F4
Salt Lake City	81	E8
Salta	94	A3
Saltillo ...	84	B4
Salto	94	C5
Salto → ...	20	C4
Salton Sea ..	82	D5
Salvador ...	93	E6
Salween → .	41	J11
Salzach → .	15	D7
Salzburg ...	15	E7
Salzgitter ...	14	B6
Salzwedel ..	15	B6
Sama de Langreo ..	18	A3
Samar	38	B3
Samara ...	24	C7
Samarinda .	37	E5
Samarqand .	29	F7
Sambalpur .	40	G5
Sambhal ...	42	E11
Sambhar ...	42	F9
Sambiase ..	21	E6
Sambir ...	17	D6
Sámos ...	23	F6
Samothráki, *Évros, Greece* .	23	D5
Samothráki, *Kérkira, Greece* .	23	E2
Samsun ...	46	B4
San → ...	16	C5
San Agustin, C.	38	C3
San Angelo .	78	D3
San Antonio, *Spain* ...	19	C6
San Antonio, U.S.A. ...	78	E4
San Benedetto del Tronto	20	C4
San Bernardino	82	C4
San Bernardino Str.	38	B2
San Diego ..	82	D4
San Feliu de Guixols ..	19	B7
San Fernando, *Spain* ...	18	D2
San Fernando, U.S.A. ...	82	C3
San Francisco	82	B1
San Gottardo, P. del ...	13	C8
San Joaquin →	82	A2
San Jorge, G.	95	F3
San Jorge, G. de	19	B6
San José, *Costa Rica*	86	E3
San Jose, U.S.A. ...	82	B2
San Juan, *Argentina* .	94	C3
San Juan, *Puerto Rico*	87	C6
San Juan Mts.	83	B9
San Leandro	82	B1
San Lucas, C.	84	C2
San Luis Obispo .	82	C2
San Luis Potosí ...	84	C4
San Marino ■	20	C4
San Matías, G.	95	E4
San Miguel de Tucumán .	94	B3
San Pedro Sula	85	D7
San Pieto ..	21	E2
San Rafael .	80	G2
San Remo ..	20	C1
San Roque .	18	D3
San Salvador	85	E7
San Salvador de Jujuy .	94	A4
San Sebastián	19	A5
San Severo .	20	D5
San Vicente de la Barquera .	18	A3
Saná	49	D3
Sana → ...	20	B6
Sancy, Puy de	13	D5
Sandakan ..	36	C5
Sanday ...	10	B5
Sandikli ...	46	C2
Sandusky ..	72	D4
Sandy L. ...	71	C10
Sanford, *Fla.*, U.S.A. ...	75	E7
Sanford, *N.C.*, U.S.A. ...	75	B8
Sanford, Mt.	71	B5
Sangerhausen	15	C6
Sangihe, P. .	39	D3
Sangli	43	L9
Sangre de Cristo Mts.	78	A1
Sankt Gallen	13	C8
Sankt Moritz	13	C8
Sankt- Peterburg .	24	B3
Sankt Pölten	15	D8
Sanliurfa ...	46	C4
Sanlúcar de Barrameda	18	D2
Sannicandro Gargánico .	20	D5
Santa Ana .	82	D4
Santa Barbara	82	C3
Santa Catalina I. .	82	D3
Santa Clara .	86	B4
Santa Coloma de Gramanet .	19	B7
Santa Cruz, *Bolivia* .	91	G6
Santa Cruz, U.S.A. ...	82	B1
Santa Cruz de Tenerife .	54	C1
Santa Fe, *Argentina* .	94	C4
Santa Fe, U.S.A. ...	83	C10
Santa Lucia Range ...	82	C2
Santa Maria, *Brazil* .	94	B6
Santa Maria, U.S.A. ...	82	C2
Santa Maria di Leuca, C.	23	E2
Santa Marta	90	A4
Santa Marta, Sierra Nevada de	90	A4
Santa Rosa .	80	F2
Santander ..	18	A4
Sant'Antíoco	21	E2

Santarém, Brazil	92	C3
Santarém, Portugal	18	C1
Santiago	94	C2
Santiago de Compostela	18	A1
Santiago de Cuba	86	C4
Santiago de los Cabelleros	87	C5
Santo Domingo	87	C6
Santoña	18	A4
Santorini = Thira	23	F5
Santos	94	A7
São Francisco →	93	E6
São João da Madeira	18	B1
São José do Rio Prêto	94	A7
São Luís	92	C5
São Paulo	94	A7
São Roque, C. de	92	D6
São Tomé & Principe ■	51	F4
São Vicente, C. de	18	D1
Saône →	13	D6
Sapporo	32	F12
Sapulpa	79	B5
Sar Planina	22	C3
Sarada →	40	D3
Sarajevo	20	C7
Sarangani B.	38	C3
Saransk	24	C6
Sarasota	75	F6
Saratov	24	C6
Sarawak □	37	D4
Saray	22	D6
Sarayköy	23	F7
Sardegna □	21	D2
Sardinia = Sardegna □	21	D2
Sardis	23	E7
Sargodha	42	C8
Sarh	53	G2
Sangöl	23	E7
Sarikamiş	46	B5
Sark	11	G5
Şarköy	23	D6
Sarlat-la-Canéda	12	D4
Sarnia	69	D2
Sarny	24	C2
Saronikós Kólpos	23	F4
Sarreguemines	13	B7
Sarthe →	12	C3
Sasebo	32	C1
Saser	42	B10
Saskatchewan □	71	C9
Saskatchewan →	71	C9
Saskatoon	71	C9
Sássari	21	D2
Sassnitz	15	A7
Sassuolo	20	B3
Sasyk, Ozero	17	F9
Sata-Misaki	33	D2
Satmala Hills	43	J9
Satna	40	E4
Satpura Ra.	43	J10
Satu Mare	17	E6
Saudi Arabia ■	47	F6
Sauerland	14	C4
Sault Ste. Marie, Canada	69	D2
Sault Ste. Marie, U.S.A.	72	A3
Saumur	12	C3
Sava →	22	B3
Savanna la Mar	86	C4
Savannah	75	C7
Savannah →	75	C7
Savoie □	13	D7
Savona	20	B2
Sawahlunto	37	E2
Sawara	32	B7
Sawatch Mts.	83	A9
Sawu	39	F2
Sawu Sea	39	F2
Saxony, Lower = Niedersachsen □	14	B5
Sayan, Zapadnyy	30	D7
Saydā	46	D3
Săzava →	16	D2
Scandicci	20	C3
Scandinavia	8	F10
Scarborough	11	D6
Schaffhausen	13	C8
Schefferville	69	C4
Schelde →	14	C3
Schenectady	73	C9
Schiermonnikoog	14	B4
Schio	20	B3
Schleswig	14	A5
Schleswig-Holstein □	14	A5
Schwäbische Alb	14	D5
Schwaner, Pegunungan	37	E4
Schwarzwald	14	D5
Schwedt	15	B8
Schweinfurt	14	C6
Schwerin	15	B6
Schwyz	13	C8
Sciacca	21	F4
Scilla	21	E5
Scilly, Isles of	11	G3
Scotland □	10	C4
Scott Inlet	68	A3
Scottsbluff	76	E3
Scranton	73	D8
Scunthorpe	11	D6
Seattle	80	B2
Şebinkarahisar	46	B4
Sedalia	77	F8
Sedan	13	B6
Seeheim	58	D3
Seferihisar	23	E6
Segesta	21	F4
Segovia	18	B3
Segre →	19	B6
Segura →	19	C5
Sehore	43	H10
Seine →	12	B4
Sekondi-Takoradi	55	H4
Selaru	39	F4
Selçuk	23	F6
Sele →	21	D5
Selemdzha →	31	C10
Selenga →	32	A5
Selkirk	71	C10
Selkirk Mts.	71	C8
Selma	75	B8
Selvas	91	E5
Semarang	37	F4
Semey	29	D9
Semisopochnoi I.	71	C1
Semmering P.	15	E8
Sendai, Kagoshima, Japan	32	D2
Sendai, Miyagi, Japan	33	G12
Senegal ■	55	F2
Senegal →	55	E1
Senigállia	20	C4
Senj	20	B5
Senja	8	E11
Senlis	13	B5
Senneterre	69	D3
Sens	13	B5
Seo de Urgel	19	A6
Seremban	37	D2
Serbia □	22	C3
Sérifos	23	F5
Serowe	59	C5
Serpukhov	24	C4
Sérrai	22	D4
Sète	13	E5
Sétif	54	A6
Seto	32	B5
Settat	54	B3
Setúbal	18	C1
Setúbal, B. de	18	C1
Sevana Lich	25	E6
Sevastopol	25	E3
Severn →, Canada	69	C2
Severn →, U.K.	11	F5
Severnaya Zemlya	30	B7
Sevilla	18	D2
Seward	71	B5
Seward Pen.	71	B3
Seychelles ■	26	K9
Sfax	52	B1
Sfîntu Gheorghe	17	F7
Shaanxi □	35	C5
Shaba □	57	F4
Shache	34	C2
Shahjahanpur	42	F11
Shajapur	43	H10
Shakhty	25	D5
Shaki	55	G5
Shan □	41	G12
Shandong □	35	C6
Shanghai	35	C7
Shangrao	35	D6
Shannon →	11	E2
Shantou	35	D6
Shanxi □	35	C6
Shaoguan	35	D6
Shaoyang	35	D6
Sharon	72	D5
Shasta, Mt.	80	E2
Shatt al'Arab →	47	E7
Shaunavon	71	D7
Shawinigan	69	D3
Shawnee	78	B5
Sheboygan	72	C2
Sheffield	11	E6
Shelburne	69	D4
Shelby	75	B7
Shelbyville	74	B4
Shellharbour	63	B5
Shenandoah →	73	E7
Shenyang	35	B7
Shepetivka	17	C8
Shepparton	63	C4
Sherbrooke	69	D3
Sheridan	81	C10
Sherman	79	C5
Sherridon	71	C9
Shetland Is.	10	A6
Shijiazhuang	35	C6
Shikarpur	42	F6
Shikoku	32	C3
Shikoku □	33	H10
Shikoku-Sanchi	32	C3
Shiliguri	40	D7
Shillong	41	E8
Shimada	32	B6
Shimizu	32	B6
Shimoga	43	N9
Shimonoseki	32	C2
Shinano →	32	A6
Shingū	32	C4
Shirane-San	32	A6
Shīrāz	44	D3
Shire →	59	B7
Shiretoko-Misaki	32	F13
Shiriya-Zaki	32	F12
Shivpuri	43	G10
Shizuoka	32	B6
Shklow	17	A10
Shkodra	22	C2
Shoshone Mts.	80	F5
Shoshong	59	C5
Shreveport	79	C7
Shrewsbury	11	E5
Shuangyashan	35	B8
Shumagin Is.	71	C4
Shungnak	71	B4
Shwebo	41	F10
Shymkent	29	E7
Sialkot	42	C9
Šiauliai	24	B1
Šibenik	20	C5
Siberut	37	E1
Sibi	42	E5
Sibiu	17	F7
Sibolga	37	D1
Sibu	37	D4
Sibuyan	38	B2
Sichuan □	34	C5
Sicilia	21	F5
Siedlce	17	B6
Sieg →	14	C4
Siegen	14	C5
Siena	20	C3
Sierra Leone ■	55	G2
Sífnos	23	F5
Sigüenza	19	B4
Siirt	46	C5
Sikar	42	F9
Sikhote Alin, Khrebet	31	E11
Sikinos	23	F5
Sikkim □	40	D7
Sil →	18	A2
Silesia = Śląsk	16	C3
Silifke	46	C3
Silistra	22	B6
Silivri	22	D7
Simav	23	E7
Simbirsk	24	C6
Simeulue	37	D1
Simferopol	25	E3
Simi	23	F6
Simla	42	D10
Simplon P.	13	C8
Simpson Desert	60	F6
Sinai, Mt. = Mûsa, G.	47	E3
Sind □	42	F6
Sind Sagar Doab	42	D7
Sines	18	D1
Sines, C. de	18	D1
Singapore ■	37	D2
Singitikós Kólpos	23	D5
Sinni →	21	D6
Sinop	46	B3
Sintra	18	C1
Sion	13	C7
Sioux City	77	D6
Sioux Falls	76	D6
Sioux Lookout	71	C10
Siping	35	B7
Sipura	37	E1
Siracusa	21	F5
Sirajganj	41	E7
Sirohi	43	G8
Síros	23	F5
Sirsa	42	E9
Sisak	20	B6
Sitapur	40	D3
Sitges	19	B6
Sitia	23	G6
Sitka	71	C6
Sittwe	41	G9
Sivas	46	C4
Siverek	46	C4
Sivrihisar	46	C2
Siwan	40	D5
Sjælland	9	G10
Skagerrak	9	G9
Skagway	71	C6
Skala-Podilska	17	D8
Skalat	17	D7
Skardu	42	B9
Skeena →	70	C6
Skegness	11	E7
Skellefte älv →	8	F12
Skellefteå	8	F12
Skíathos	23	E4
Skien	9	G9
Skikda	54	A6
Skíros	23	E5
Skole	17	D6
Skópelos	23	E4
Skopje	22	C3
Skvyra	17	D9
Skye	10	C3
Slamet	37	F3
Śląsk	16	C3
Slatina	22	B5
Slave →	70	B8
Slavonski Brod	20	B7
Slavuta	17	C8
Slawharad	17	B10
Sleeper Is.	68	C2
Sligo	11	D2
Sliven	22	C6
Slonim	17	B7
Slough	11	F6
Slovak Rep. ■	16	D5
Slovenia ■	20	B5
Slovenské Rudohorie	16	D4
Slovyansk	25	D4
Sluch →	17	C8
Slutsk	17	B8
Smarhon	17	A8
Smederevo	22	B3
Smith Arm	70	B7
Smolensk	24	C3
Smolikas, Óros	23	D3
Smyrna = İzmir	23	E6
Snake →	80	B4
Snake River Plain	81	D7
Sneek	14	B3

Snøhetta ... 8 F9
Snowdon ... 11 E4
Snowdrift .. 70 B8
Snowy Mts. .. 63 C4
Snyatyn ... 17 D7
Snyder 78 C3
Sobral 92 C5
Sochi 25 E4
Société, Is. de
la 65 L15
Socotra 49 E5
Söderhamn . 8 F11
Sofiya 22 C4
Sognefjorden . 8 F9
Sohâg 52 C5
Soissons ... 13 B5
Sokal 17 C7
Söke 23 F6
Sokhumi ... 25 E5
Sokoto 55 F6
Solapur ... 43 L9
Solingen .. 14 C4
Sóller 19 C7
Sologne ... 12 C4
Solomon
Is. ■ 64 K10
Solothurn . 13 C7
Šolta 20 C6
Solunska
Glava 22 D3
Soma 23 E6
Somali
Rep. ■ 49 F4
Somerset
East 59 E5
Somerset I. . 70 A10
Somme → 12 A4
Somosierra,
Puerto de . 18 B4
Somport,
Puerto de . 12 E3
Søndre
Strømfjord 68 B5
Sóndrio ... 20 A2
Songkhla .. 36 C2
Sopot 16 A4
Sorel 69 D3
Sorgono ... 21 D2
Soria 19 B4
Soroca 17 D9
Sorong 39 E4
Sørøya 8 D12
Sorsogon .. 38 B2
Sosnowiec . 16 C4
Soúdhas,
Kólpos ... 23 G5
Sŏul 35 C7
Souris 71 D9
Souris → .. 71 D10
Sousse 52 A1
South
Africa ■ .. 58 E4
South
Australia □ 62 B2
South Bend . 72 D2
South
Carolina □ 75 C7
South China
Sea 36 C4
South
Dakota □ . 76 C4
South I. ... 65 E3
South
Magnetic
Pole 96 A13
South
Nahanni → 70 B7
South Orkney
Is. 96 A4
South
Platte → .. 76 E2
South Pole . 96 C
South
Ronaldsay 10 B5

South
Saskatchewan →
.... 71 C9
South
Shetland Is. 96 A4
South Shields 11 D6
South Uist .. 10 C3
Southampton 11 F6
Southampton
I. 68 B2
Southend-on-
Sea 11 F7
Southern Alps 65 E4
Southern
Indian L. .. 71 C10
Southern
Uplands .. 10 D5
Söya-Misaki 32 E12
Sozh → ... 17 C10
Spain ■ ... 18 C4
Spanish Town 86 C4
Spartanburg 75 B7
Spárti 23 F4
Spartivento,
C., Calabria,
Italy 21 F6
Spartivento,
C., Sard.,
Italy 21 E2
Spátha, Ákra 23 G4
Spence Bay . 70 B10
Spencer G. . 62 B2
Spey → ... 10 C5
Speyer 14 D5
Split 20 C6
Spokane ... 80 B5
Spoleto ... 20 C4
Spree → .. 15 B7
Springbok . 58 D3
Springfield,
Ill., U.S.A. 77 F10
Springfield,
Mass.,
U.S.A. ... 73 C9
Springfield,
Mo., U.S.A. 79 A7
Springfield,
Ohio,
U.S.A. ... 72 E4
Springfield,
Oreg.,
U.S.A. ... 80 C2
Springfontein 59 E5
Springhill .. 69 D4
Springs ... 59 D5
Squamish .. 71 D7
Srebrnica .. 20 B7
Sredinnyy
Khrebet . 31 D14
Sri Lanka ■ . 43 R12
Srikakulam . 40 H4
Srinagar .. 42 B9
Stade 14 B5
Stadlandet . 8 F9
Stafford ... 11 E5
Stakhanov . 25 D4
Stamford ... 73 D9
Stanley,
Canada .. 71 C9
Stanley,
Falk. Is. . 95 G5
Stanovoy
Khrebet . 31 D10
Stara Planina 22 C4
Stara Zagora 22 C5
Starokonstyantyniv
.... 17 D8
Staryy
Chartoriysk 17 C7
State College 73 D7
Statesville .. 75 B7
Stavanger .. 9 G9
Stavropol ... 25 D5

Steiermark □ 15 E8
Steinkjer .. 8 F10
Stellenbosch 58 E3
Stendal ... 15 B6
Sterlitamak . 29 D6
Stettiner Haff 15 B8
Stettler ... 71 C8
Steubenville 72 D5
Stevenage . 11 F6
Stewart ... 70 B6
Stewart I. .. 65 G2
Steyr 15 D8
Stillwater .. 78 A5
Štip 22 D4
Stirling ... 10 C5
Stockerau .. 15 D9
Stockholm . 9 G11
Stockport .. 11 E5
Stockton .. 82 B2
Stockton-on-
Tees 11 D6
Stoke on
Trent 11 E5
Stolac 20 C6
Stolin 17 C8
Stonehaven . 10 C5
Stonewall .. 71 C10
Stora
Lulevatten 8 E11
Storavan .. 8 E11
Store Bælt . 9 G10
Storm B. ... 62 D4
Stormberge . 59 E5
Stornoway .. 10 B3
Storozhynets 17 D7
Storsjön .. 8 F10
Storuman .. 8 E11
Stowbtsy .. 17 B8
Stralsund .. 15 A7
Strand 58 E3
Stranraer .. 11 D4
Strasbourg . 13 B7
Stratford .. 69 D2
Straubing .. 15 D7
Strimón → . 23 D4
Strimonikós
Kólpos ... 23 D5
Strómboli .. 21 E5
Stronsay .. 10 B5
Strumica .. 22 D4
Stryy 17 D6
Stutterheim . 59 E5
Stuttgart ... 14 D5
Subotica .. 16 E4
Suceava .. 17 E8
Sucre 91 G5
Sudan ■ .. 53 E4
Sudbury ... 69 D2
Sudety 16 C3
Sueca 19 C5
Suez = El
Suweis ... 52 C5
Suhl 14 C6
Sukkur 42 F6
Sulaiman
Range 42 D6
Sulawesi □ . 39 E2
Sulitjelma . 8 E11
Sulu Arch. .. 38 C2
Sulu Sea ... 38 C2
Sumatera □ . 37 D2
Sumba 39 F1
Sumbawa .. 37 F5
Summerside 69 D4
Sumperk ... 16 D3
Sumter 75 C7
Sumy 24 C3
Sunda, Selat 37 F3
Sundarbans,
The 41 G7
Sunderland . 11 D6
Sundsvall .. 8 F11
Sungurlu .. 46 B3
Sunnyvale .. 82 B1

Superior ... 77 B8
Superior, L. . 69 D2
Suphan Dağı 46 C5
Supiori ... 39 E5
Sūr 46 D3
Surabaya ... 37 F4
Surakarta ... 37 F4
Surat 43 J8
Surgut 29 C8
Surinam ■ . 92 B2
Suruga-Wan 32 B6
Susanville .. 80 E3
Susquehanna →
.... 73 E7
Susurluk ... 23 E7
Sutlej → ... 42 E7
Suva 64 L12
Suwałki ... 17 A6
Suzhou 35 C7
Suzu-Misaki . 32 A5
Svealand □ . 9 G10
Sverdlovsk =
Yekaterinburg
.... 29 D7
Svislach ... 17 B7
Svyetlahorsk 17 B9
Swakopmund 58 C2
Swan Hill .. 62 C3
Swansea ... 11 F5
Swaziland ■ . 59 D6
Sweden ■ ■ . 9 G10
Sweetwater . 78 C3
Swellendam 58 E4
Swift Current 71 C9
Swindon .. 11 F6
Switzerland ■ 13 C8
Sydney,
Australia . 63 B5
Sydney,
Canada .. 69 D4
Syktyvkar .. 28 C6
Sylhet 41 E8
Sylt 14 A5
Syracuse .. 73 C7
Syrdarya → 29 E7
Syria ■ ... 46 D4
Syzran 24 D6
Szczecin .. 16 B2
Szechwan =
Sichuan □ 34 C5
Szeged ... 16 E5
Székesfehérvár
.... 16 E4
Szekszárd . 16 E4
Szolnok ... 16 E5
Szombathely 16 E3

Tabas 44 C4
Tablas 38 B2
Table Mt. .. 58 E3
Tábor 16 D2
Tabora 57 F6
Tabriz 46 C6
Tacloban ... 38 B2
Tacna 91 G4
Tacoma 80 B2
Tacuarembó 94 C5
Tadoussac . 69 D4
Tadzhikistan =
Tajikistan ■ 29 F8
Taegu 35 C7
Taejŏn 35 C7
Tafalla 19 A5
Tafelbaai .. 58 E3
Taganrog ... 25 D4
Tagish 70 B6
Tagish L. ... 70 B6
Tagus =
Tejo → ... 18 C1
Tahiti 65 L16

Tahoe, L. .. 80 F3
Taibei 35 D7
Tain 10 C4
Tainan 35 D7
Tainaron,
Ákra 23 F4
T'aipei =
Taibei ... 35 D7
Taiping ... 36 D2
Taiwan ■ .. 35 D7
Taïyetos Óros 23 F4
Taiyuan ... 35 C6
Taizhong .. 35 D7
Ta'izz 49 E3
Tajikistan ■ . 29 F8
Tak 36 A1
Takada 32 A6
Takamatsu . 32 B4
Takaoka ... 32 A5
Takapuna .. 64 B6
Takasaki ... 32 A6
Takatsuki .. 32 B4
Takayama .. 32 A5
Takefu 32 B5
Talaud,
Kepulauan 38 D3
Talavera de la
Reina ... 18 C3
Talca 94 D2
Talcahuano . 94 D2
Talladega .. 74 C4
Tallahassee . 75 D5
Tallinn 24 B1
Tamale ... 55 G4
Tambov ... 24 C5
Tamega → . 18 B1
Tamil Nadu □ 43 P10
Tamo Abu,
Pegunungan
.... 37 D5
Tampa 75 F6
Tampere ... 8 F12
Tampico ... 84 C5
Tamworth .. 63 B5
Tana → ... 8 D13
Tana, L. ... 53 F6
Tanami
Desert ... 60 D5
Tanana ... 71 B4
Tanana → . 71 B4
Tánaro → .. 20 B2
Tando Adam 42 G6
Tane-ga-
Shima ... 33 D2
Tanga 57 F7
Tanganyika,
L. 57 F5
Tanger 54 A3
Tangshan .. 35 C6
Tanimbar,
Kepulauan 39 F4
Tanjungbalai 37 D1
Tanjungkarang
Telukbetung
.... 37 F3
Tanzania ■ . 57 F6
Tapajós → . 92 C3
Tapi → ... 43 J8
Tarabagatay,
Khrebet . 29 E9
Tarābulus,
Lebanon . 46 D3
Tarābulus,
Libya 52 B1
Tarakan ... 37 D5
Taranaki □ . 64 C6
Tarancón .. 19 B4
Táranto ... 21 D6
Táranto, G. di 21 D6
Tarashcha . 17 D10
Tarazona .. 19 B5
Tarbes 12 E4
Taree 63 B5
Tarifa 18 D3

Tarim Pendi	34	C3
Tarkhankut, Mys	25	D3
Tarn →	12	D4
Tarnów	16	C5
Tarragona	19	B6
Tarrasa	19	B7
Tarsus	46	C3
Tartu	24	B2
Taschereau	69	D3
Tashkent = Toshkent	29	E7
Tasman B.	65	D5
Tasmania □	62	D4
Tatarbunary	17	F9
Tatarsk	29	D8
Tatarstan □	29	D6
Tateyama	32	B6
Tatry	16	D4
Tatta	43	G5
Tatvan	46	C5
Tauern	15	E7
Taunton	11	F5
Taunus	14	C5
Taupo	64	C7
Taupo, L.	64	C6
Tauranga	64	B7
Taurianova	21	E6
Taurus Mts. = Toros Dağlan	46	C3
Tavira	18	D2
Tavoy	36	B1
Tawau	36	D5
Tay →	10	C5
Taymyr, Poluostrov	30	B7
Tbilisi	25	E5
Tchad = Chad ■	53	E2
Tchad, L.	53	F1
Te Anau, L.	65	F2
Te Aroha	64	B6
Tebingtinggi	37	D1
Tegal	37	F3
Tegucigalpa	85	E7
Tehachapi	82	C3
Tehrān	44	C2
Tehuantepec, G. de	85	D5
Tehuantepec, Istmo de	85	D6
Tejo →	18	C1
Tekirdağ	22	D6
Tel Aviv-Yafo	46	D3
Telavi	25	E6
Telford	11	E5
Telukbutun	37	D3
Tema	55	G4
Temirtau	29	D8
Temora	63	B4
Tempe	83	D7
Temple	78	D5
Tenali	40	J3
Tenda, Col di	20	B1
Tenerife	54	C1
Tennessee □	74	B4
Tennessee →	72	F1
Tenryū-Gawa →	32	B5
Teófilo Otoni	93	F5
Tepic	84	C4
Teplice	16	C1
Ter →	19	A7
Téramo	20	C4
Terebovlya	17	D7
Teresina	92	D5
Términi Imerese	21	F4
Térmoli	20	C5
Ternate	39	D3
Terni	20	C4
Ternopil	17	D7
Terracina	20	D4
Terralba	21	E2
Terre Haute	72	E2
Terschelling	14	B3
Teruel	19	B5
Teshio-Gawa →	32	F12
Teslin	70	B6
Tetterev →	17	C10
Tetiyev	17	D9
Tétouan	54	A3
Tetovo	22	C3
Teutoburger Wald	14	B5
Tévere →	20	D4
Texarkana	79	C6
Texas □	78	D4
Texas City	79	E6
Texel	14	B3
Tezpur	41	D9
Thabana Ntlenyana	59	D5
Thabazimbi	59	C5
Thailand ■	36	A2
Thailand, G. of	36	B2
Thal	42	C7
Thames →	11	F7
Thane	43	K8
Thar Desert	42	F7
Thásos	23	D5
The Pas	71	C9
Thermaïkós Kólpos	23	D4
Thermopylae P.	23	E4
Thessaloníki	23	D4
Thetford	11	E7
Thetford Mines	69	D3
Thiers	13	D5
Thies	55	F1
Thimphu	41	D7
Thionville	13	B7
Thíra	23	F5
Thívai	23	E4
Thomasville, Ga., U.S.A.	75	D6
Thomasville, N.C., U.S.A.	75	B7
Thompson	71	C10
Thrace	22	D6
Thun	13	C7
Thunder Bay	69	D2
Thüringer Wald	14	C6
Thurles	11	E3
Thurso	10	C5
Tian Shan	34	B3
Tianjin	35	C6
Tianshui	35	C5
Tiber = Tévere →	20	D4
Tibesti	52	D2
Tibet = Xizang □	34	C3
Ticino →	20	B2
Tierra de Campos	18	A3
Tierra del Fuego, I. Gr. de	95	G3
Tiétar →	18	C2
Tighina	17	E9
Tignish	69	D4
Tigris = Dijlah, Nahr →	47	E6
Tijuana	84	A1
Tiksi	30	B10
Tilburg	14	C3
Tilos	23	F6
Timaru	65	F4
Timbuktu = Tombouctou	55	E4
Timişoara	16	F5
Timmins	69	D2
Timor	39	F2
Tinaca Pt.	38	C3
Tinos	23	F5
Tipperary	11	E2
Tirana	22	D2
Tiraspol	17	E9
Tire	23	E6
Tirebolu	46	B4
Tiree	10	C3
Tîrgoviște	22	B5
Tirgu-Jiu	17	F6
Tirgu Mureş	17	E7
Tirich Mir	42	A7
Tîrnavos	23	E4
Tirol □	14	E6
Tirso →	21	E2
Tiruchchirappalli	43	P11
Tirunelveli	43	Q10
Tisa →	22	B3
Tisdale	71	C9
Titicaca, L.	91	G5
Titov Veles	22	D3
Tívoli	20	D4
Tizi-Ouzou	54	A5
Toamasina	59	H9
Toba	37	D1
Toba Kakar	42	D6
Tobago	87	D7
Tobermory	10	C3
Tobol →	29	D7
Tocantins →	92	C4
Tochigi	32	A6
Togliatti	24	C6
Togo ■	55	G5
Tōkamachi	32	A6
Tokat	46	B4
Tokelau Is.	65	K13
Tokushima	32	B4
Tokuyama	32	B2
Tōkyō	32	B6
Toledo, Spain	18	C3
Toledo, U.S.A.	72	D4
Toledo, Montes de	18	C3
Toliara	59	J8
Toluca	84	D5
Tomakomai	32	F12
Tomar	18	C1
Tomaszów Mazowiecki	16	C4
Tombouctou	55	E4
Tomelloso	18	C4
Tomini, Teluk	39	E2
Tomsk	29	D9
Tonawanda	73	C6
Tonga ■	65	L13
Tonga Trench	65	L13
Tongue →	76	B2
Tonk	42	F9
Tonkin, G. of	36	D5
Tonlé Sap	36	B2
Toowoomba	63	A5
Topeka	77	F7
Torbalı	23	E6
Torbay	11	F5
Tordesillas	18	B3
Torgau	15	C7
Torino	20	B1
Tormes →	18	B2
Torne älv →	8	E12
Torneträsk	8	E11
Tornio	8	E12
Toroníios Kólpos	23	D4
Toronto	69	D3
Toros Dağlan	46	C3
Tôrre de Moncorvo	18	B2
Torre del Greco	21	D5
Torrejón de Ardoz	18	B4
Torrelavega	18	A3
Torremolinos	18	D3
Torrens, L.	62	B2
Torrente	19	C5
Torreón	84	B4
Torres Vedras	18	C1
Torrevieja	19	D5
Tortosa	19	B6
Tortosa, C. de	19	B6
Toruń	16	B4
Tosa-Wan	32	C3
Toscana □	20	C3
Toshkent	29	E7
Tosya	46	B3
Toteng	58	C4
Tottori	32	B4
Toul	13	B6
Toulon	13	E6
Toulouse	12	E4
Touraine	12	C4
Tourcoing	13	A5
Touriñán, C.	18	A1
Tournai	14	C2
Tournon	13	D6
Tours	12	C4
Townsville	61	D8
Toyama	32	A5
Toyohashi	32	B5
Toyonaka	32	B4
Toyooka	32	B4
Toyota	32	B5
Trabzon	46	B4
Trafalgar, C.	18	D2
Trail	71	D8
Tralee	11	E2
Trang	36	C1
Trangan	39	F4
Trani	20	D6
Transantarctic Mts.	96	C3
Transilvania	17	F7
Trápani	21	E4
Traralgon	63	C4
Trasimeno, L.	20	C4
Traun	15	D8
Travemünde	15	B6
Travnik	20	B6
Trebič	16	D2
Trebinje	20	C7
Tremp	19	A6
Trent →	11	E6
Trento	20	A3
Trenton	73	D8
Trepassey	69	D5
Treviso	20	B4
Trier	14	D4
Trieste	20	B4
Triglav	20	A4
Trikkala	23	E3
Trinidad □	78	A1
Trinidad & Tobago ■	87	D7
Trinity →	79	E6
Trinity B.	69	D5
Trinity Range	80	E4
Tripoli = Tarābulus	52	B1
Trípolis	23	F4
Tripura □	41	F8
Trivandrum	43	Q10
Trnava	16	D3
Troglav	20	C6
Trois-Rivières	69	D3
Trollhättan	9	G10
Trondheim	8	F10
Trondheimsfjorden	8	F10
Trout L.	70	B7
Trouville-sur-Mer	12	B4
Troy, Turkey	23	E6
Troy, Ala., U.S.A.	74	D5
Troy, N.Y., U.S.A.	73	C9
Troyes	13	B6
Trujillo, Peru	91	E3
Trujillo, Spain	18	C3
Truk	64	J10
Truro, Canada	69	D4
Truro, U.K.	11	F4
Truskavets	17	D6
Trutnov	16	C2
Tsau	58	C4
Tshabong	58	D4
Tshane	58	C4
Tshwane	58	C4
Tsimlyanskoye Vdkhr.	25	D5
Tskhinvali	25	E5
Tsu	32	B5
Tsuchiura	32	A7
Tsugaru-Kaikyō	32	F12
Tsumis	58	C3
Tsuruga	32	B5
Tsurugi-San	32	C4
Tsuruoka	33	G11
Tsyelyakhany	17	B7
Tuamotu Is.	65	L16
Tübingen	14	D5
Tubuai Is.	65	M16
Tucson	83	D7
Tucumcari	78	B2
Tudela	19	A5
Tuktoyaktuk	70	B6
Tula	24	C4
Tulare	82	B3
Tulcán	90	C3
Tulcea	17	F9
Tulchyn	17	D9
Tullamore	11	E3
Tulle	12	D4
Tulsa	79	A6
Tulua	90	C3
Tumaco	90	C3
Tunguska, Nizhnyaya →	30	C6
Tunis	54	A2
Tunisia ■	54	B6
Tunja	90	B4
Tupelo	74	B3
Turabah	47	E5
Turgutlu	23	E6
Turhal	46	B4
Turia →	19	C5
Turin = Torino	20	B1
Turkana, L.	57	D7
Turkey ■	46	C3
Turkmenistan ■	29	F6
Turks & Caicos Is. ■	87	B5
Turku	9	F12
Turnhout	14	C3
Tuscaloosa	74	C4
Tuscany = Toscana □	20	C3
Tuticorin	43	Q11
Tuttlingen	14	E5
Tuxtla Gutiérrez	85	D6
Tuy	18	A1
Tuz Gölü	46	C3
Tuzla	20	B7
Tver	24	B4
Twillingate	69	D5
Twin Falls	81	D6

Tyachiv 17 D6
Tychy 16 C4
Tyler 79 C6
Tyrrhenian
  Sea 21 E4
Tyumen 29 D7
Tzaneen 59 C6

Ube 32 C2
Ubeda 18 C4
Uberaba ... 93 F4
Uberlândia . 93 F4
Ubort → .. 17 B9
Ucayali → . 90 D4
Uchiura-Wan 32 F12
Udaipur ... 43 G8
Udaipur Garhi 40 D6
Údine 20 B4
Udmurtia □ . 28 D6
Udon Thani . 36 A2
Ueda 32 A6
Uelzen 14 B6
Ufa 29 D6
Uganda ■ .. 57 D6
Ugljane 20 B5
Uinta Mts. .. 81 E8
Uitenhage .. 59 E5
Ujjain 43 H9
Ujung
  Pandang . 39 F1
Ukraine ■ .. 25 D3
Ulaanbaatar 35 B5
Ulan Ude ... 30 D8
Ulhasnagar . 43 K8
Ullapool ... 10 C4
Ulm 14 D5
Ulster □ ... 11 D3
Ulubat Gölü . 23 D7
Uludağ 23 D7
Ulyasutay .. 34 B4
Uman 17 D10
Ume älv → . 8 F12
Umeå 8 F12
Umnak I. ... 71 C3
Umtata 59 E5
Una → 20 B6
Unalaska ... 71 C3
Ungava B. .. 68 C4
Ungava Pen. 68 B3
Ungheni ... 17 E8
Unimak I. .. 71 C3
United Arab
  Emirates ■ 44 F3
United
  Kingdom ■ 11 E5
United States
  of
  America ■ 67 F10
Unst 10 A6
Ünye 46 B4
Upington ... 58 D4
Uppsala 9 G11
Ural →
  Zhayyq → 29 E6
Ural Mts. =
  Uralskie
  Gory ... 28 D6
Uralskie Gory 28 D6
Urawa 32 B6
Urbana 72 D1
Urbino 20 C4
Urbión, Picos
  de 19 A4
Urganch ... 29 E7
Urla 23 E6
Urmia, L. =
  Orūmiyeh,
  Daryācheh-
  ye 46 C6
Uruguay ■ . 94 C5
Uruguay → . 94 C5
Ürümqi 34 B3
Usakos 58 C2

Usedom 15 B8
Üsküdar ... 25 E2
Ussuriysk .. 31 E11
Ústí nad
  Labem ... 16 C2
Ustica 21 E4
Ustyurt,
  Plateau .. 29 E6
Usuki 32 C2
Utah □ 81 F8
Utica 73 C8
Utrecht ... 14 B3
Utrera 18 D3
Utsunomiya 32 A6
Uttar
  Pradesh □ 42 F11
Uttaradit .. 36 A2
Uusikaupunki 8 F12
Uwajima ... 32 C3
Uzbekistan ■ 29 E7
Uzerche ... 12 D4
Uzh → 17 C10
Uzhhorod .. 17 D6
Uzunköprü .. 22 D6

Vaal → 58 D4
Vaasa 8 F12
Vadodara .. 43 H8
Vadsø 8 D13
Vaduz 13 C8
Vah → 16 D3
Val d'Or ... 69 D3
Valahia 22 B5
Valandovo .. 22 D4
Valdepeñas . 18 C4
Valdés, Pen. 95 E4
Valdez 71 B5
Valdivia ... 95 D2
Valdosta ... 75 D6
Valence ... 13 D6
Valencia,
  Spain ... 19 C5
Valencia,
  Venezuela 90 A5
Valencia □ .. 19 C5
Valencia, G.
  de 19 C6
Valencia de
  Alcántara . 18 C2
Valencia I. .. 11 F1
Valenciennes 13 A5
Vall de Uxó . 19 C5
Valladolid .. 18 B3
Valledupar .. 90 A4
Valletta ... 80 F2
Valletta ... 21 G5
Valls 19 B6
Valognes .. 12 B3
Valozhyn ... 17 A8
Valparaíso .. 94 C2
Valverde del
  Camino .. 18 D2
Van 46 C5
Van Gölü .. 46 C5
Vanadzor .. 25 E5
Vancouver,
  Canada .. 71 D7
Vancouver,
  U.S.A. ... 80 C2
Vancouver I. 71 D7
Vänern 9 G10
Vännäs ... 8 F11
Vannes ... 12 C2
Vanrhynsdorp 58 E3
Vanua Levu . 64 L12
Vanuatu ■ .. 64 L11
Vapnyarka .. 17 D9
Varanasi ... 40 E4
Varangerfjorden
  .... 8 D13
Varaždin .. 20 A6
Varberg ... 9 G10
Varese 20 B2

Varna 22 C6
Vasilevichi .. 17 B9
Västerås ... 9 G11
Västervik .. 9 G11
Vasto 20 C5
Vasylkiv ... 17 C10
Vatican City ■ 20 D4
Vättern ... 9 G10
Vawkavysk . 17 B7
Vega 8 E10
Vegreville . 71 C8
Vejer de la
  Frontera .. 18 D3
  Planina ... 20 B5
Vélez Málaga 18 D3
Vélez Rubio . 19 D4
Velika Kapela 20 B5
Velletri 20 D4
Vellore 43 N11
Vendée □ .. 12 C3
Vendôme .. 12 C4
Venézia ... 20 B4
Venézia, G. di 20 B4
Venezuela ■ 90 B5
Venice =
  Venézia .. 20 B4
Ventotene .. 21 D4
Ventoux, Mt. 13 D6
Ventspils ... 24 B1
Vera 19 D5
Veracruz .. 84 D5
Veraval ... 43 J7
Verbánia .. 20 B2
Vercelli ... 20 B2
Verden ... 14 B5
Verdun 13 B6
Vereeniging . 59 D5
Verín 18 B2
Verkhoyansk 31 C11
Verkhoyanskiy
  Khrebet .. 31 C10
Vermilion .. 71 C8
Vermont □ . 73 C9
Vernon,
  Canada .. 71 C8
Vernon,
  U.S.A. ... 78 B4
Véroia ... 23 D4
Verona ... 20 B3
Versailles .. 12 B5
Vert, C. ... 55 F1
Verviers ... 14 C3
Vesoul ... 13 C7
Vesterålen .. 8 E11
Vestfjorden . 8 E10
Vesuvio ... 21 D5
Veszprém .. 16 E3
Vettore, Mte. 20 C4
Viana do
  Alentejo .. 18 C2
Viana do
  Castelo .. 18 B1
Viareggio .. 20 C3
Vibo Valéntia 21 E6
Vicenza ... 20 B3
Vich 19 B7
Vichy 13 C5
Vicksburg .. 79 C8
Victoria ... 71 D7
Victoria □ .. 62 C3
Victoria, L. .. 57 E6
Victoria Beach 71 C10
Victoria de
  Durango =
  Durango .. 84 C4
Victoria Falls 59 B5
Victoria I. .. 70 A8
Victoria Ld. . 96 B14
Victoria West 58 E4
Vienna =
  Wien 15 D9
Vienne 13 D6

Vienne → .. 12 C4
Vientiane .. 36 A2
Vierzon ... 12 C5
Vietnam ■ .. 36 A3
Vigévano .. 20 B2
Vigo 18 A1
Vijayawada . 40 J3
Vikna 8 F10
Vila do Bispo 18 D1
Vila Franca de
  Xira 18 C1
Vila Nova de
  Gaia 18 B1
Vila Real .. 18 B2
Vila Real de
  Santo
  António .. 18 D2
Vilaine → .. 12 C2
Vileyka ... 17 A8
Vilhelmina . 8 F11
Villacarrillo . 18 C4
Villach 15 E7
Villagarcía de
  Arosa ... 18 A1
Villahermosa 85 D6
Villajoyosa .. 19 C5
Villalba ... 18 A2
Villanueva de
  la Serena . 18 C3
Villanueva y
  Geltrú ... 19 B6
Villarreal .. 19 C5
Villarrobledo 19 C4
Villaviciosa . 18 A3
Villena 19 C5
Villeneuve-
  d'Ascq .. 13 A5
Villeneuve-
  sur-Lot .. 12 D4
Villingen-
  Schwenningen
  .... 14 D5
Vilnius 24 C2
Vilyuy → .. 31 C10
Vilyuysk ... 31 C10
Viña del Mar 94 C2
Vinaroz ... 19 B6
Vindhya Ra.. 43 H10
Vineland ... 73 E8
Vinkovci ... 20 B7
Vinnytsya .. 17 D9
Viranşehir . 46 C4
Virden 71 D9
Vire 12 B3
Virgin Is.
  (British) ■ 87 C7
Virginia □ .. 73 F6
Virginia
  Beach ... 73 F8
Virovitica .. 20 B6
Vis 20 C6
Visalia 82 B3
Visby 9 G11
Višegrad ... 20 C7
Viseu 18 B2
Vishakhapatnam
  .... 40 J4
Viso, Mte. .. 20 B1
Vistula =
  Wisła → .. 16 A4
Viterbo ... 20 C4
Viti Levu .. 64 L12
Vitigudino .. 18 B2
Vitória, Brazil 93 G5
Vitoria, Spain 19 A4
Vitória da
  Conquista 93 E5
Vitsyebsk .. 24 B3
Vittória ... 21 F5
Vittório
  Véneto ... 20 B4
Vivero 18 A2
Vize 22 D6
Vladikavkaz . 25 E5

Vladimir ... 24 B5
Vladivostok . 31 E11
Vlissingen .. 14 C2
Vlóra 23 D2
Vltava → .. 16 C2
Vogelsberg . 14 C5
Voghera ... 20 B2
Voiron 13 D6
Vojvodina □ 22 B2
Volga → ... 25 D6
Volgograd .. 25 D5
Volodymyr-
  Volynskyy 17 C7
Vologda ... 24 B4
Vólos 23 E4
Volovets ... 17 D6
Volta ■ → . 55 G5
Volta, L. .. 55 G5
Volta
  Redonda . 93 G5
Volterra ... 20 C3
Volturno → 20 D4
Volzhskiy .. 25 D5
Voríai
  Sporádhes 23 E4
Vorkuta ... 28 C7
Voronezh .. 24 C4
Vosges ... 13 B7
Vouga → .. 18 B1
Voznesensk . 25 D3
Vrangelya,
  Ostrov .. 31 B15
Vrbas → ... 20 B6
Vrede 59 D5
Vredenburg . 58 E3
Vryburg ... 58 D4
Vryheid ... 59 D6
Vukovar ... 20 B7
Vulcanești .. 17 F9
Vulcano ... 21 E5
Vychodné
  Beskydy . 17 D5
Vylkove ... 17 F9
Vynohradiv . 17 D6
Vyškov 16 D3

Waal → ... 14 C3
Wabash → . 72 F1
Waco 78 D5
Wâd Medani 53 F5
Waddington,
  Mt. 71 C7
Wager B. .. 68 B2
Wager Bay . 68 B1
Wagga
  Wagga .. 63 C4
Wah 42 C8
Waigeo ... 39 E4
Wainganga →
  .... 43 K11
Waingapu .. 39 F2
Wainwright,
  Canada .. 71 C8
Wainwright,
  U.S.A. ... 71 A3
Waipara ... 65 E5
Waitaki → .. 65 F4
Wajima ... 32 A5
Wakasa-Wan 32 B4
Wakatipu, L. 65 F3
Wakayama . 32 B4
Wakkanai .. 32 E12
Wałbrzych . 16 C3
Wales □ ... 11 E4
Walgett ... 63 A4
Walla Walla . 80 B4
Wallis &
  Futuna, Is. 64 L13
Wallowa Mts. 80 C5
Walvisbaai . 58 C2
Wanganui .. 64 C6
Wangaratta . 63 C4
Wangerooge 14 B4

Warangal ...	43	L11
Wardha → .	43	K11
Warmbad ..	59	C5
Warner Mts. .	80	E3
Warrego → .	63	B4
Warrenton .	58	D4
Warrington, U.K.	11	E5
Warrington, U.S.A. .	74	D4
Warrnambool	62	C3
Warsaw = Warszawa	16	B5
Warszawa .	16	B5
Warta → ..	16	B2
Warwick ..	63	A5
Wasatch Ra.	81	E8
Wash, The .	11	E7
Washington .	73	E7
Washington □	80	B3
Washington, Mt.	73	B10
Waskaganish	69	C3
Wasserkuppe	14	C5
Waterbury .	73	D9
Waterford ..	11	E3
Waterloo ...	77	D8
Waterton-Glacier International Peace Park	81	A6
Watertown .	73	C8
Waterville .	73	B11
Watford ...	11	F6
Watrous ...	71	C9
Watson Lake	70	B7
Watsónville .	82	B2
Watubela, Kepulauan	39	E4
Waukegan .	72	C2
Waukesha .	72	C1
Wausau ...	77	C10
Wauwatosa .	72	C2
Waxahachie	79	C5
Waycross ...	75	D6
Wazirabad .	42	C9
Weddell Sea	96	A4
Weiden ...	15	D7
Weifang ...	35	C6
Weimar ...	15	C6
Welkom ...	59	D5
Wellesley Is.	60	D6
Wellington, Australia .	63	B4
Wellington, N.Z.	65	D6
Wellington, I.	95	F1
Wels	15	D8
Welshpool ..	11	E5
Wemindji ...	69	C3
Wenatchee .	80	B3
Wenzhou ...	35	D7
Werra → ..	14	C5
Werribee ...	63	C3
Weser → ..	14	B5
West Bengal □ .	40	F7
West Palm Beach ...	75	F7
West Virginia □ .	72	E5
West Wyalong .	63	B4
Westerland .	14	A5
Western Australia □	60	F3
Western Ghats ..	43	N9
Western Sahara ■ .	54	D2
Western Samoa ■ .	65	L13
Westerwald .	14	C4
Westland Bight ...	65	E4
Weston-super-Mare	11	F5
Westport, Ireland ..	11	E2
Westport, N.Z.	65	D4
Westray ...	10	B5
Wetar	39	F3
Wetaskiwin .	71	C8
Wetzlar ...	14	C5
Wexford ...	11	E3
Weyburn ...	71	D9
Weymouth ..	11	F5
Whakatane .	64	B7
Whale → ..	68	C4
Whale Cove .	70	B10
Whales, B. of	96	B16
Whangarei .	64	A6
Wheeling ..	72	D5
White →, Ark., U.S.A.	79	C8
White →, Ind., U.S.A.	72	E2
White Nile = Nil el Abyad → .	53	E5
White Russia = Belarus ■ .	24	C2
White Sea = Beloye More	28	C4
Whitehaven .	11	D5
Whitehorse .	70	B6
Whitney, Mt.	82	B3
Wholdaia L. .	70	B9
Whyalla ...	62	B2
Wichita ...	78	A5
Wichita Falls	78	C4
Wick	10	B5
Wicklow Mts.	11	E3
Wien	15	D9
Wiener Neustadt .	15	E9
Wiesbaden .	14	C5
Wilhelmshaven	14	B5
Wilkes-Barre	73	D8
Wille	11	C9
Willemstad .	87	D6
Williams Lake	71	C7
Williamsburg	73	F7
Williamsport	73	D7
Williamstown	63	C3
Williston ..	76	A3
Willowmore	58	E4
Wilmington, Del., U.S.A.	73	E8
Wilmington, N.C., U.S.A.	75	B9
Wilson → ..	75	B9
Wilsons Promontory	63	C4
Wimmera →	62	C3
Winchester .	11	F6
Wind River Range ...	81	D9
Windhoek ..	58	C3
Windsor, N.S., Canada ..	69	D4
Windsor, Ont., Canada ..	69	D2
Wingham ..	69	D2
Winisk → ..	69	C2
Winnipeg ..	71	D10
Winnipeg, L.	71	C10
Winnipegosis L.	71	C9
Winona ...	77	C9
Winston-Salem ...	75	A7
Winterthur .	13	C8
Wisconsin □	77	C10
Wisła → ..	16	A4
Wismar ...	15	B6
Witbank ...	59	D5
Wittenberg .	15	C6
Wittenberge	15	B6
Wkra → ..	16	B5
Włocławek ..	16	B4
Wodonga ...	63	C4
Wokam ...	39	F4
Wolfsberg .	15	E8
Wolfsburg ..	15	B6
Wollaston Pen. ...	70	B8
Wollongong	63	B5
Wolverhampton	11	E5
Wŏnsan ...	35	C7
Woodland .	80	F3
Woods, L. of the	71	D10
Woodstock .	69	D4
Worcester, S. Africa .	58	E3
Worcester, U.K.	11	E5
Worcester, U.S.A. .	73	C10
Workington .	11	D5
Worms ...	14	D5
Worthing ..	11	F6
Wrangell ..	71	C6
Wrangell Mts.	71	B5
Wrath, C. .	10	B4
Wrexham ..	11	E5
Wrigley ...	70	B7
Wrocław ..	16	C3
Wuhan ...	35	C6
Wuhu	35	C6
Wuppertal .	14	C4
Würzburg ..	14	D5
Wutongqiao	34	D5
Wuxi	35	C7
Wuzhou ...	35	D6
Wyandotte .	72	C4
Wyndham .	60	D4
Wyoming □ .	81	D10
Xánthi	22	D5
Xiaguan ...	34	D5
Xiamen ...	35	D6
Xi'an	35	C5
Xiangfan ..	35	C6
Xiangtan ..	35	D6
Xingu → ..	92	C3
Xining ...	34	C5
Xinjiang Uygur Zizhiqu □ .	34	B3
Xizang □ ..	34	C3
Xuzhou ...	35	C6
Yablonovyy Khrebet ..	31	D9
Yakima ...	80	B3
Yakutat ...	71	C6
Yakutsk ...	31	C10
Yalova ...	22	D7
Yalta	25	E3
Yam Kinneret	46	D3
Yamagata .	33	G12
Yamaguchi .	32	B2
Yamal, Poluostrov	28	B8
Yambol ...	22	C6
Yamdena ...	39	F4
Yamethin ..	41	G11
Yampil ...	17	D9
Yamuna → .	40	E3
Yana → ...	31	B11
Yanbu 'al Bahr ...	47	F4
Yantai ...	35	C7
Yanji	35	B7
Yantai ...	35	C7
Yapen ...	39	E5
Yaremcha .	17	D7
Yarkhun → .	42	A8
Yaroslavl ..	24	B4
Yaselda ...	17	B8
Yasinya ...	17	D7
Yatağan ..	23	F7
Yathkyed L. .	70	B10
Yatsushiro .	32	C2
Yavoriv ...	17	D6
Yawatahama	32	C3
Yazd	44	D3
Yazoo → ..	79	C8
Yecla	19	C5
Yekaterinburg	29	D7
Yell	10	A6
Yellow Sea .	35	C7
Yellowhead Pass ...	71	C8
Yellowknife .	70	B8
Yellowknife →	70	B8
Yellowstone →	76	B3
Yellowstone National Park ...	81	C8
Yelsk	17	C9
Yemen ■ ..	49	E3
Venice ...	23	E6
Yenisey → .	28	B9
Yeniseysk .	30	D7
Yeola ...	43	J9
Yeovil ...	11	F5
Yerevan ...	25	E5
Yeu, I. d' ..	12	C2
Yevpatoriya	25	D3
Yiannitsa ..	23	D4
Yibin	35	D5
Yichang ...	35	C6
Yichun ...	34	B7
Yinchuan ..	34	C5
Yingkou ...	35	B7
Yogyakarta	37	F4
Yokkaichi ..	32	B5
Yokohama .	32	B6
Yokosuka ..	32	B6
Yonago ...	32	B3
Yonkers ...	73	D9
Yonne → .	13	B5
York, U.K. .	11	E6
York, U.S.A.	73	E7
Yorkton ...	71	C9
Yosemite National Park	82	B3
Yoshkar Ola	24	B6
Youghal ...	11	F3
Youngstown	72	D5
Yozgat ...	46	C3
Yuan Jiang → .	35	D6
Yuba City ..	80	F3
Yübari ...	32	F12
Yucatán, Canal de .	85	C7
Yucatán, Peninsula de	85	D7
Yugoslavia ■	22	B3
Yukon → ..	71	B3
Yukon Territory □	70	B6
Yuma	82	D5
Yunnan □ ..	34	D5
Yuzhno-Sakhalinsk	31	E12
Yvetot ...	12	B4
Zabrze	16	C4
Zadar	20	B5
Zafra	18	C2
Zagreb ...	20	B6
Zagros Mts. = Kühhā-ye .	44	C2
Zagros, Kühhā-ye .	44	C2
Zähedän ..	45	D5
Zahlah ...	46	D3
Zaïre = Congo, Democratic Republic of the ■ ...	56	E4
Zaïre → ...	56	F2
Zákinthos .	23	F3
Zalishchyky .	17	D7
Zambeze →	59	B7
Zambia ■ ..	59	B5
Zamboanga .	38	C2
Zamora ...	18	B3
Zamość ...	17	C6
Zanesville .	72	E4
Zanjän ...	46	C7
Zante = Zákinthos .	23	F3
Zanzibar ...	57	F7
Západné Beskydy .	16	D4
Zaporizhzhya	25	D4
Zara	46	C4
Zaragoza ..	19	B5
Zaria	55	F6
Zaskar Mts. .	42	C10
Zbarazh ...	17	D7
Zdolbuniv .	17	C8
Zeebrugge .	14	C2
Zeerust ...	59	D5
Zeitz	15	C7
Zenica ...	20	B6
Žepče ...	20	B7
Zêzere → .	18	C1
Zhabinka ..	17	B7
Zhambyl ...	29	E8
Zhangjiakou	35	B6
Zhangzhou .	35	D6
Zhanjiang .	35	D6
Zhashkiv ...	17	D10
Zhayyq → .	29	E6
Zhejiang □ .	35	D7
Zhengzhou .	35	C6
Zhigansk ..	30	C10
Zhlobin ...	17	B10
Zhmerynka .	17	D9
Zhodzina ..	17	A9
Zhytomyr ..	17	C9
Zibo	35	C6
Zielona Góra	16	C2
Zigong ...	35	D5
Ziguinchor .	55	F1
Zile	46	B3
Žilina ...	16	D4
Zimbabwe ■	59	B5
Zion National Park	83	B6
Zlatoust ...	29	D6
Zlin	16	D3
Znojmo ...	16	D3
Zolochiv ...	17	D7
Zonguldak .	46	B2
Zrenjanin ..	22	B3
Zug	13	C8
Zugspitze ..	14	E6
Zunyi	35	D5
Zürich ...	13	C8
Zwettl ...	15	D8
Zwickau ...	15	C7
Zwolle ...	14	B4